Flannery O'Connor

The Obedient Imagination

Flannery O'Connor

The Obedient Imagination

Sarah Gordon

The University of Georgia Press | Athens and London

© 2000 by the University of Georgia Press

Athens, Georgia 30602

All rights reserved

Designed by Kathi Dailey Morgan

Set in 10 on 14 Electra by G&S Typesetters

Printed and bound by Thomson-Shore

The paper in this book meets the guidelines for

permanence and durability of the Committee on

Production Guidelines for Book Longevity of the

Council on Library Resources.

Printed in the United States of America

04 03 02 01 00 C 5 4 3 2 1

Library of Congress Cataloging-in-Publication Data

Gordon, Sarah, 1941–

   Flannery O'Connor : the obedient imagination / Sarah Gordon.

   p. cm.

   Includes bibliographical references and index.

   ISBN 0-8203-2203-2 (alk. paper)

   1. O'Connor, Flannery — Criticism and interpretation.

   2. Women and literature — Southern States — History — 20th century.

   3. Imagination in literature. 4. Authority in literature. I. Title

   PS3565.C57 Z6796 2000

   813'.54—dc21   00-021654

British Library Cataloging-in-Publication Data available

Acknowledgments for previously published material appear

on pages x–xi, which constitute an extension of the

copyright page.

This book is dedicated to the memory of Margaret I. Raynal, professor of English at Randolph-Macon Woman's College, 1960–91. Her enthusiastic devotion to literature and to the life of the mind continues to inspire those of us who were her students.

Contents

Acknowledgments

Because of other obligations, most notably my continuing editorial work on the *Flannery O'Connor Bulletin*, I have seemed to make rather slow progress on this book. In the academic year 1990–91, Georgia College & State University, then Georgia College, granted me a faculty research grant for study leave to begin my work on this project. For that grant and for the hospitality of Sarah Shearouse on St. Simons Island, Georgia, I am extremely grateful. During that year, with time to read and to think, I made considerable headway. In the ensuing years I have worked sometimes intensely and sometimes sporadically, but always with the goal of completing my book. The ongoing conversations on O'Connor that I have enjoyed with my many O'Connor "connections" have spurred me on, particularly in times when my teaching schedule and other assignments would seem to have prohibited me from ever completing my task. Louise Westling, Margaret Whitt, Ralph Wood, Bruce Gentry, Virginia Wray, Rick Asals, Martha Stephens, Georgia Newman, and Sura Rath have been especially challenging in provoking me to consider and reconsider—and to laugh, a prime requisite for serious readers of O'Connor. I extend my sincere thanks to Nancy Davis Bray, special collections librarian of the O'Connor Collection in Russell Library at Georgia College & State University, for her help in locating research materials. Man Martin, my former student whose imagination and sense of humor know no bounds, created "The Flannery O'Connor Computer" when he was in my O'Connor class and has allowed me to publish it. My good friend Lucy Underwood has always provided me with steady support, and for that I am ever thankful.

✳ ✳ ✳

Reprinted by permission of Farrar, Straus & Giroux, Inc.:

Excerpts from "The Crop," "The Barber," "Wildcat," "The Geranium," and "The Turkey" from *The Complete Stories* by Flannery O'Connor. Copyright © 1971 by the Estate of Mary Flannery O'Connor.

Excerpts from "Everything That Rises Must Converge," "Greenleaf," "The Enduring Chill," "The Lame Shall Enter First," "Revelation," and "Parker's Back" from *Everything That Rises Must Converge* by Flannery O'Connor. Copyright © 1965 by the Estate of Mary Flannery O'Connor. Copyright renewed © 1993 by Regina O'Connor.

Excerpts from *The Habit of Being: Letters of Flannery O'Connor*, edited by Sally Fitzgerald. Copyright © 1979 by Regina O'Connor.

Excerpts from "The Church and the Fiction Writer," "The Nature and Aim of Fiction," "The Regional Writer," "The Fiction Writer and His Country," "Writing Short Stories," "The Grotesque in Southern Fiction," "Introduction to *A Memoir of Mary Ann*," and "On Her Own Work" from *Mystery and Manners: Occasional Prose* by Flannery O'Connor, selected and edited by Sally and Robert Fitzgerald. Copyright © 1969 by the Estate of Mary Flannery O'Connor.

Excerpts from *The Violent Bear It Away* by Flannery O'Connor. Copyright © 1960 by Flannery O'Connor. Copyright renewed © 1988 by Regina O'Connor.

Excerpts from the unpublished work of Flannery O'Connor are used by permission of the literary executor, Robert Giroux. Copyright © 2000 by the Estate of Flannery O'Connor.

The aesthetic object is never fully grasped but is rather an act of understanding that is not yet completely understood. Like other deeds, it lives by that which it is not yet. Any attempt to limit art to its brute form treats art as if it were over, as if it were a thing and not a deed. —Katerina Clark and Michael Holquist, *Mikhail Bakhtin*

Introduction

In the thirty years that I have been reading and teaching the fiction of Flannery O'Connor, I have been heartened by the steady increase in her readership. In my first year of teaching at Georgia College & State University, O'Connor's alma mater then known as Georgia State College for Women, I was appalled by the lack of knowledge about—and, even worse, the apparent lack of interest in—O'Connor's strange, funny, deeply haunting tales. At that time the O'Connor Collection in the college library consisted primarily of an assortment of photographs of the author and a cardboard box filled with clippings of O'Connor's achievements, mostly from Georgia newspapers. O'Connor's books were not stocked in the college bookstore, the manager's excuse being that he had no real call for them. Except for her popularity in the college English department and among a handful of local enthusiasts, Flannery O'Connor was dismissed as "Regina's daughter who wrote those peculiar stories," a local aberration, actually one of many in Milledgeville, a city with perhaps more than its share of the bizarre and the grotesque, the homely and the historic. At least since the work of Josephine Hendin, all serious students of O'Connor are profoundly aware of the complex and mannered society in this central Georgia town, miraculously spared by Sherman in his March to the Sea, home to what was once the largest mental institution in the world, home now to a women's prison, a boys' reformatory, and Georgia College & State University.

Although we O'Connor readers in the late 1960s and 1970s sometimes liked to console ourselves — perhaps a bit condescendingly — with the words of the writer of the Gospel of Matthew, "A prophet is not without honor, save in his own country," we were convinced that O'Connor would inevitably find her readership and that even locally she would be recognized. Our hopes have certainly been fulfilled. Milledgeville and GC&SU now receive each year numbers of visitors from throughout the world; the university, repository of the writer's manuscripts and private library, is the scene of much scholarly activity; and the college bookstore finds it profitable to keep primary and secondary sources in stock, as well as a supply of O'Connor T-shirts and Milledgeville memorabilia. The university has hosted four successful O'Connor symposia over the last twenty years, the last one in 1994 attracting some five hundred visitors from thirty states and five foreign countries. Indeed, shod in all shoe sizes and types, O'Connor's readers assemble in the waiting room, all eyes on Mary Grace, hunched fiercely over her text, biding her time.

As for this aging reader of O'Connor, with the passing of the seasons have come, along with the recurring delights of the fiction, serious questions, many of which maintain a tenacious hold. Some of these questions have been raised by critical articles in the *Flannery O'Connor Bulletin*, published by our college since 1972, or in other books and articles on O'Connor's work. However, most of my concerns derive from my own encounters over the years with the texts themselves, as I have taught O'Connor and engaged in research, both for the *Flannery O'Connor Bulletin* and for my own projects;

certainly, changing trends in literary criticism have intensified the old questions and served as the catalyst for new ones. Moreover, because the process of reading the primary sources, mercifully, never allows us to remain fixed in our reactions, I have found my own responses to O'Connor's fiction changing as I have changed over the years. To be sure, these changes have never caused me to think that my previous readings of the O'Connor texts are completely invalid, nor have they caused any diminution of the appeal of O'Connor's work for me. Although I do not want to overstate the influence of feminist criticism, reader response criticism, or the dialogic theory of Mikhail Bakhtin, for example, on my current approach to O'Connor, I am aware that many of the issues that trouble me today were nonexistent or, at least, hidden from me in the late 1960s and 1970s. Quite honestly, I have had despairing moments over the years in which I have almost wished to return to my state of near innocence. Would it not be salutary simply to be able to laugh at Ruby Turpin's foolishness and be done with it? Such a return to the unfallen state is, of course, impossible, and the questions of the day inevitably lope along beside me into the classroom. I comfort myself with the recognition that such questioning and rethinking testifies to the enduring vitality of the fiction.

Because I was schooled in the New Criticism, my habit when teaching literature has always been to admit honestly when the text appears problematic. Through the years I have tried to hold to that tenet especially strongly when teaching or talking about Flannery O'Connor. I believe that my students at Georgia College & State University are particularly appreciative of such candor, for they often enter the O'Connor class with the idea that the posture of the adoring fan is the attitude most likely to please the teacher, here at O'Connor's alma mater. I am certain that Flannery O'Connor herself would despise such a notion and that, although she certainly had strong reservations about the way literature was taught at the college level, she would never have countenanced anything less than the most thorough and informed appraisal of her work.

If I am asked whether the primary audience for this book is the teacher or the student of O'Connor's works, I would have to hedge in my answer. I do have the teacher in mind, of course, as she or he tries to present O'Connor judiciously and sensitively in the classroom setting, and certainly there are some scholarly approaches to which I feel compelled to respond. I hope that these readers will find a measure of satisfaction in my efforts. In my mind also, however, is the perplexed reader wherever he or she is found. I think of my own late mother, for example, who had a number of cogent questions about O'Connor's fictional world, questions that she was not able to phrase in literary language but ones that nevertheless signaled important issues in the fiction.

Literature matters. If those of us who serve as guides to others in the study of books do not espouse that simple truth, we are sounding brass and clanging symbol. If we with our rather sophisticated reading skills and techniques still manage to miss the meanings, our enterprise is futile. Of course, we must admit that much of our critical language and thought these days is freighted with difficulty, that often in naming the parts or the angles of viewing and the myriad possibilities for reading author and text, we seem to lose the sense of what we are about. On the other hand, we admit that sometimes, just when we think our critical universes are nicely settled and populated, a new planet swims into our ken — or is thrust there by a Marxist, a feminist, or a deconstructionist. That is as it should be. The very life of literature depends on such disturbance.

My own reading of Flannery O'Connor began in 1966 with my simple delight in her sense of humor. At that time I was a displaced southerner, two years out of college, living in Columbia, Missouri, where I was working on a master's degree, and feeling more than a little superior to the (then increasingly publicized) provincialism of the South. I was, quite frankly, elated to find in O'Connor's fiction such scathing attacks on the frivolous and superficial thinking of some of my southern compatriots. At that time I believed that I knew exactly the world that O'Connor described: the post–Civil War South in which too often ignorant, self-serving, smug white folks set themselves up as paragons of hard work and decency and use other people for their own ends, usually social respectability or financial gain. As O'Connor presented this world, her central characters, certain of their own superiority, overflowed with clichés that often disguised their own need for control and power. I knew Mrs. Cope and Mrs. McIntyre or their like, and I was glad to see them humbled at the story's close. If I didn't always recognize that the arrogant, superior intellectuals and would-be writers were also receiving their comeuppance, perhaps I simply did not want to see that O'Connor was, in her wildly humorous way, indicting us all. O'Connor's relentless attacks on narrow-mindedness, smugness, and pride drew this young southerner like a magnet. I found O'Connor hilarious. I was hooked.

Nevertheless, as the years have passed, my laughter has become tempered, has even halted from time to time, as other concerns have risen to the fore. For example, is O'Connor's world a narrow and limited one, as many critics allege? Why does O'Connor inevitably paint so bleak a world? Why are family relationships inevitably distorted, even horrible? Why are the blacks such marginal and stereotypical characters? Was O'Connor a racist? Is O'Connor's laughter mean or cruel, always making the joke at somebody else's expense? Where is evidence of the goodness and love, or even the possibility for these feelings, that we associate with Christian hope? Is the feminine or the female all too often the object of O'Connor's scorn? These matters and others have demanded my attention, as they have demanded the attention of other serious readers of O'Connor over the years. Because I believe that my concerns are not unique and that my thoughts and even my tentative conclusions — in those cases in which I am able to draw a conclusion — may be of interest or help to other students of O'Connor, I am arranging this book around those questions. Especially helpful to me have been Mikhail Bakhtin's ideas that the aesthetic object is never completed and that the aesthetic experience, which is found in the totality of the relationships among author, reader, and text, is an endless process. As the epigraph to this introduction suggests, Bakhtinian theory is antithetical to the formalist criticism in which I and many of my contemporaries were schooled, and for this reason, I have had to shed (and am still shedding) a good bit of the rather rigid critical baggage of my past. I confess, moreover, that I have not much minded the loss, for it has enabled me to maintain a certain openness in my approach to O'Connor. In spite of my long association with Georgia College & State University and the *Flannery O'Connor Bulletin* and in spite of the frequent assumption that I speak the "party line" or, to use another familiar metaphor, serve as a keeper of the flame, I have tried to resist stringently parochial readings of O'Connor, particularly in recent years when literary theory has seemed to suggest so many new ways of thinking. If, in my own writing about O'Connor in the past, I have been guilty of rigidity or of a kind of literary absolutism, I can only say, with Bakhtin and others, that the critic's position is also in process, constantly evolving. Finally, I acknowledge that my approach may not be meaningful or convincing to some readers. To certain readers my comments may appear too loose; to others, too limiting. I should add, furthermore, that on some points—the conscious grounding of O'Connor's fiction in her devout Catholicism or the brilliant skill and craft of that fiction, for example—I cannot be budged. If to some readers that measure of inflexibility is troubling, I apologize ahead of time.

Be assured, however, that even as this book is completed, I feel myself privileged to be, still, reading Flannery O'Connor.

Like George Eliot, [Virginia] Woolf strives to dissociate herself from silly lady readers and silly lady writers. Indeed, her voyeuristic visions of adoptive foremothers are shadowed by a few virulent essays, virtually poison pen letters, in which she definitively distances herself from "scribbling women." —Sandra Gilbert and Susan Gubar, *The War of the Words*

When I became aware [in college] of my "wrong" experience, I chose fantasy. Convinced I had no real experience of life, since my own obviously wasn't part of Great Literature, I decided consciously that I'd write of things nobody knew anything about, dammit. So I wrote realism disguised as fantasy, that is, science fiction. —Joanna Russ, *How to Suppress Women's Writing*

1 Questions of Power and Authority

Throughout history women writers have developed a number of strategies by which they are able to muster a measure of control over their material and their careers.[1] Overlooked, mocked, even reviled, they have managed to conceal their identities, disguise themselves in male pseudonyms, and subvert the patriarchal status quo in work that often appears on the surface to affirm that status quo. As Mary Jacobus notes, writing has "a quietly subversive power . . . to destabilize the ground on which we stand" (59). Women writers, even in the male tradition, "work ceaselessly" to "write what cannot be written" (52). Even a writer like Flannery O'Connor, who in her prime writes boldly and confidently, clearly grappled in her formative years with questions of power and authority. This fact is evident in the stories in the master's thesis, and these concerns continue to manifest themselves to some extent in later work as well.

O'Connor would doubtless have been chagrined to see her master's thesis stories included in the 1971 volume *The Complete Stories*. That thesis, *The Geranium: A Collection of Short Stories*, was completed in 1947, dedicated to her teacher at the University of Iowa, Paul Engle, and largely put behind her as O'Connor moved on to complete *Wise Blood*. While it is true that O'Connor used a later version of "The Train" as the opening chapter in *Wise Blood* and continued to rewrite her first published story and the first story in the collection, "The Geranium," until the end of her life, the other four stories in the thesis collection are slight, clearly the work of a young writer experimenting with form and voice. Indeed, until the late 1970s, critics largely ignored the six thesis stories, although their inclusion in the 1971 collection with its illuminating introduction by Robert Giroux would seem to have whetted scholars' interest. To this day most commentators note the uncharacteristic absence of O'Connor's religious themes in these stories, citing "The Turkey" (and its later, more successful version, "An Afternoon in the Park") as the most indicative of fictional interests and strategies of the mature writer. Although several commentaries on the thesis stories had appeared before 1982, Frederick Asals's *Flannery O'Connor: The Imagination of Extremity* was perhaps the most noteworthy discussion of the apprentice stories, attempting to connect subject, theme, and technique of these stories to the later work.

Among the thesis stories, only "The Geranium," "The Turkey," and "The Train" were published in O'Connor's lifetime. "The Barber," "Wildcat," and "The Crop" were published in the early 1970s by permission of the author's literary executor at the time, Robert Fitzgerald, who, in the case of both "The Barber" and "The Crop," appended a note explaining that the stories' shortcomings obviously resulted from their being early works. "The Barber" is largely of interest to critics because of the early satire of the liberal intellectual, a theme that dominated the later work, while "Wildcat," with its obvious indebtedness to Faulkner's "That Evening Sun," is usually cited as indicative of the young O'Connor's search for subject and voice. "The

Crop," which has received no extended critical attention, may well be the most important story in the thesis collection.

On one draft of "The Crop" O'Connor herself scrawled, "UNPUBLISH-ABLE/FOC 1953" (Dunn and Driggers 8), certainly a clear indication that the maturing writer saw the limitations of this early story. In 1948, however, O'Connor had tried to get the story published; she notes, in a letter to Elizabeth McKee, that the story is "for sale to the unparticular" (*Habit of Being* 6), and later in that same year when the revised story had been rejected, she wrote to McKee, "I should not write stories in the middle of a novel" (7). In his note to the posthumous publication of the story (1971), however, Fitzgerald observed that "although it is obviously far from her best work, 'The Crop' would never be mistaken for anyone else's production," adding that "we enjoy a small caricature of that shady type, the imaginative artist," and that the "exacting art, the stringent spirit, and the sheer kick of her mature work are promised here" (*Complete Stories* 551).

Few would claim that the choice of subject matter in "The Crop" is propitious; in fact, a hallmark of the novice storyteller is the attempt to write about writers and writing, perhaps a necessary though self-conscious step in the evolution of self-confidence. Of course, western literature is filled with successful examples of such writerly self-consciousness, and O'Connor was certainly familiar with many of them. Joyce's *A Portrait of the Artist as a Young Man*, for example, exerted great influence on O'Connor, most particularly in her satiric portrait of the artist Asbury in "The Enduring Chill." In fact, O'Connor's scathing attack on her "artist" figure in that story is a subversion of the Joycean religion of art and the artist and of the romantic figure of the intense, sensitive, and alienated writer, superior to his surroundings and to the claims of family and familial duty. "The Enduring Chill," the work of the mature and focused O'Connor, is anticipated by "The Crop," the only O'Connor story that presents the artist as female. In spite of its superficial texture, this thesis story is noteworthy as a revelation of O'Connor's acknowledgment of the forces over which the female artist must have control; in some measure O'Connor is here revising Woolf's *A Room of One's Own*. If the genuine confidence of a writer emanates from a real sense of control over material, the apprentice's story of the writer grappling with subject matter and with the basic questions of the relationship of art to life can be seen as an implicit acknowledgment of the territory to be conquered.

Flannery O'Connor's "The Crop," although a sharply satirical account of the would-be artist, is just such an acknowledgment. Furthermore, this story suggests many of the dilemmas of the southern female artist in the middle of the twentieth century by implying the author's own questions of range, form, and content.

At the conclusion of "The Crop," we are certain that Miss Willerton will never complete a story. Having discarded several quite fanciful plots, including one in which she herself becomes involved as a character, Miss Willerton is ready to take up the subject of the Irish. We see clearly from the last sentence that she knows no more about the Irish than she knows about the foreign bakers, teachers, or sharecroppers she has earlier considered for her subject matter: "Miss Willerton had always admired the Irish. Their brogue, she thought, was full of music; and their history—splendid! And the people, she mused, the Irish people! They were full of spirit—red-haired, with broad shoulders and great, drooping mustaches" (*Flannery O'Connor: Collected Works*, 740, hereafter referred to as *O'Connor*). As we smile at the superficiality of Miss Willerton's knowledge of the Irish, we note also that the Irish "people" are present in her mind as a stereotype that is male. The author is probably not satirizing Miss Willerton's neglect of the female population of Ireland; O'Connor herself obviously thought in terms of the primacy of the male, a point to which I shall return later.

Here O'Connor is satirically delineating the problems of a writer who, with little knowledge or experience of the world, nonetheless seeks to write about it. Moreover, she indirectly attacks the emphasis in mid-twentieth-century fiction on social and economic realism, especially as exemplified in the work of a fellow Georgian, Erskine Caldwell. Caldwell's stories of sharecroppers and other impoverished characters would certainly have fulfilled Miss Willerton's ideal: "Miss Willerton had never been intimately connected with sharecroppers but, she reflected, they would make as arty a subject as any, and they would give her that air of social concern which was so valuable to have in the circles she was hoping to travel!" (*O'Connor* 733). Early on in the story we perceive Miss Willerton as a ludicrous figure, shallow and unfulfilled, preferring to escape to the dream life momentarily afforded her by her own fanciful creation, the story of Lot Motun.

Asals observes that "The Crop" points up the age-old theme of the difference between art and life; that, although Miss Willerton "is no more than a stock character" (16), she is nevertheless the first of the "comic authorial self-projections" presented throughout her fiction by O'Connor; and that the story finally hints at O'Connor's own rejection of both "fashionable 'subjects,' elaborated by free-floating fantasy" (17) and the subject matter of everyday life *anywhere* (16–17). Asals's observations are certainly valid ones, but, in my view, they do not go far enough. As I indicated earlier, the fact that this story concerns a female writer, or would-be writer, is crucial, for although one can argue that O'Connor's scathing attack on Miss Willerton later culminates in such characters as Joy/Hulga Hopewell of "Good Country People," Julian in "Everything That Rises Must Converge," and Asbury in "The Enduring Chill," we do well to remember that Joy/Hulga is not a writer, or even a would-be writer, and that Julian and Asbury are male. To be sure, Mary Elizabeth, Calhoun's double in "The Partridge Festival," is an aspiring writer, but Miss Willerton is the only female artist given center stage. As O'Connor's only treatment of the myriad problems of the woman writer, "The Crop" forecasts O'Connor's adoption of the patrilineal literary heritage.

I believe that this story constitutes an early dialogue with herself on O'Connor's part, for it is a powerful statement of the author's attempt to exert some control over her own textuality, even as it describes, albeit in fiercely humorous fashion, the attempt of a woman writer to exert that same control. And just as Miss Willerton "kills off" the female protagonist in the sharecropper story in order that she may enter the plot as the replacement of that female character (an obvious attack on the notion of art as therapy or fulfillment for the emotionally starved), so Miss Willerton's imaginative vision is "killed off" by the interruption of Lucia, who asks "Willie" to go to the store and thus thrusts her back into reality. Finally, in our minds as well as in her own, O'Connor "kills off" Miss Willerton by making her a completely foolish figure: Our laughter, elicited by O'Connor's relentless attack, is the killing blow. Thus, from the deathblow she gives to Miss Willerton's idea of art and the artist and on the basis of our dismissal of Miss Willerton as a character not to be taken seriously, we see Flannery O'Connor deconstructing in order to construct. If we look carefully, we may see O'Connor's acute awareness of limitation, restraint, and possibility in the female artist's situation, perhaps especially in the South. Furthermore, we see O'Connor's rejection of what Gilbert and Gubar call the matrilineal heritage, a rejection entailing more than O'Connor's dismissal of those silly "lady" writers and "lady" readers alluded to in the first epigraph to this chapter.

If O'Connor had been asked whether this story was concerned with the specific problems of the *woman* writer, she would very likely have ridiculed such an idea. She was certainly not a feminist, and she would never have claimed that the difficulties of the female writer are in any significant way different from those of the male writer. After all, O'Connor wrote her disclaimer to "A" in 1956: "On the subject of the feminist business, I just never think, that is never think of qualities which are specifically feminine or masculine. I suppose I divide people into two classes: the Irksome and the Non-Irksome without regard to sex. Yes and there are the Medium Irksome and the Rare Irksome" (*Habit of Being* 176). Surely, as we read her letters, we see no indication that O'Connor felt restricted as an artist because she was a woman. Like Eudora Welty, O'Connor in her public statements seems to deny the need for attention to a writer's gender. As Welty said to Alice Walker in a 1973 interview, "Of course, I haven't any bones to pick, myself. A writer never has the problem to face. Being a woman has never kept me from writing or from finding publication for my work" (Prenshaw 136). That statement is contradicted by the fact that *Esquire* magazine rejected "Petrified Man" in 1941 because it did not publish fiction by women. Both Welty and O'Connor appear to have been less than thoughtful or realistic on the subject of the plight of the woman writer. Although we might excuse them on the grounds of ignorance of the historic struggle of women writers, of which feminist critics have made us acutely aware in the last twenty years, both women seem resistant and defensive with respect to this subject.

Perhaps not surprisingly, O'Connor's insightful and instructive comments about the writing process are usually stated in the most authoritative and objective terms, at least when she is writing to young or inexperienced writers who have sought her advice and opinions. As a writer schooled in the New Criticism and thereby greatly influenced by notions of the objective, impersonal artist found in the work of Eliot and others, O'Connor would have decried any apparently self-indulgent or self-serving analysis of writing difficulties. She believed that writing talent is a gift of God and that it must be developed with discipline and responsibility. Indeed, her letters reiterate the necessity for the writer to struggle and to do without, almost in the manner of priestly self-denial, in the process of creation. She wrote to "A" in 1956, "There is a great deal that has to either be given up or be taken away from you if you are going to succeed in writing a body of work," and she added, in an unusual personal revelation, "There seem to be other conditions in life that demand celibacy besides the priesthood" (*Habit of Being* 176). Moreover, the stringency of her opinions and the authority with which she writes seem to place O'Connor in that "priesthood of critics" established by Eliot (Bonnie Kime Scott 12). We should note that Eliot, in his qualified admiration of Djuna Barnes and Marianne Moore—the two female writers to whom he gives any critical attention—concentrates on those elements in their work that are in keeping with the "tradition" of the canonical writers, ignoring aspects of their work—especially that of Barnes—not easily assimilated into the "tradition" that was "European, white, and male" (Gish 140). O'Connor's statements about writing, in her essays and letters, are not tentative and offer little of the experimentation with idea and the flexibility of approach that we associate with Virginia Woolf or other female critics. Writing, for O'Connor, involves struggle and difficulty, which can be overcome only through self-denial and discipline.

One of her friends in graduate school at the University of Iowa, Barbara Tunnicliff Hamilton, testifies to O'Connor's dedication to her craft: "As I recall Flannery's mode of life, she kept things plain and simple. She did not want curtains at the windows, for instance, because they would be distracting. When she was alone in the room she would often pull the window shades so that it would be dark in there. And she would sit at her typewriter turning out yellow sheets of paper—writing and rewriting and rewriting. She told me she wrote because she 'had to.' And whenever she wasn't writing, she was reading" (1). Hamilton continues, "I think those of us who lived with Flannery were a little in awe of her what-you-might-call sense of destiny. She knew she was a 'great writer.' She was not pompous or boastful about it, she just knew she was" (2). In 1957, in a letter to "A," who as a writer herself was apparently in need of a good bit of caution and corrective, O'Connor wrote, "In my whole time of writing the only parts that have come easy for me were Enoch Emery and Hulga; the rest has been pushing a stone uphill with my nose" (*Habit of Being* 241). "[A]ll writing is painful and . . . if it is not painful then it is not worth doing" (242). And in 1960, in yet another long letter to "A" on writerly concerns, O'Connor authoritatively stated, "You do not write the best you can for the sake of art but for the sake of returning your talent increased to the invisible God to use or not use as he sees fit" (*Habit of Being* 419). In this last statement, of course, O'Connor separates herself from Joyce and the fin de siècle idea of autonomous art as an article of faith and replaces it with the conservative Christian view of art espoused by Eliot's later poetry and criticism.

In her letters in *The Habit of Being* and in her essays or lectures first published as *Mystery and Manners*, O'Connor writes (or speaks) with great conviction on two subjects: writing and faith. To be sure, in the case of the authoritative letter and lecture or essay, she is usually addressing herself to an audience of "seekers," whether writers or critics and/or the spiritually hungry, and we might expect such conclusiveness and certainty. A teacher, after all, may fear that she will lose her effectiveness if she admits uncertainty or doubt about the subject matter. The possibility, however, is very real that those who have read a great deal of O'Connor's nonfiction will be somewhat discomfited by her self-assurance and even suspect her of covering her own doubt with dogmatism. As we read the letters, we may notice that after our laughter at O'Connor's anecdotes has subsided a bit and after we have perhaps even underscored certain of her memorable and pithy statements about life and faith, we recognize the significant absence of something we are accustomed to finding in our own letters, namely, the evidence of our common human questions, doubts, and uncertainties. We may eventually realize that the admirable firmness with which the twenty-five-year-old O'Connor stands up to John Selby, her editor at Holt Rinehart, asserting that *Wise Blood* is not intended to be a conventional novel, is only a harbinger of the authorial firmness to come.

Although we may continue marking those pithy admonitions, what we may want is the assurance that Flannery O'Connor is flesh and blood like the rest of us and that, at least from time to time, she experienced uncertainty and doubt—about her faith and about her talent. Rarely, however, does such an admission occur in the letters. Thus when we find, in a 1962 letter to Father McCown, O'Connor's request that the priest pray that God will send her some more stories, we may feel curiously gratified by her candor: "I've been writing for sixteen years and I have the sense of having exhausted my original potentiality and being now in need of the kind of grace that deepens perception, a new shot of life or something" (*Habit of Being* 468). That unusual admission stands in sharp contrast to O'Connor's characteristic objectivity and toughness, especially concerning matters of writing and faith. I believe that the beginnings of that objectivity and toughness are evident in "The Crop." And as I shall demonstrate in later chapters, that objectivity and impersonality derive in large measure from prevalent attitudes toward the female at the time, especially as those attitudes were embodied in O'Connor's literary education.

As one perhaps might expect in an early story, "The Crop" is sketchy in certain details. Critics generally assume — incorrectly — that Miss Willerton lives in a boardinghouse, although there is no statement in the text to that effect. Furthermore, O'Connor lets us infer that the forty-four-year-old spinster has no full-time employment and that her "writing" is the means of wish-fulfillment for a person who has never really entered into life. We are easily led into these assumptions, I believe, because the condition of the "redundant woman" is such a familiar one to us. After all, the foolish old maid who is emotionally and sexually deprived is traditionally the brunt of jokes and, in the South at least, reputedly goes to her grave denying the facts of life. She is therefore an easy target for O'Connor. Additional comedy is provided for us in this case, however, when O'Connor at the outset of the story demonstrates Miss Willerton's apparent uselessness: "Miss Willerton always crumbed the table. It was her particular household accomplishment and she did it with great thoroughness" (*O'Connor* 732). These opening sentences anticipate a motif that underlies this story and much of O'Connor's later fiction — an implicit reaction against, perhaps even contempt for, those domestic and social duties usually associated with the "feminine" and womanly, especially in the traditional South. Indeed, a bit later Miss Willerton, in contemplating the niceties of style, remembers a talk she has given to the United Daughters of the Colonies in which she discussed "phonetic art" (734). Here O'Connor clearly has great fun with Miss Willerton's preoccupation with the sound of her writing, for she had hardly arrived at her subject (the sharecropper Lot Motun and his dog) when she was pleased to be able to strike the two "Lot's" in one paragraph because such repetition is displeasing to the ear. Before the assembled ladies Miss Willerton is obviously more taken with the sound of her voice uttering its writerly platitudes than she has been seized by the will to write. In her view, style — or, as Miss Willerton defines it, "tonal quality" — is the essence of writing. Although in her own story she finds the opening sentence, "Lot Motun called his dog," to be "biting and sharp," she cannot proceed because of her ignorance of what sharecroppers actually do. Might they not be "reasonably . . . expected to roll over in the mud?" (734). Her dilemma is captured in E. M. Forster's lecture on Virginia Woolf after her death, when Forster asserted that Woolf was not a great writer "because she had no great cause at heart" and that she "despised the working class" and was a "lady" (qtd. in Russ 73).

What was the appropriate subject matter for a female writer? Miss Willerton has read in clandestine fashion a book so shocking that when Lucia found it in Miss Willerton's bureau, she concluded that Garner had put it there as a joke. When Lucia tells Miss Willerton that she has felt it necessary to burn the book, Miss Willerton "was sure it could be none other's than hers but she hesitated in claiming the distinction. She had ordered it from the publisher because she didn't want to ask for it at the library. It had cost her $3.75 with the postage and she had not finished the last four chapters. At least, she had got enough from it, though, to be able to say that Lot Motun might reasonably roll over in the mud with his dog" (*O'Connor* 735). Her "knowledge" of the world and hence her subject matter will have to come from her secret reading in material that is considered unladylike, to say the least. Garner, a privileged male, may read this book or have it in his possession, but Miss Willerton may not. Furthermore, given her exclusion as a woman from the corridors of power (perhaps a double exclusion when we consider that she is also a spinster), where is her subject matter to come from? Interestingly enough, Lucia has come upon the forbidden book while she is performing her domestic duty of cleaning, and as a female conditioned by the patriarchy, she denies Miss Willerton possession of it. (She, too, would have had to sneak a look at the book, of course, in order to be able to say, "It was awful. . . . I burned it.") Evidently, such "awful" material, the raw facts of life, is the privilege and province of the male; to the female writer, therefore, are relegated whatever "crumbs" she can secretly collect of that awful real life and matters of "style," harmless enough and certainly appropriate feminine concerns. As Joanna Russ describes the process, using the terminology of Jane Marcus, the woman writer must perform a sort of "mental hysterectomy" and create an art that is nonthreatening (99).

Perhaps not surprisingly, then, Miss Willerton's story concerns a male protagonist, although she recognizes that "[t]here had to be a woman" (735), correctly assuming that the "real world," the world of "social problems," centers around men. Miss Willerton will provide the requisite femme fatale, recognizing, of course, that "[t]hat type of woman" will have to be killed off: "Now she would plan her action. There had to be a woman, of course. Perhaps Lot could kill her. That type of woman always started trouble. She might even goad him on to kill her because of her wantonness and then he would be pursued by his conscience maybe" (*O'Connor* 735). The components of this plot are revealing. The story that our Miss Willerton will tell, in spite of her propriety, is the archetypal one of a man goaded into killing a woman because she is sexually promiscuous. Like Eve, "that type of woman" inevitably instigates trouble; *perhaps* the male is only doing his duty and might be "pursued by his conscience." Therefore, in godlike fashion, Miss Willerton considers the creation of her own Garden of Eden, in which, in proper order, the man exists with his dog and then is joined by the woman, who will lead the man to sin, specifically murder. Our creator feels that it will be easy to give the man "principles," although combining principles with "all the love interest there'd have to be" (735) would doubtless be difficult. Seemingly delighting in these fictional problems, Miss Willerton recognizes that she will have to create "passionate scenes," and although she likes to "plan" them, "when she came to write them, she always began to feel peculiar and to wonder what the family would say when they read them" (735). We are reminded here, of course, of Virginia Woolf's "Angel in the House," the emblem of the powerful conditioning that hovers over the shoulder of all women writers urging them to cut out, to censor, to avoid offending. Woolf cautions the woman writer that she will never be free to create until she has killed both the "Angel in the House" and the notion that her work must *please* ("Professions for Women" 238–41).

The sentences that immediately follow Miss Willerton's concern for her family's reaction to her scenes of passion seem to suggest that Miss Willerton does not, in fact, live in a boardinghouse but that Garner, Bertha, and Lucia are members of her family. She wonders what they will say when they read her passionate passages:

> Garner would snap his fingers and wink at her at every opportunity; Bertha would think she was terrible; and Lucia would say in that silly voice of hers, "What have you been keeping from us, Willie? What have you been keeping from us?" and titter like she always did. But Miss Willerton couldn't think about that now; she had to plan her characters. (*O'Connor* 735–36)

Just what are the relationships among the characters in "The Crop"? Was the young O'Connor simply less than painstaking in providing expository material to explain Miss Willerton's situation? Or was that situation simply not clear in O'Connor's own mind? An apparent contradiction of this sort is common enough among young writers, although we might have expected

Paul Engle or other readers of O'Connor's thesis to have discerned the problem. Fragments and drafts of this story in the O'Connor Collection at Georgia College & State University do not suggest changes in setting or any real
explanation of Miss Willerton's situation. In several fragments, we should
note, Miss Willerton is "Miss Medger," she has been a writer since the age
of ten, and she "instantly begins imagining an acceptance from *Harper's*
whenever her thoughts become impure" (Collection 7).[2] Thus, regardless of
her failure to provide details of setting or background, O'Connor seems to
have had on her mind, from the beginning of her work on the story, problems
of the writer's use of "impure" subject matter. Moreover, one fragment suggests that acceptance of her story by a reputable magazine would go a long
way toward nullifying Miss Medger's impure thoughts.

That O'Connor herself had misgivings about the response to her fiction
on the part of her own family and her community is not surprising. In Milledgeville, stories abound to the effect that the local gentry were appalled by
the contents of *Wise Blood*, that O'Connor's own relatives could not imagine
where she had gotten her ideas (as one reportedly put it, "Mary Flannery
always associated with *her own kind*"), and that some of her relatives, and
most emphatically her mother, wanted her to produce another *Gone with
the Wind* (a fact confirmed by O'Connor's comments in *The Habit of Being*
and echoed in "The Enduring Chill"). Sometimes in the letters O'Connor
expressed her own misgivings humorously and at other times seriously. Even
rather late in her career, for example, she was quite concerned with the local
reaction to "The Partridge Festival," not a sexually explicit story but one
based on a shooting spree that actually took place in Milledgeville. She wrote
Cecil Dawkins in 1960 that she had finished the story ("that farce") and
added that, although she had "made it less objectionable from the local
standpoint," her mother "still didn't want [her] to publish it where it would
be read around [Milledgeville]" (*Habit of Being* 404–5). O'Connor seems
relieved to report that the story was accepted for the first issue of a new
Catholic magazine, a fact that would have seemed to guarantee that then
largely Protestant Milledgeville would not have had access to it.

Thus the dramatization of Miss Willerton's concern over the reaction of
her "family" to her depiction of scenes of passion suggests O'Connor's own
concern and the concern of women writers for centuries. In this century
feminist writers and critics — from Virginia Woolf to Adrienne Rich, Sandra
Gilbert, Susan Gubar, Carolyn Heilbrun, and Louise Westling — have not

ceased to remind us of this limitation of subject matter and the audacity of women writers in defying such limitation. In *Sacred Groves and Ravaged Gardens: The Fiction of Eudora Welty, Flannery O'Connor, and Carson McCullers,* Westling addresses the special dilemma of the white female southern writer, focusing on the courage involved in any southern woman's decision to write. As Westling and others easily demonstrate, the ideal of southern womanhood, with its emphasis on "doing pretty" and supporting the white patriarchal power structure by refusing to utter a discouraging word (or a smart or an unpretty one) would seem to have precluded a woman's choice of the writer's life: "How could a person brought up to be soft and yielding, warm and self-sacrificing, dare to intrude herself upon the public mind? How could she presume?" (Westling 54)

Moreover, intruding herself upon the public mind is only the first step. As we have seen, if the woman writer is to succeed in pursuing her own vision and thereby establish control of her text, she must be as free as possible from societal (including familial) pressure to "do pretty." In "A Good Man Is Hard to Find," the concern of the grandmother with maintaining the appearance of a lady and her desperate attempt to assure herself and the Misfit—who is amazingly polite, even chivalrous to his victims—that he is a good man who comes from nice people are obviously O'Connor's fierce attacks on such superficial notions of goodness and worth. Commentators on southern culture such as W. J. Cash and Anne Firor Scott have underscored the powerful antebellum image of the "soft, submissive, perfect [white] woman" (Scott 21), an image that maintained its hold well into the twentieth century and one that is clearly embedded in the grandmother's consciousness, preoccupied as she is with ladylike appearance and with Tara-like plantations containing secret vaults. There is every indication, of course, that Flannery O'Connor was rebelling against that silly image in her characterization of many of her female characters. Although she would undoubtedly be horrified at such a comparison, O'Connor might well be allied with Margaret Mitchell in her refusal to allow her female protagonists to follow the script for acceptable behavior. The popular Scarlett O'Hara, passionate and headstrong, may seem worlds apart from the grandmother, Joy/Hulga Hopewell, Lucynell Crater, Sally Poker Sash, or Ruby Turpin, but all of these characters reflect their author's subversion of the ideal of the docile, submissive "lady," whose motto "Pretty is as pretty does" was put to many of us who grew up as females in the twentieth-century South. The female child protagonists in both "A Temple of the Holy Ghost" and "A Circle in the Fire" enact the anger and rebellion many of us experienced as adolescents in a region in which "doing pretty" and *pleasing* our mothers and young men counted above nearly everything. Moreover, in countering the ideal of the pretty, sweet, docile female, O'Connor is in a significant way freeing herself, perhaps in the only way her situation allowed.

Many southern writers have left home, both literally and imaginatively, in order to be free. Lucinda MacKethan observes that the actual act of writing itself is often tantamount to a woman's separating herself from the familiar and the secure. In discussing the works of Catherine Hammond and Harriet Jacobs, nineteenth-century southern writers, MacKethan asserts that "language led [Hammond and Jacobs] away from the patriarch's home, toward themselves," obviously implying that such women writers could not get to themselves without such a distancing and adding that "we can view the act of writing as an act of separation, an act of leaving home" (37). The implications of these last metaphors — for a woman, writing as separation, leaving home — are serious ones when we consider that Flannery O'Connor's literal time away from home was severely curtailed because of illness. We might even conclude that O'Connor never really left home at all, for the primary relationship of her life was that with her mother.

Like Emily Dickinson, O'Connor remained a daughter in her parent's house. Barbara Mossberg writes that Dickinson "never progressed beyond her primary identity as a daughter functioning in reference to her parents: she never left home" (10). O'Connor clearly intended to leave home and had begun the process of forming strong friendships in New York and Connecticut when illness necessitated a permanent return to Milledgeville and her mother's household. From this point on, her old friendships were maintained and new ones formed primarily through correspondence. The only child, the only daughter, O'Connor may indeed have found serenity and identity only through the solitary activity of writing, a way of "leaving home" and separating herself when literal mobility and independence became impossible. O'Connor's "room" on the first floor of the farmhouse at Andalusia was certainly her own, and we sense that books and writing gave her, if not total financial independence, a measure of solvency and freedom. The fact, however, that O'Connor was actually separated from her mother only briefly is crucial to our understanding of her fiction.

Also like Emily Dickinson, O'Connor clearly rejected the values of the mother. Mossberg describes Dickinson as rejecting the masculine or patriarchal ideal of femininity and motherhood embodied in her mother; she notes that Dickinson's mother is "largely absent from her chronicles of her intellectual and spiritual life" (43) but that when the mother does appear, "it is with gentle humor as [Dickinson] records and makes fun of her mother's use of clichés: *cold as ice, like a bird, turn over a new leaf* " as she asserts "her independence and disapproval of her mother's limited mental and moral conventionality, especially regarding expectations for women which the other tries to enforce" (43). *The Habit of Being* is filled, of course, with O'Connor's own humorous depictions of Regina O'Connor, complete with O'Connor's account of actual conversational exchanges. In these letters Regina emerges as the practical businesswoman absorbed in the affairs of life on the farm and removed from the realm of literature and ideas that occupied her daughter, although we hasten to add that O'Connor's comical stories about her mother are a large part of the success of the letters. It is as though the daughter is often the straight man for the humor Regina provides; O'Connor's "gentle humor" (and when we compare the tone of these anecdotes to the fierce humor of the stories, indeed it may appear gentle) seems to be her way of distancing herself from her mother's undeniable obstinacy and domination.

As Catherine Moirai, a Milledgeville acquaintance and fellow communicant at Sacred Heart Church in the late 1950s, remembers that relationship, it was not by any means ideal: "Rather, what I remember is a tenseness. The expression I remember on Regina's face as she watched Flannery was often something I identified as impatience and irritation; Flannery usually looked withdrawn or carefully, deliberately, politely controlled. I took it for granted that there was a good bit of friction between them" (140). Moirai even considers the jokes about Regina in O'Connor's letters to be characterized by "sting" and concludes that the relationship was "mixed with some resentment" (140). She comments that reading O'Connor's letters "reminded [her] of what 'home' in the patriarchy meant . . . the loneliness, the repression, the internal and external violence," noting the difficulty of leaving home emotionally: "Most of us will be unlearning home for the rest of our lives" (146). While I hasten to add that the relationship between Flannery and Regina O'Connor cannot and should not be oversimplified, replete as it is with both affection and rebellion on the daughter's part (the only version of the relationship on record), the evidence is plain that O'Connor did use both her fiction and her letters as a means of breaking away from the parent's values, of separating herself— of "leaving home" in the only way she could. Paradoxically, however, O'Connor's fiction in many ways adopts masculinist or patriarchal values in its style, tone, and subject matter; both O'Connor's literary education and religious convictions caused her to ally herself with the very masculinist modern tradition, at the same time that some rebellion against the patriarchal view of woman is clearly evident within the fiction itself.

We should note that in the most profound sense of all, Flannery O'Connor never left her Father's house: Although we have reason to believe that O'Connor did experience moments of spiritual questioning and resistance, especially in her early years, she remained a devout Catholic, indeed a compelling apologist for the faith. Furthermore, because the patriarchal Church imposes its own set of constraints, many of which have to do with the subordination and denial of the flesh, O'Connor would seem not to have found the kind of freedom Virginia Woolf and others advocate for the woman writer. O'Connor was, after all, an apologist for a church that forbade its parishioners to read certain books on the basis of their sexual and moral content. We are, ironically enough, here reminded of Lucia's comment to Miss Willerton on the discovery of that unacceptable book in her bureau: "It was awful. . . . I burned it. . . . I was sure it couldn't be yours" (735). Here Lucia, not the Church, seems to function as the censoring agent and seems motivated by society's expectations of ladylike propriety. One could well argue, perhaps, that O'Connor never felt a lack of the kind of freedom that Woolf and others suggest is essential for the woman writer; her letters and essays, as we have noted, testify to an individual apparently secure in her beliefs. To those readers and friends who would suggest that her imaginative freedom is restrained by the Catholic Church, O'Connor would undoubtedly say, as she did in the essay "The Church and the Fiction Writer" (published in the Catholic magazine *America* in 1957), "When people have told me that because I am a Catholic, I cannot be an artist, I have had to reply, ruefully, that because I am a Catholic, I cannot afford to be less than an artist" (*Mystery and Manners* 146). "It is when the individual's faith is weak, not when it is strong, that he will be afraid of an honest fictional representation of life; and when there is a tendency to compartmentalize the spiritual and make it resident in a certain type of life only, the supernatural is apt to be lost" (*Mystery and Manners* 151).

To the Catholic audience of this essay, O'Connor argues that the Church demands O'Connor's utmost in the use of her talent and that when the spiritual becomes separate from the flesh in what she, on another occasion, terms "the Pious Style," the supernatural may be lost. We observe, however, that although she appears to be making a case for the necessary freedom of the Catholic artist, O'Connor in this same essay argues in favor of the Church's policy of censorship:

> The business of protecting souls from dangerous literature belongs properly to the Church. All fiction, even when it satisfies the requirements of art, will not turn out to be suitable for everyone's consumption, and if in some instance the Church sees fit to forbid the faithful to read a work without permission, the author, if he is a Catholic, will be thankful that the Church is willing to perform this service for him. It means that he can limit himself to the demands of art. (*Mystery and Manners* 149)

Clearly O'Connor is walking a fine line here, arguing that the Catholic writer must describe "truthfully what he sees from where he is" (*Mystery and Manners* 150), that only those of weak faith will be fearful of "an honest fictional representation of life" (151) and, on the other hand, that the Church provides a real service for the Catholic writer (and, of course, any Catholic reader) by determining which works of literature are fit for her "consumption." Furthermore, O'Connor argues that the writer should be grateful for such a service. Although we acknowledge that one of O'Connor's aims in this essay is certainly to admonish Catholic readers about their lack of the "fundamental equipment" necessary for reading some kinds of literature (151), we may be awed, if not dismayed, by O'Connor's confident support of the Church's power to censor. We may be equally dismayed by her willingness to allow the Church (an institution governed, we are to assume, by individuals who do possess the "fundamental equipment" necessary for sophisticated reading) to restrain the artist's freedom to explore, at least inasmuch as freedom to read what she pleases is essential to that freedom of exploration. O'Connor, incidentally, was thirty-two years old when "The Church and the Fiction Writer" was published. We may stand in awe of her authority at this age; we may be appalled by it.

In this consideration of O'Connor's own attitude toward artistic freedom, we should not forget Miss Willerton. Unlike later and more characteristic efforts, "The Crop" contains no overt religious theme. Furthermore, the conclusions of "The Church and the Fiction Writer" come some ten years after O'Connor's thesis stories, perhaps suggesting that O'Connor's commitment as a Christian writer was not fully established at the time of her graduate study. Sally Fitzgerald notes in an interview in 1996 that through her recent access to a notebook O'Connor kept when she was eighteen, she believes that O'Connor at that time had a sense of herself as a person with "a particular destiny" and that she then "began to understand her vocation" ("An Interview with Sally Fitzgerald" 9). That vocation as a Christian writer, however, is certainly not evident in the thesis stories, with the possible exception of "The Turkey." Miss Willerton's problems as a writer, exaggerated and frivolous as they may appear, are not resolved by the Church's doctrine, the intervention of the supernatural, or the humbling of the protagonist as she recognizes her mortal frailty. Thus in a sense this story provides us with an unusual glimpse of O'Connor in that it outlines in comic fashion only the dilemma of the female artist, specifically with regard to her subject matter; O'Connor does not imply a solution, although she suggests that Miss Willerton's inability to understand either what she reads or what she experiences is a major stumbling block. The limitations of her sensibility appear related to her limited experience and to her idealization of writers deriving from that limited experience. Of course, the question is which comes first, limited sensibility or limited experience? I suspect that O'Connor herself saw Miss Willerton largely in terms of an innately limited sensibility, perhaps an ultimately impenetrable obtuseness. That view is consonant with the writings of the "mature" O'Connor, who as a Christian writer holds that our limited, mortal natures are our downfall. Joy/Hulga in "Good Country People," Asbury in "The Enduring Chill," and Thomas in "The Comforts of Home" are surely Miss Willerton's mortal relatives. To see these and other O'Connor characters as of the family of sinners is to read O'Connor as she has been read by many very discerning critics, who often relate the theme of human frailty in the master's thesis stories to the emphasis on original sin in the work of the more mature writer.

On the other hand, to read Miss Willerton's limitations as at least partly the result of her status as unmarried woman in a society that devalues and even ridicules the unmarried female is also possible. The story certainly testifies to the marginal experience of this unmarried woman, as well as demonstrating O'Connor's own internalizing of the scorn directed at such a marginal and ultimately "useless" existence. Yet—after the laughter subsides — serious questions about woman as writer remain, and O'Connor raises these questions. I believe that in creating Miss Willerton, O'Connor at least unconsciously acknowledges her own limitation of experience and therefore her own likely difficulties as an aspiring woman writer. Forster's condemnation of Woolf is again appropriate here; for Forster, Woolf's writing lacked a "great cause."

One imagines that Henry James's advice to the writer to "be one of the people on whom nothing is lost" has limited meaning for women, whose lack of exposure to the world beyond the domestic has certainly circumscribed their experience. Although James has previously stated that the young woman living in a village "has only to be a damsel upon whom nothing is lost to make it quite unfair (as it seems to me) to declare to her that she shall have nothing to say about the military" (1478), James seems unable to understand the traditional constraints of women writers. These women, after all, have until very recently had severe problems with subject matter because they have been denied access to the realms of politics, world affairs, and education. Perhaps most damaging of all, because their work was frequently concerned with the domestic, it was often dismissed as trivial. Even Miss Willerton recognizes the problem when, near the end of the story, she contemplates the women in the grocery store and their limited lives:

> Silly that a grocery should depress one — nothing in it but trifling domestic doings — women buying beans — riding children in those grocery go-carts — higgling about an eighth of a pound more or less of squash — what did they get out of it? Miss Willerton wondered. Where was there any chance for self-expression, for creation, for art? All around her it was the same — sidewalks full of people scurrying about with their hands full of little packages and their minds full of little packages — that woman there with the child on the leash, pulling him, jerking him, dragging him away from a window with a jack-o-lantern in it; she would probably be pulling and jerking him the rest of her life. And there was another, dropping a shopping bag all over the street, and another wiping a child's nose, and up the street an old woman was coming with three grandchildren jumping all over her, and behind them was a couple walking too close for refinement. (*O'Connor* 740)

While O'Connor is obviously having fun here with Miss Willerton's superiority and condescension to the lives of ordinary women (note that the "people" in the street are mostly female, or so Miss Willerton perceives the scene), she also acknowledges, albeit in caricature, the problems for the woman writer described by Woolf and others early in the century. We might say that O'Connor is poking fun at Miss Willerton's assimilation of the ideas of feminists like Virginia Woolf, while indirectly acknowledging, in the thematic emphasis of the total story, the truth of those ideas. Although critics such as John May, Carter Martin, and Frederick Asals point out that "The Crop" is "a thoroughly delightful spoof of the pitfalls of the creative writer" (May 29), none of these critics treats the story as a depiction of the distinct dilemma of the writer who is female. Yet how can we overlook the fact of femaleness here?

O'Connor grew up in a largely matriarchal, protective society. As accounts of her early years in Savannah attest, O'Connor's childhood was for the most part spent in the company of female relatives. Even though she attended parochial school and associated primarily with children from Irish Catholic families in Savannah, her mother carefully supervised her playmates. According to one perhaps apocryphal report, Mrs. O'Connor kept a list of approved playmates and on at least one occasion sent a child home who was not on that list. Although the young O'Connor enjoyed a very close and loving relationship with her father, his employment difficulties and, later, his illness and premature death ensured that Regina O'Connor would be the dominant adult in O'Connor's adolescence. Furthermore, the Cline house in Milledgeville, where O'Connor spent her high school and college years, was, after the father's death, essentially a female household, consisting of O'Connor, her mother, and several aunts. Peabody Laboratory School (her high school) was female, as was Georgia State College for Women, from which O'Connor graduated in 1945. Surely O'Connor, well apprised of the expectations for white women in her society, was acutely aware of the courage that would be necessary for any woman who determined to be a writer. As Catherine Moirai put it,

> "Pretty is as pretty does" was one of my grandmother's expressions, and I heard it often. . . . Like most girls being reared to be middle-class ladies, I learned the lesson that expression encapsulated: a lady never causes a disturbance, raises her voice, or is conspicuous in any way; the best way to do anything is quietly and politely. (133)

The woman writer, however, is almost obligated to rebel against such quietness and politeness, and she must be willing, if necessary, to cause a disturbance.

Louise Westling, Lucinda MacKethan, and others have specifically applied the conclusions of Sandra Gilbert and Susan Gubar to the southern locale in describing the sheer gall required of a woman who genuinely wishes to be a writer; that is to say, a woman who wishes to control her own text. The respectable southern white woman, as we have mentioned, is controlled by a script that calls for her submission to the ideal of southern womanhood, an ideal that does not include the freedom to think for herself, to imagine other worlds, to set about inscribing those worlds. Flannery O'Connor absorbed that milieu and grappled with it in "The Crop," a story that can be read, to say the least, as subversive of niceness and propriety. And in this instance, she subverts the conventional without recourse to the teachings of the Church. We may need to be reminded, also, that this story was written at the same time that she was working on *Wise Blood*, a fact that O'Connor believed accounted for the weakness of "The Crop." To be sure, *Wise Blood*, with its male protagonist and obviously Christian themes, would seem a far cry from the concerns of "The Crop," yet the drafts of *Wise Blood* suggest that O'Connor was intensely involved in questions of femaleness as she worked on the novel as well.

In "The Crop," then, O'Connor is defining for herself what a woman writer is by delineating what she is not or cannot be. This effete, finicky woman, who cannot face reality—warts and all—is no artist. We are amused by the apparent fastidiousness of a "writer" who has yet to write the first scene of passion (there is no indication that she has actually *written* anything beyond the first three sentences), and we may suspect that her hesitation has a great deal to do with her own inability to deal with the realities of the flesh. On her trip to the store, for example, Miss Willerton makes note of the couple walking "too close for refinement." Earlier, the account of childbirth in her fantasy demonstrates real naiveté and is clearly intended to point up her foolishness. Willie, who has become the character in her own story, awakens with what she describes as "a soft, green pain with purple lights running through it" and "her head rolled from side to side and there were droning shapes grinding boulders in it" (738). The pain of childbirth, apparently something like a bad headache, is increasingly mingled with the "drone," which turns out to be the sound of raindrops, a fact that Willie recognizes just as she is delivered of a daughter. Miss Willerton's aversion to the reality of the physical is clearly demonstrated in the end of the story when she is confronted by her characters in the flesh (fat ankles, mottled skin, stooped shoulders, and all) and can only be repelled: "'Ugh,' she shuddered" (740). If we continue to read this story somewhat autobiographically — or at least as O'Connor the youthful writer facing her own situation — we may conclude that Miss Willerton's simultaneous attraction to and repulsion from matters of the physical in some measure reflect O'Connor's own conflict. That conflict was common among women writers of the mid-twentieth century, given the misogyny of the literary establishment and the understandable ambivalence of the woman writer. I shall have more to say about this in a later chapter.

Eudora Welty's story "A Memory," included in her 1941 collection, *A Curtain of Green*, is remarkably similar to "The Crop" in its thematic concerns. The first-person narrator of Welty's story is clearly the young artist coming to terms with the disparity between her dreams and reality. Acknowledging that "[e]ver since I had begun taking painting lessons, I had made small frames with my fingers, to look out at everything" (75), the narrator forms judgments about everything, and whenever a "person, or a happening, seemed to me not in keeping with my opinion, I was terrified by a vision of abandonment and wildness which tore my heart with a kind of sorrow" (75). The intrusion of inescapable reality strikes her most excruciatingly when the young man on whom her heart has rested has a nosebleed: "I remember with exact clarity the day in Latin class when the boy I loved (whom I watched constantly) bent suddenly over and brought his handkerchief to his face. I saw red — vermilion — blood flow over the handkerchief and his square-shaped hand; his nose had begun to bleed" (75). This moment precipitates her concern that her lover's house "might be slovenly and unpainted, hidden by tall trees, that his mother and father might be shabby — dishonest — crippled — dead" (76). On another occasion this fastidious apprentice-artist visits the beach and is quietly horrified by a family of "common" people, who "wore old and faded bathing suits which did not hide either the energy or the fatigue of their bodies, but showed it exactly" (77). The reality of their appearance and their actions appalls the girl: "I saw the man lift his hand filled with crumbling sand, shaking it as the woman laughed, and pour it down inside her bathing suit between her bulbous descending breasts. There it hung, brown and shapeless, making them all laugh" (78).

Welty effectively juxtaposes the young girl's idealistic fantasy about her boyfriend with the vulgar antics of the family on the beach to point up the inevitable compromises we as individuals and artists have to make: "Once when I looked up, the fat woman was standing opposite the smiling man. She bent over and in a condescending way pulled down the front of her bathing suit, turning it outward, so that the lumps of mashed and folded sand came emptying out. I felt a peak of horror, as though her breasts themselves had turned to sand, as though they were of no importance at all and she did not care" (79). This story is clearly an important predecessor of "The Crop," whether O'Connor knew the work or not. O'Connor does state in a 1955 letter to "A" that in graduate school in Iowa she read "the best southern writers like Faulkner and the Tates, K. A. Porter, Eudora Welty and Peter Taylor" (*Habit of Being* 98). It seems likely that O'Connor read *A Curtain of Green*, Welty's first published work. "The Crop" might then be viewed as a response to Welty's story, especially to its overwhelming lyricism. Like Miss Willerton, the young narrator/artist in "A Memory" has grave difficulty accepting the world in all its power and ugliness: "I saw that they were all resigned to each other's daring and ugliness" (78). She, of course, resolves never to be so resigned.

Matters of sexuality also figure in both stories, although, as I have indicated, Welty only suggests the girl's dilemma in accepting fleshly reality. In O'Connor's story, the tone of which is markedly satiric rather than gracefully suggestive of the conflict, she presents a "grown-up" version of Welty's adolescent artist. O'Connor implies the need for tough-mindedness, an outlook only hinted at by Welty. Although Miss Willerton wants to write of a relationship between the sexes, certainly a great part of the essence of real life, she is unable to, for several reasons. First, as we have seen, she fears actually writing about passion. Second, she becomes so much a part of her own plot that it amounts to little more than wish-fulfillment of a very idealized sort. Finally, when she encounters in the grocery store the very characters she has created, she is repelled by them. "The Crop" can therefore be read as (albeit playful) self-mockery, serving as a kind of objectification of many of the uncertainties O'Connor herself felt in her decision to be a writer. In this connection, we may find that Miss Willerton's nickname, Willie (sometimes in the drafts spelled Willy), not only mocks Miss Willerton's lack of will but also suggests those androgynous names which many aspiring women writers throughout history and especially in the nineteenth century adopted in order to hide their femaleness from male publishers' discriminating eyes. Interestingly enough, in one of the drafts of "The Crop," O'Connor allows her character, here named Miss Medger, to consider using a pseudonym:

> This novel was a terrific thing. She really didn't know, if it got published, what her friends would say to her. They were all in it. What she had decided to do was use a pen name. Medger was not a good name for a novelist — particularly Edith wasn't, which was her first name. What she really thought about doing was to use a man's name[.] Hilary & Ralph were her two favorite names — she didn't know whether she would use Ralph Hilary or Hilery [sic] Ralph. The first was more normal sounding but the more she thought about it, the more she really thought the other would be better. (Collection 15a, 2)

Here the writer's concern seems to be with her friends' opinions of what she will write; she will not reveal that she is the author of "Swept from the Heart" (15a, 3), a title certainly suggestive of inappropriate subject matter for a woman author in the 1940s.

At least two of O'Connor's own undergraduate efforts were signed with pseudonyms (the silly female names of "Jane Shorebanks" and "Gertrude Beachlock," as found in folders 4b and 4c in the O'Connor Collection), indicating, at the least, the author's early name-consciousness. Moreover, Sally Fitzgerald notes that in 1942 O'Connor dropped her first name, Mary, on her college assignments (*O'Connor* 1239). Her work in the *Corinthian*, the college literary magazine, was signed "M. F. O'Connor," an act that certainly suggests O'Connor's intention to resist the feminizing and softening associated with the southern tradition of double names for girls. Despite its euphonious lilt, "Mary Flannery" is hardly a name that would connote strength and authority or lend itself to a book jacket. I believe that, in giving herself a new name, O'Connor was in a certain measure creating a new self, her own text, and claiming her own territory, one apart from the scripted one for dutiful southern daughters. And in typical O'Connor fashion, she is not above mocking her own action in "Good Country People," in which Joy changes her name to "Hulga" to spite her mother. Significantly, just as Mrs. Hopewell agonizes that Joy is a "poor stout girl in her thirties who [has] never danced a step or had any *normal* good times," Mrs. Hopewell thinks that Joy has deliberately chosen "the ugliest name in any language"; indeed, whenever she thinks of the name, she pictures "the broad blank hull of a battleship" (*O'Connor* 266). The name, therefore, is clearly associated in Mrs. Hopewell's mind with her daughter's rebellion against "normal" good times. For her part, Joy/Hulga is obviously aware of her rebellion; she views the name Hulga "as the name of her highest creative act" and is gratified that the change of name has prevented her mother from turning "her dust into Joy" (267). In accordance with the less-than-pleasing, less-than-feminine sound of the name, Joy dresses "in a six-year-old skirt and a yellow sweat shirt with a faded cowboy embossed on it" and, much to Mrs. Hopewell's chagrin, she appears amused by her own get-up. From Mrs. Hopewell's point of view, each year Joy "grew less like other people and more like herself—bloated, rude, and squint-eyed" (268).

"Good Country People," which at its center is a mockery of the archetypal comedy of seduction, is as close as O'Connor ever comes to treating sexual passion directly; it contains the most moving, though brief, treatment of passion to be found in her published fiction. Furthermore, much of the success of that treatment depends upon O'Connor's harshly satirical portrait of southern womanhood. It is as though O'Connor by this time has determined that the flesh — including matters of passion — that both attracted and repelled Miss Willerton can best be dealt with in terms of relentless satire and the blackest of humor. As I will suggest later, O'Connor's attitude toward female sexuality is an adoption of the male modernist position into which she was educated by the powerful academic and spiritual institutions of the patriarchy.

Clearly, Joy/Hulga's rebellion is against her own mother and all that she stands for. Glynese and Carramae, Mrs. Freeman's two "normal" daughters, become "Glycerin" and "Caramel" to Joy/Hulga, who is obviously weary of her mother's use of these girls to point up her daughter's failure to have "normal" good times, although she is also perversely fascinated by Mrs. Freeman's morning reports of her daughters' activities. For Joy/Hulga, rebellion against the scripted behavior for "normal" females has several sources: her sense of physical unattractiveness as the result of the wooden leg, her feeling that her mother has not really confronted her physical deformity (she is not "normal"), and her belief that her own superior intellect elevates her above others' conventional beliefs and expectations. Furthermore, we suspect that her cultivation of the intellect and her pride in it may be compensatory for all that she has suffered as the result of her deformity. Thus, when the Bible salesman appears to be interested in her, she is ambivalent. She is secretly pleased at the prospect of this date, perhaps flattered by the attention she is receiving, and simultaneously contemptuous of Manley Pointer's narrow mind and limited outlook. She plans to seduce him (thus maintaining control of the script and again mocking traditional expectations of appropriate behavior for a lady), exulting in the fact that, afterward, she will have to contend with his Christian remorse. Of course, Joy/Hulga receives her comeuppance. The passionate feelings she experiences for the first time in her life lead her to lose control and to be willing to reveal to Manley Pointer that most fragile and intimate part of herself, the "secret" of her wooden leg's connection.

The Bible salesman's name certainly suggests his sexuality and at least one way that the encounter with him is to be significant to Joy/Hulga: the reminder that she is flesh and that she is capable of losing control. Through the fact of her femaleness, then, Joy/Hulga is opened to the fact of her creatureliness and to the possibility for change, a recognition essential to O'Connor's Christian emphasis on the need for conversion. However, without denying O'Connor's conscious intention as a Catholic writer, Louise Westling asserts that O'Connor often uses female characters whose autonomy is "continually punished by masculine assaults" (172) and that, especially in the "complex and troubling presentation of mothers and daughters in the farm stories," she "has inadvertently presented a poignant and often excruciating picture of the problems these women have in living together, of female self-loathing, powerlessness, and justified fear of masculine attack" (174). If we consider O'Connor's place in twentieth-century literary history, however, her attacks on female culture should not be surprising.

In their brilliant collaborative analysis of the twentieth-century woman writer, Sandra Gilbert and Susan Gubar establish the difficult place of that writer as she finds herself in a culture dominated by the male modernist fear of the female, especially as the suffrage movement and related social changes empowered woman to consider herself man's equal. Such influential figures as Ezra Pound, T. S. Eliot, D. H. Lawrence, Wyndham Lewis, James Joyce, Ernest Hemingway, and William Faulkner consistently express revulsion at female power and often retreat to the dark, destructive stereotypes of the femme fatale, capable of paralyzing, if not annihilating, male creativity. Gilbert and Gubar cite the misogyny of such works as Eliot's early unpublished poem "The Love Song of St. Sebastian," which prefigures the "far more subdued" hostility toward the female of "The Love Song of J. Alfred Prufrock" and *The Waste Land*, Lawrence's *Women in Love*, Faulkner's *Light in August*, and Hemingway's "The Short Happy Life of Francis Macomber," to assert that modernism was not just a reaction to "the grain of Victorian male precursors, not just in the shadow of a shattered God, but . . . an integral . . . complex response to female precursors and contemporaries" (*War of the Words* 156). Postmodernist writers also established "their artistic integrity in opposition to either the literary incompetence or the aesthetic hysteria they associated with women" (157).

The presence of women writers in the public eye from the nineteenth into the first decades of the twentieth century created such fear and loathing on the part of the powerful male literary establishment that their works are pervaded by satiric attacks on and mockery of "the ladies." In *The Adventures of Huckleberry Finn*, Mark Twain's humorously satirical treatment of Emmeline Grangerford, that tender, young, nauseatingly sentimental poetess, is a case in point. Her silly "mortuary" verse, ground out "with fatal fluency," is certainly one of the comic high points of the novel (*War of the Words* 144). The tradition of literature in English, then, privileged and honored the male with access to education and to powerful economic and political institutions, reflecting his necessary concern with matters of ultimate urgency and importance. Gilbert and Gubar assert that in literary criticism and literary education the resonant voices of Eliot, Lawrence, and the New Critics—John Crowe Ransom, Allen Tate, and Robert Penn Warren, among others—established a kind of invisible fencing whereby women's voices and women's experience were excluded. The breadth of evidence provided by these feminist critics is convincing; their argument, persuasive.

Most significantly, perhaps, Gilbert and Gubar posit that women writers' responses to their place in literary history in the first half of our century may be described by a Freudian model. Citing Freud's 1931 essay "Female Sexuality," they remind us of the three paths of development a growing girl may follow as she "confronts the fact of her femininity" (*War of the Words* 167): She may completely turn her back on sexuality, in fear of being compared to the male; she may "cling in obstinate self-assertion to her threatened masculinity," this "'masculinity complex' [resulting] in a manifestly homosexual object-choice"; or she may "arrive at the ultimate normal feminine attitude in which she takes her father as love-object, and thus arrives at the Oedipus complex in its feminine form" (Freud qtd. in *War of the Words* 168). In literary terms, therefore, the struggle with what Gilbert and Gubar call "the female affiliation complex" in the woman writer is central to her development as she vacillates between matrilineage and patrilineage (168). For Freud, of course, the healthiest response is the third-named possibility. Although Gilbert and Gubar would obviously question the "health" and desirability of the third-named choice, they acknowledge that "for Freud, clearly, the appropriate female developmental strategy entails a repression of the 'pre-Oedipal' desire for the mother and an elaboration of the wish for the phallus (which possesses the mother) into a desire for the father, the man who possesses the phallus (and hence the mother)" (169). Nineteenth-century women writers for the most part employed this strategy, writing in interaction with the male tradition. Such writers as Maria Edgeworth, Charlotte Brontë, George Eliot, and Emily Dickinson, according to Gilbert and Gubar, embody this "revisionary erotic transference" and in their careers did battle with "the master-muse, even as they sought an invasion of his influence" (169–70).

However, in the twentieth century, a "paradigm of ambivalent affiliation" developed, emphasizing the "intertwined attitudes of anxiety and exuberance about creativity" on the part of the woman writer (*War of the Words* 170). The dilemma of the twentieth-century woman writer is a complicated one, in which she must confront the fact of the newly emerging maternal tradition and affiliate with that or affiliate with the paternal tradition. She is often understandably ambivalent toward both traditions, and the most "mature" move that Freud described—her move toward desire for the power and authority of the father—was problematic. As Gilbert and Gubar assert, the healthy or "mature" move toward the father "sometimes becomes in our own era a vexed, nostalgic, and guilt-ridden service to sustain his name and fame, sometimes becomes an unpremeditated usurpation of his primacy, and sometimes becomes a fearful and guilty propitiation of his outraged authority" (171). They even suggest that Freud's setting up the daughter's return to the father as "normative" may be viewed as his effort to bolster the patriarchal family in view of the appearance of the "New Woman" and to counter cultural instability caused by newly empowered intellectual women (180). Be that as it may, the Freudian construct seems a credible way of presenting the women writer's choices in the aftermath of the "New Woman," the suffrage movement, and the increase in the numbers of women writers and the knowledge about them.

For such writers as Gertrude Stein, Renée Vivien, Djuna Barnes, and Radclyffe Hall, the need to connect with the matrilineal tradition, though sometimes complicated by their attacks on what they considered the triviality of much "women's fiction," is evident. Certainly the undisguised lesbianism of all of these writers would ally them with Freud's second possible course of development, the girl's clinging to her "threatened masculinity." Gilbert and Gubar argue that these writers "liberate aesthetic energy" by "recovering and reconstituting the child's primordial, pre-Oedipal desire for the mother as an inspiring eroticism" (186). The case of other writers is less easily described, although Gilbert and Gubar are convinced that Virginia Woolf, more than any other modernist writer, presents the "problems and possibilities of matrilineal (literary) affiliation" (196). In Woolf's "deliberately imprudent and impudent essay" entitled "Indiscretions," these critics find an account of

> the multiple binds in which the twentieth-century woman writer feels herself to be caught when she confronts the new reality of her female literary inheritance. First, she sees the pain her precursors experienced and wishes to renounce it: to become a woman writer may be, she fears, to become an invisible star in male sunshine—to be, in other words, marginalized, dispossessed, alienated; or, worse, it may be to sniff and bicker—that is, to become a jealous neurotic or even a madwoman. In addition, though, she acknowledges the power her precursors achieved and worries that she may not be able to equal it: to become a woman writer may be to have to find a way of coming to terms with the accomplishments of other women writers. Finally, however, she fears the consequences of both renunciation and rivalry: to renounce her precursors' pain or to refuse to try to rival them may be to relinquish the originatory authority their achievements represent and to isolate oneself forever in the secondary and belated position of the voyeur. (*War of the Words* 198–99)

At the risk of belaboring Gilbert and Gubar's analysis and, simultaneously, of oversimplifying their rich and complex argument, I find their insights into the outlook of the twentieth-century woman writer instructive as I seek to understand the choices Flannery O'Connor made as a writer. Obviously O'Connor did not embrace the matrilineal tradition, either in literature or in life; instead, she appears to have followed the route that Freud (not Gilbert and Gubar) describes as normative: that of embracing the male tradition, taking the father, as it were, as love object. "The Crop" therefore may be viewed as O'Connor's condemnation of the woman writer who seems to trivialize her literary ambition because she is so repelled by reality that she can only seek escape in another fantasy. Miss Willerton is another version of Emmeline Grangerford, whose feminine sensibility is mocked by Mark Twain. O'Connor, in other words, seems as imbued with the threat of the female, of those "scribbling women" decried by Hawthorne, as her male predecessors and models. She mocks the trivial and trivializing Miss Willerton and, in so doing, challenges herself to embrace the father in order to assume his authority and his power. This stance reveals at least an unconscious decision that, I believe, accounts for the disturbing quality of O'Connor's fiction — that is to say, the toughness of the narrative style and subject matter and the boldness of the vision. We should not be surprised that O'Connor so closely allies herself with male masters — T. S. Eliot, Nathanael West, and James Joyce, for example.[3] They become her models and the source of her authority, even as she dismisses the work of Erskine Caldwell, judged by the critical establishment to be, at best, second-rate. Moreover, O'Connor's profound commitment as a Christian writer, evident in her mature work, is based in large measure on the strongly misogynistic tradition of the Roman Catholic Church; in this important part of her life, O'Connor also embraces the authority of the "father."

I believe that the need to establish her own textual territory apart from the expectations of appropriate female behavior and to assume the authority and power of the patrilineal inheritance was crucial for O'Connor and that, at the same time, she intended her mature fiction to reflect the Christian emphasis on humanity's fallen nature, the need for belief. One may wonder, however, if it is possible for a writer both to seek authority and control over her own text — creating in O'Connor's case a deliberately harsh and punishing realm where ugliness seems a matter of course — and to seek to demonstrate within that fiction the foolishness of just such attempts at attaining power and control? Does O'Connor not repeatedly demonstrate in her fiction that those who separate themselves from Hawthorne's "magnetic chain of humanity," desiring desperately to be in control (in her own case, to assume the authority of the father), risk damnation for their arrogant and often manipulative behavior? Joy/Hulga, Asbury, Mrs. McIntyre, Ruby Turpin, Julian, the grandmother, Mrs. Cope, Sheppard — these and many other O'Connor characters run such a risk, as, by extension, does O'Connor herself.

Therefore, the conflict between O'Connor's own situation as a southern white woman who — though she wanted to leave home to write and thereby create her own territory apart from conventional social expectations and in so doing to reject the matrilineal in favor of the power and authority of the patrilineal — could not leave home, and her strong belief that her art must be used in the service of her faith is, I believe, largely responsible for the shape and content as well as the tension of her fiction. In fact, O'Connor's large and startling figures are to some extent the measure of the conflict within the artist who sought to control her text as a means of asserting her power through alliance with the patrilineal, of moving away from the nice and the pretty, all the while, of course, dramatizing, in her fictional territory, the limits of such power. Unlike Miss Willerton, O'Connor will not shudder when she looks at the mottled skin and fat ankles of people in the real world; instead, she will incorporate those details and much more that is ungainly, unexpected — even grotesque — into her fiction. Thus her Christian vision will be manifested in a distinctive and bold style that some readers still consider shocking and perhaps inappropriate for a woman writer.

O'Connor creates a language for a universe filled with shrunken objects, smelling remarkably like a chicken coop. — Josephine Hendin, *The World of Flannery O'Connor*

Meanwhile, I have hit on a new approach to the works of Chanda Bell. I am trying to read them sideways. — James Thurber, "A Final Note on Chanda Bell," in *Thurber Country*

2 The Case of the Fierce Narrator

Since the publication of O'Connor's first book, *Wise Blood* (1952), many critics and reviewers have been stymied by the severity of O'Connor's vision and have repeatedly addressed the matter of style. Nearly every critical approach — biographical, psychological, feminist, deconstructionist, or Bakhtinian — has been used to account for O'Connor's relentlessly harsh vision. If we are not reading the works of O'Connor sideways, we appear to be coming close to it. Style, of course, must be understood as a far more encompassing matter than Miss Willerton's idea of what is pleasing and euphonious in the choice and arrangement of words on the page. In point of fact, literary theorists today would question any discussion of style that does not consider such questions as narrative reliability, mimesis and diegesis, dialogue, and structure and arrangement.

The elusive matter of style has elicited copious commentary of late. British critic David Lodge, for example, espouses Bakhtin's idea that "there is no such thing as *the* style, *the* language of a novel, because a novel is a medley of many styles, many languages — or, if you like, voices" (6). How, then, can we generalize at all about a writer's style? Must we forgo the custom of alluding to characteristic styles — Dickensian, Chekhovian, Faulknerian, for example?

Without attempting to summarize the many sides of the current critical debate, I believe that, at the very least, we can agree that just as Faulkner's and Hemingway's fictive worlds are inseparable from what traditional critics might have termed the fullness or leanness of their respective strategies, so O'Connor's fiction is often accepted or rejected on the basis of a reader's response to the harshness of her presentation. In his astute introduction to *Critical Essays on Flannery O'Connor* (1985), Melvin J. Friedman, one of the earliest students of O'Connor's work, puts a positive gloss on the matter: "[O'Connor's] lean, understated prose offers a determined stylistic accompaniment to her grim, Augustinian faith" (2). Although we may not agree that O'Connor's prose is understated, Friedman's view is typical of the most common approach to O'Connor's style to date — namely, that the finely honed sentences conveying an often unflinchingly brutal view of reality serve primarily as the means of conveying O'Connor's faith through her fiction. In this way of thinking, form follows content, which follows intent. Critics using this line of argument invariably quote at length from O'Connor's essays, lectures, and letters to demonstrate that she consciously intended the stringent style and wildly unconventional plots to jolt a numbed, secular audience out of its complacency and unbelief and to offer the possibility of the soul's confrontation with limitation as a necessary first step to conversion. Anticipated by the work of such early critics as Carter Martin, John May, Kathleen Feeley, Gilbert Muller, and Marion Montgomery, the best examples from the abundance of O'Connor criticism are the works of Ralph C. Wood, Edward Kessler, John Desmond, Brian Abel Ragen, Richard Giannone, and

Robert Brinkmeyer. Sally Fitzgerald remains, of course, the most powerful advocate of an unequivocally Catholic reading of the fiction. Clearly such critics must walk a fine line to avoid treating fiction as dogma or polemic or even as message-centered, for underscoring message or arguing dogma might well suggest O'Connor's weakness as an artist.

While the theological approach has dominated O'Connor scholarship, more secular critics—not all of whom, incidentally, are antithetical to O'Connor's theology—have taken upon themselves the task of demonstrating that O'Connor's art is indeed art, not homiletic. In so doing, they have tended to focus on the author's ability to tell a story, citing her debt to the southern storytelling tradition in general and to the southwest humorists in particular. Furthermore, in the tradition of the late lamented New Critics, they comment on such matters as structural arrangement, character development, and symbolic unity to assert the integrity of the story *as story*. At the 1977 O'Connor symposium at Georgia College, Louis D. Rubin Jr. stunned some in the audience by reading a paper entitled "Flannery O'Connor's Company of Southerners; or, 'The Artificial Nigger' Read as Fiction Rather than Theology," a clear attempt to rescue the story and O'Connor's fiction in general from those who would use it, in Rubin's words, "as a weapon for belaboring the heathen" (47). Concerned that "[t]here has grown up in recent years a kind of cult, made up principally of well-bred young acolytes who regret the fall of Richmond in 1865 and the fall of Man some years earlier than that," Rubin proceeded to demonstrate that O'Connor's knowledge of the "Georgia plain folk" is as essential to her fiction as her theology is essential (47). That Rubin, one of the foremost critics of southern literature, felt compelled to take so blunt a stand testifies to the extent of the critical dilemma twenty years ago.

Today the controversy has not abated. From the early sixties to the present time, readers resistant to the theological readings—in varying degrees of objection to such readings—include John Hawkes, Josephine Hendin, Martha Stephens, Claire Katz Kahane, Carol Shloss, and Clara Claiborne Park. Hawkes's early essay "Flannery O'Connor's Devil" (1962) in many ways anticipated later approaches in his assertion that O'Connor's use of symbol and image is "mildly perverse" and that "the other side of [O'Connor's] imagination," that is to say, "the demonic" (405), enables her to escape the bonds of "a constraining realism" (398). Although Hawkes, a friend of O'Connor, admits that she sharply disagreed with his reading, he argues that just as the creative process threatens the Holy throughout Flannery O'Connor's fiction by generating a paradoxical fusion of improbability and passion out of the Protestant "do-it-yourself" evangelism of the South, and thereby raises the pitch of apocalyptic experience when it finally appears; so too, throughout this fiction, the creative process transforms the writer's objective Catholic knowledge of the devil into an authorial attitude in itself some measure diabolical. (400–401)

Noteworthy in this statement, of course, is the assumption that the author's creative talent in a sense takes over her theological function, perhaps not to edge it out of the picture but at least to transform theological intent to its opposite number. Of course, Hawkes makes no distinction between the author of the stories and the narrative voice; they are, in his treatment, one and the same. Hawkes's controversial essay is also significant for its focus on the relationship of style — apparently defined by Hawkes as the total effect of O'Connor's world as it is crafted in sentence, word choice, image, metaphor, symbol — to O'Connor's vision. For example, intending a compliment, Hawkes writes, "Certainly Flannery O'Connor reveals what can only be called brilliant creative perversity when she brings to life a denuded *actuality* and writes about a 'cat-faced baby' or a confidence man with 'an honest look that fitted into his face like a set of false teeth' or an automobile horn that makes 'a sound like a goat's laugh cut off with a buzz saw.' This much, I should think, is happily on the side of the devil" (406). Setting aside for a time the fact that the author was evidently not complimented, we observe that Hawkes's statement has in common with the most recent O'Connor commentary the matter of the rhetorical sharpness or, more precisely, the nearly unremitting ugliness of the world O'Connor presents, her "denuded *actuality.*" Following Hawkes's lead, the latest commentary has employed the newest, most fashionable critical tools, such as those of psychoanalytical criticism, deconstruction, feminism, and reader response, to cope with narrative style. Starting from an essentially secular base, Hendin, Stephens, Asals, Shloss, Kahane, Westling, Park, and Bleikasten are among the commentators applying these diverse approaches to confront what Kahane has called the "rage" of O'Connor's vision.

In a lengthy feature essay in a 1990 *New York Review of Books*, Frederick Crews presents a broad survey of the abundance of O'Connor commentary to date, his only significant omission being the work of any of the feminist critics. Despite that omission, Crews's essay is for the most part a cogent evaluation of the history and current status of the criticism, including some of the "new" methodology. When we remember that Crews is the author of *The Pooh Perplex,* an early satirical slashing of the literary establishment and a book of which O'Connor was quite fond, we are not surprised to find in this review a strong indictment of academe's propensity to answer questions of textual difficulty by means of a new methodology. Crews writes,

> Academic second thoughts about O'Connor already appear to be astir, although, curiously, it is her would-be protectors who chiefly manifest them. Here and there, one notices, her penchant for settled judgments is being treated as a worrisome problem. But today, no less than in the prime of the New Criticism, the professorial instinct when a difficulty looms is not to face it squarely but to reach for a methodological wand that can make it disappear. In the Fifties that protective principle was "organic unity" or "ironic vision"; now it is some form of deconstructive loosening whereby the offensive content can be represented as neutralized or altogether negated by subversive textual forces. (49)

Certainly Crews's point is well taken, and I myself might indeed qualify as one of the "would-be protectors," one who, to Crews's way of thinking, might be altogether too eager to find that cure-all theory which will wash my doubts away or, at the very least, give words to, provide language for, my misgivings about the text. In my own work with O'Connor readers over the years, I have continued to hear doubt and misgiving expressed, often enough by high school and university teachers who must contend with the O'Connor texts in a quotidian context, year in and year out. Most of the problems, as I have indicated, concern the harshness of the world O'Connor presents and the compatibility of that worldview with traditional Christian or Catholic teaching. Thus, who can blame the theorists or their proponents for hoping that theirs is the explanation that will ultimately satisfy us all, if not thereby to erase the mystery, at least to describe it more precisely? Who can fault the simple urge to understand, even though that urge for understanding demands constant rereading, rethinking, and reformulating?

Crews is correct in reminding us that O'Connor herself would be more than mildly amused at our critical shenanigans. I suspect, however, that she who said she would be willing to wait a hundred years for her work to be understood would not begrudge us our theories as long as those theories do not cause us to lose sight of the fiction itself. Her professed skepticism about the critical "establishment" to the contrary notwithstanding, O'Connor was an avid student of theory, whether theological, philosophical, or literary, and although she might have had to repress the urge to create savage caricature, she would doubtless have been more than mildly interested in the current debate. Now, having engaged in such speculation, I must nonetheless add that the author's permission is not necessary in order for us to proceed; what is necessary is an open mind and dissatisfaction with any approach that diminishes the complexity of the fiction, for it is obvious that O'Connor's fiction is far more complex than much of the early commentary allowed.

One essential question for the critics continues to concern narrative stance: Is the usually harsh, often biting voice of the narrator the voice of O'Connor herself? If so, why so negative, so unloving a worldview? If not O'Connor, who *is* the narrator? I want to suggest a complex of early influences on O'Connor's technique — in addition to the literary and theological sources cited in O'Connor criticism over the years — that may have helped to shape O'Connor's distinctive narrative strategies.

Until rather recently O'Connor commentators, like John Hawkes, appear to have assumed that the voice of the narrator was that of O'Connor herself, or at least their commentary seems to be undergirded by that often unstated assumption. Thus the critics emphasizing the Christian basis of the fiction argued that O'Connor was depicting the ugliness of the world as the result of the Fall and that her "large and startling figures" were intended as distortions whereby the secular, atheistic, or just plain slumbering twentieth-century reader would experience epiphany of the most profound sort. Basing their approach primarily on the author's public statements of intention, these critics argue a kind of Christian necessity: Because we are, in Eliot's words, "distracted from distraction by distraction," O'Connor must raise her voice, she must shout. The publication in 1970 of Josephine Hendin's *World of Flannery O'Connor*, however, marked a turning point in the consideration of style.

To the surprise and dismay of conservative O'Connor critics and to the horror of the local Milledgeville community, which had extended its hospitality to Hendin as she engaged in her research, she argued that readers ought not "to lose sight of the believer behind the belief" in O'Connor's work (17), that O'Connor's work cannot be interpreted solely in light of her Catholicism, and that John Hawkes "does not go far enough" (20) in arguing that O'Connor is of the devil's party:

I think O'Connor is best when writing like a devil of reduction, most convincing when most literal and least convincing when consciously symbolic. In Hawkes's words, in the process of using the devil's voice for satire, O'Connor becomes the devil herself, speaking most authentically when using his voice. In effect this destroys the balance between the satiric and the real, the literal and the metaphoric, the actual and the symbolic. Consequently, much of O'Connor's work tends to remain literal and never reach a symbolic or even allegoric plane. While some of her suns become Eucharistic, most of them remain merely suns or are reduced to "fat yellow roosts" with chickens on them. The latter is the symbolizing process in reverse: a foreshortening of meaning that reduces significance instead of expanding it. What is immense and expansive is made to appear minute. O'Connor creates a language for a universe filled with shrunken objects, smelling remarkably like a chicken coop. This whittling abrasive impulse is much more than a vagary of literary style; it is one of the most powerful and most ignored expressions of O'Connor's relation to her work and of the quality of life in her fiction. (20–21)

Following Hawkes's lead, Hendin makes no separation between author and narrator; she maintains that even as the author elects to use "the devil's voice for satire," she "becomes the devil herself." Hendin then concludes that the narrative voice is O'Connor "speaking most authentically." Hendin's focus on O'Connor's "whittling abrasive impulse" and her later assertion that this impulse and the universe it creates are largely the result of O'Connor's resentment of and resistance to the social expectations of life in Milledgeville as Regina O'Connor's daughter were surely controversial at the time of the book's publication. Some time before feminist critics began to insist formally on such considerations, Hendin succeeded in calling attention to the writer behind the writing and clearly established the need to cope with the intensity and power of the narrative voice — as reflective of the dilemma of the artist herself. The "universe filled with shrunken objects, smelling . . . like a chicken coop," Hendin argued, is for the most part the result of O'Connor's own torment as a rebellious daughter of the South; the fiction serves as a kind of release of the rebellion that O'Connor dared not demonstrate in actual life. Never mind, Hendin concludes, that O'Connor's apparent acquiescence to the social status quo only increased the power of the despised system: O'Connor rebelled in the only way that she could. Today Hendin's quasi-psychoanalytic approach seems to have been ahead of its time, anticipating the work of Frederick Asals, Clare Kahane, and Louise Westling and certainly providing me with perspective in my reading of "The Crop" in chapter 1.

Although Hendin clearly sees the fierce narrator as O'Connor herself, or at least as a strongly rebellious, even embittered side of the author's personality, the Bakhtinian critics Marshall Bruce Gentry and Robert Brinkmeyer treat the matter of the narrator with little emphasis on the personal life of the author, focusing instead on what might be called narrative tension. Gentry argues, for example, that O'Connor's characters are in conflict with an authoritarian narrator, presumably not O'Connor herself; their victory over the narrator ensures their salvation. Robert Brinkmeyer joins other commentators in objecting to the absence of divine grace in Gentry's account of the characters' salvation but proceeds with his own Bakhtinian reading to argue, perhaps more astonishingly, that the narrative voice in O'Connor's fiction is the voice of fundamentalism. He believes that the Catholic O'Connor was intensely drawn to Protestant fundamentalism and that her way of working out that attraction was through the most intense dialogue between herself as author and a fundamentalist narrative voice. Brinkmeyer seeks to explain the ferocity, the often eviscerating humor, the grim shape of O'Connor's narrative, in light of the writer's Christian commitment. Here again the narrative voice is the center of attention.

Brinkmeyer's argument may appear a compelling one, especially to the reader who remains disturbed by the stringency of O'Connor's vision, and a summary of its essential points may be useful. Moreover, reviewing Brinkmeyer's argument will allow us to examine the ideas of Mikhail Bakhtin concerning the dialogic imagination and to suggest another Bakhtinian perspective on O'Connor's work, one significantly different from that presented by Brinkmeyer.

Beginning quite appropriately with a discussion of Bakhtin's theory that the dialogic imagination is responsible for truly great literature, Brinkmeyer proceeds to argue that O'Connor's imagination is indeed dialogic in the Bakhtinian sense; that is to say, it is open to the consciousness of others, fully aware of "the impossibility of the existence of a single consciousness" (Bakhtin qtd. in Brinkmeyer 15) and resistant therefore to "solipsistic tendencies" that are stultifying to individual freedom and growth. The gifted (dialogic) artist is fully engaged by the world of his creation and through that engagement enters into a "dialogic encounter with the self, because frequently the consciousnesses of the characters created embody voices from within the artist's own consciousness." Thus, "the artist's encounter with the art is an encounter with the otherness of the artist's multi-voiced self" (17). For Bakhtin, Dostoevsky is the dialogic artist par excellence. Dostoevsky is able, in his fiction, to see the world through the eyes of many others, that is, through many consciousnesses. As Clark and Holquist observe, "Dostoevsky is able to create such simultaneity and diversity because he opens his characters to each other. Like the underground man, he is aware that there is no final truth about people as long as they are alive. The root desire of individuals to upset all finalizing definitions of their selfhood is what Dostoevsky calls 'living life' or 'the man in man,' and he stresses this quality in each of his characters" (Clark and Holquist 241).

Dostoevsky, then, creates "a polyphonic world" in contrast to the "monologic (homophonic) European novel" (Bahktin qtd. in Clark and Holquist 241–42). He is thereby able to create in his fiction a nearly perfect alterity, the process by which the artist sees the other "both as a subject and as an object" (Clark and Holquist 78). In explaining the necessary alterity for the dialogic (polyphonic) artist, Clark and Holquist offer as an example the perception of another's suffering:

> The classical example is how I perceive an other's suffering. I see her pain but do not feel it, or at least not in the same way that she experiences her own pain. But I can conceptually enter her cognitive space and perceive through her eyes that the world's appearance is colored in all its aspects by the sensation of suffering. When the sufferer sees the trees surrounding us, she perceives suffering trees, as it were; when she sees other persons, she perceives them too through the optic of her pain. The world is homogeneous in her perception of it. And by going out to this suffering other, I can know all this; through her eyes I can see the world as an extension of her suffering.
>
> But when I return to the time and space of my own unique place in existence, in addition to the knowledge I have gained of the sufferer's world, I can add to the catalogue of things she sees the things that she is unable to see from her situation and that can be perceived only from mine, such as the grimace on her face or the rictus of her limbs. More, I see all this in the context of the same trees she perceived through her pain. But those trees have quite a different aspect from my place. I render the other complete by the additions I make to her from my position of being both inside and outside her. (78–79)

The parallels between the individual's experience of alterity and the artist's experience of it as that artist engages the created consciousnesses of the fictional world are clear. As Brinkmeyer observes, "The characters in a dialogic work frequently embody the subjective perspectives by which the author views the world; their creation in fiction thus liberates the author from preconceived ways of seeing" (17).

On the other hand, the monologic artist, according to Bakhtin, yields to the "centripetal forces" that "seek to enclose the world in system" and shuts out the claim of "centrifugal forces that battle completeness in order to keep the world open to becoming" (Clark and Holquist 79–80). As we might imagine, any system positing that it alone possesses the truth denies the possibility for alterity, for growth and becoming. Thus Bakhtin saw the early centuries of the Christian community as vastly different from the Middle Ages, which he described as "a monologic period of calm and unity":

> The creative, founding figure of the prophet and miracle worker who preached outside the appointed, ritual times and places, who came from the folk and not the priestly class, who consorted with known prostitutes and was sympathetic to thieves, who preached in private homes or from the deck of a ship, was associated with the first period. The epigonic follower, the copier of old texts, the celebrator of stasis, the medieval monk, was typical of the second age. At the outset of Christianity, a vibrant, engaged man appeared, a voice alive and in dialogue with other persons and other voices. But in the following centuries there was a calcification of the founder's living word, a loss of his most engaged, fullest and most present meaning. (Clark and Holquist 250)

Thus, in Bakhtin's view, the period of the great flourishing of the Church, the Middle Ages, was a stifling time, a period characterized by stasis and loss of the vibrancy of Christ's dialogism. Although a believer himself, Bakhtin deplored the stringency of the Church's monologic position, as indeed he deplored the monologism of a political system that refused alterity. After all, in his own life Bakhtin had experienced the repressiveness of such a system in Soviet Russia; his development of a dialogic theory that applied to all aspects of life — politics, literature, belief — and his continued vehement defense of that theory over the years are certainly understandable.

Robert Brinkmeyer appears to have understood Bakhtin's dialogism, and therefore it is surprising that he attempts to argue the dialogism of Flannery O'Connor's imagination. As is the case with many of the recent readings of O'Connor, Brinkmeyer's argument is grounded in O'Connor's statements in the essays and letters indicating her aversion to literature as dogma and to the Pious Style. Asserting that O'Connor's faith was a struggling one, profoundly ill at ease with facile piety, Brinkmeyer maintains that O'Connor "believed that embracing religious faith did not mean escape from, and denial of, the problems and challenges of the contemporary world but a fuller experience of the world" (23) and that her search for other perspectives led her to dialogism. More specifically, Brinkmeyer argues that O'Connor as author engaged her own attraction to fundamentalism through the creation of a fundamentalist narrator to tell her stories.

And just what are the values of that fundamentalist narrator, values to which O'Connor is drawn but which, in Brinkmeyer's view, she must renounce? Relying on Schneidau's definition of the Yahwist vision as that which underlies the "radical alienation" of the Hebrew prophets (31), Brinkmeyer notes that the "central tenet [of the Yahwist vision] is that an absolute gulf separates humanity from an all-powerful God" and thus "humanity and all of its works" are "totally devalued" (29). The Hebrew prophets, "displaced and decentered, alienated not only from those about them but also from their own selves," engaged in a critique essential to "a larger and more enlightened vision" by seeing their own insignificance: "Whatever significance and value the prophets located in their individual consciousnesses the Yahwist perspective reduced to the empty dreams of vanity and pride: to gain insight into their own insignificance, the prophets, in a sense, stepped free from themselves, seeing themselves from the perspective of the ultimate other—Yahweh" (31). Brinkmeyer asserts that because O'Connor was familiar with and drawn to this prophetic skepticism, she found this "Yahwist thinking" most obviously in "the fundamentalist preachers of the southern backwoods" (32) and in their essential premise: "The center of all meaning resides . . . not in oneself or the world but in Jesus, and how one stands with him is, finally, the only thing that matters. Every person must make a personal choice either to accept Christ into his or her life or to reject him. There is no gray area, no room for compromise: One lives by Christ or the Devil" (33). Therefore, "one part of [O'Connor], one of the voices of her multivoiced self" becomes in her "mature" work "a narrator profoundly fundamentalist in sympathy" (34).

Crucial to the success of O'Connor's vision, by the terms of Brinkmeyer's argument, is the "interplay between the dominant voice of O'Connor's Catholicism and her fundamentalist voice — an interplay expressed most significantly in the relationship between Catholic author and her fundamentalist vision" (34). Brinkmeyer discusses four of O'Connor's stories that he considers representative of the successes and failures of O'Connor's use of the narrator. In "Everything That Rises Must Converge," he sees the narrator's fundamentalist "pressuring" of O'Connor and the story as being "undone" by the story itself; both the narrator and Julian are revealed as "cynical authority figures who stand in harsh judgment of those about them," and the humbling of Julian at the story's end "implicitly signals the narrator's [humbling], even if the narrator remains unaware of it" (72). Thus, even as the narrator destroys Julian's position at the end of the narrative, the narrator's own position is destroyed. Brinkmeyer does not attempt to say that the reader of this story is aware of the destruction of the narrator's position, a fact that would seem to suggest a serious limitation in his reading. He does posit that "The Artificial Nigger," "The Enduring Chill," and "The Lame Shall Enter First" represent a "less severe" tension between O'Connor and the narrator (67). Moreover, "The Artificial Nigger" contains a considerable weakening of the narrator's fundamentalism, "making this narrator less detached from the action and less the evangelist serving an all-demanding God" and creating "a fiction less burdened by the crushing tensions of [O'Connor's] other work and more affirmative of the human experience" (67). Perhaps not surprisingly, Brinkmeyer maintains that the narrators of the two novels, both with overtly religious concerns, are even more starkly fundamentalist, "more willing to bend and distort to drive home the significance of the religious underpinning of the story, and more eager to assert a fundamentalist and narrative authority" (99). Unlike *Wise Blood,* however, in which, Brinkmeyer argues, the conclusion, presented from Mrs. Flood's more charitable point of view, effectively balances the extreme fundamentalism of the narrator, *The Violent Bear It Away* represents the triumph of the fundamentalist narrator and thus of O'Connor's own "fanaticism" (131).

In spite of the undeniable urge that many of us have for the comfort of a single, all-encompassing theory to account for the narrator's stance, I believe that we must question Brinkmeyer's argument. First of all, both Brinkmeyer's definition of fundamentalism and his conclusion that Roman Catholicism and southern Protestant fundamentalism are essentially opposed are debatable. Brinkmeyer is guilty on more than one occasion of equating charity, openness, and tolerance with Catholicism and equating violence, "distortion," "willfulness," "a single-mindedness that closes off a good deal of reality," and "lack of charity" with fundamentalism (129). Obviously, these kinds of assumptions are questionable (and, oddly enough, they seem to deny the very openness and dialogism that Bakhtin espouses). Furthermore, O'Connor's statements in the essays and letters concerning her attraction to southern fundamentalism indicate a real affinity for the absolute terms of the fundamentalist's conviction, a fact that is not surprising when we consider the strong similarities between southern fundamentalist Protestantism and traditional Roman Catholicism, especially the stringent monologism of each. In light of that monologism, Brinkmeyer's assertion that O'Connor's imagination is dialogic seems unfounded. Although O'Connor appreciated the need for the story to be artful in its own right and not to be used as a vehicle for dogma, she herself never wavered in her Catholic faith. Indeed, she considered her writing talent the gift of God, a fact sufficient to warrant its wise use. She thus creates fiction that, regardless of its "accidents," is in essence or substance Christian, specifically Catholic, and, as Bakhtin would define it, centripetal or monologic.

Jane Marcus, writing about the work of modernist Catholic writer Antonia White, proposes that White, especially in her autobiographical work *Frost in May*, contributes to modernism the appropriation of "the authoritative third person for the female voice" (598). Marcus cites scholars of Church history who have demonstrated that "individual confession to a priest was a replacement of public confession and absolution of the congregation during mass in order to control and define female sexuality" (599), and she notes Michel Foucault's assertion that by making confession a sacrament in the fourth Lateran Council of 1215 the Church "consolidated [its] discursive power" and shifted control of individual narrative from the speaker (the penitent) to the confessor (599). For a writer like Antonia White to decide to present autobiographical material in a third-person narrative, rather than in the rather easily dismissed (because subjective) first-person, was therefore a very bold move. In Marcus's words, "White shows no narrative mercy" (599).

Flannery O'Connor was, of course, not translating autobiography into fiction. However, her use of what Jane Marcus calls "the female monologic" is, in a sense, an extremely innovative and courageous step, for O'Connor, a Catholic writer like White, was trained by the Church "in the prayerful discourse of supplication, in the woman's position of speaking in abjection on her knees" (Marcus 600). O'Connor may be commended for her boldness as she, like White, "rises to assume the stance of speaking subject" in fiction characterized by those "large and startling figures."

O'Connor's embrace of the "female monologic" vision is ironically her way of defying the accusations of subjectivity and sentimentality often associated with women's writing; in other words, it is her way of allying herself with patriarchal authority and power. Thus, whatever credit we give O'Connor for a stylistic audacity not characteristic of female writers in general, and especially not those with Christian purpose, we must remember that she writes out of a closed system, a closed worldview, whether we like that fact or not. Her work is most like the Christian fiction of Bernanos, Mauriac, Greene, and Percy; it is not Dostoevskian, except as particular works of Dostoevsky may have influenced her creation of character or situation, as, for example, the Misfit's questioning of the appropriateness of punishment to the crime is Dostoevskian. When O'Connor engages the world, she does not do so to inhabit other consciousnesses or philosophies or points of view in order to demonstrate myriad possibilities for human belief and action; she presents all secular answers, especially humanist social doctrine, in light of the one truth of Christianity. Furthermore, O'Connor would not have apologized for this monologic vision; that she wrote from the standpoint of Christian orthodoxy was, she believed, essential to the true freedom of her artistry. And even if we were to grant a measure of truth to Brinkmeyer's assertion of a fundamentalist narrator, O'Connor's vision is still monologic. Roman Catholicism and fundamentalism are surely part of the same monologic system.

Brinkmeyer's argument is worth our time and attention because it reflects the extent of the continuing concern of O'Connor commentary with the narrative voice. In attempting to explain the stringency of the narrative consciousness in terms of O'Connor's own spiritual struggle, Brinkmeyer acknowledges, indeed he underscores, the difficulty O'Connor presents to secular and Christian readers alike—how to reconcile that stark narration with Christian love and forgiveness.

The problem is further emphasized by the fact that many readers of *The Habit of Being* were relieved to find evidence there of a witty and sensible human being at times fully taken up with the mundane affairs of daily life, in contrast, they felt, to the hard-nosed voice in the fiction. Although O'Connor's authoritative comments on faith and the writing life have been at least somewhat discomfiting to readers of her letters, these letters nonetheless offer a real antidote to the harshness of the fiction. Some of O'Connor's commentators, in fact, have gone so far as to urge us to read the letters before we read the fiction. Sally Fitzgerald has advocated reading the letters to get a clear idea of O'Connor and her intentions before tackling the fiction, while Claire Claiborne Park suggests that O'Connor's most important legacy is her letters and not her fiction, fraught as the latter is, in Park's view, with meanness, frustration, and, certainly, limitation. However, there are the problems with the letters themselves. Are they the complete picture of Flannery O'Connor? Why the excisions? Exactly who was Betty Hester, until her death in 1998 known to readers of the letters as "A"? What about the *full* correspondence of O'Connor and Maryat Lee, now available to scholars in the O'Connor Collection at Georgia College & State University? Many of those letters were not included in *The Habit of Being* and have recently been the object of scholarly concern with O'Connor's alleged racism, a matter to which I shall return in chapter 5.

How do we read an author's letters? Do we read them as the voice of the author when she is most nearly herself? Or can we not find in some of O'Connor's letters, as some critics have already observed, the conscious creation of the voice of the country rube, disdainful of "interleckchuls," the northern critical establishment, and anything smacking of pretense or affectation? And how does one reconcile that voice with another voice in the letters, the authoritative words of the writer and believer, certain of herself, disciplined, articulate, sophisticated in matters of art, intellect, and spirituality?

I believe that making the letters the basis for our reading of O'Connor, as writer or person or both, is also a risky business. In writing about O'Connor's fellow Georgian Margaret Mitchell, Anne Goodwyn Jones notes that in her letters Mitchell created a persona as a means of "reconciling her desire for personal privacy with the need for some social relationships and some public statements" and that the author's letters were clearly "designed to convey to her reader the impression of a woman who is witty and sensitive but self-deprecating" (316). What Jones sees in Mitchell's letters may well be the case of the letters of Flannery O'Connor. Jones even uses the word *mask* to describe Mitchell's creation of an epistolary identity, arguing that self-deprecation was part of the recipe for southern ladylike behavior and that Mitchell, for her entire life, was torn between her need to be emancipated (her mother was, after all, a suffragist) and her need to fulfill the ideal of southern womanhood. The conflict between Melanie and Scarlett in *Gone with the Wind* can clearly be viewed in light of Mitchell's own confusion about female identity, Jones asserts, and although Mitchell "had to kill Melanie for Scarlett to live" (321), she never finally resolved the conflict. Thus Jones sees Mitchell's letters as proof of her efforts to create a public persona or mask to hide her ambivalence. Just as Jones finds that Mitchell's letters are useful up to a point, I would posit that O'Connor's letters, rich repositories though they may be, are limited in their usefulness in understanding the fiction.

The case of O'Connor's fierce narrator will not be solved simply by recourse to the letters, either as explanation for O'Connor's intentions in the fiction (as Fitzgerald would have it) or as substitution for the fiction (as Park recommends). Nor will the matter be resolved as simply as Brinkmeyer would have it resolved, with his notion of an essentially theological struggle between author and narrator.

We must acknowledge that no one camera angle on O'Connor's fiction is sufficient to present it in its fullness or complexity. Is the proposal that O'Connor was a monologic writer, however, tantamount to arguing that only one response to her fiction is correct or, for that matter, even possible? In other words, must we adopt O'Connor's stated Christian intent as the only measure of our evaluation of her success? If we do that, might we not find ourselves in the dilemma of a critic like Brinkmeyer in attempting to make everything — and especially the often disagreeable voice of the narrator — fit a Christian (Catholic) perspective? Do we not thereby reduce the fiction, flatten it out, shrink it to our size to make it fit? To be sure, a feminist reading, a psychoanalytic reading, or, for that matter, a Marxist reading might be equally reductionist or reductively monologic. Without in any way denying that O'Connor's Catholic beliefs undergird her *conscious* intent as a writer, we may be able to see that other factors are also at play — her southern upbringing, her femaleness, the early loss of her father, her serious illness, her complex relationship with her mother, her attraction to the banal and the bizarre, her sense of humor, her early interest in satire, her education in the New Criticism, her long-distance friendships, her reading in literature and theology, and, as critic Jon Lance Bacon has recently argued in *Flannery O'Connor and Cold War Culture,* her assimilation of and response to the social and political issues of the cold war. I would, of course, add to this list of influences O'Connor's embrace of the power and authority of the patriarchal tradition, a factor that undergirds other choices and other interests. The fierce narrator may well result from many of these factors, and at this stage we might be tempted to a kind of absolutist relativism and thereby to posit that, because no truth is *the* truth, we had best leave well enough alone, tipping our hats to the multifaceted, multileveled nature of the creative process, and call it a day. To do so, however, would be to misread Bakhtin and to yield to the kind of anti-intellectualism that undergirds the protests of many undergraduates when they object to literary analysis as the "ruining" of a literary work. Let us therefore plunge in, fully aware that the water is deep and the water is wide.

Whence came O'Connor's impulse to satire, with its propensity for verbal extravagance and caricature? I believe that O'Connor discovered very early in her career the possibilities of visual and verbal distortion and its suitability to her particular needs — in fact, long before her Christian intent was firmly established.

I have suggested that "The Crop" in many ways may be viewed as O'Connor's coming to terms with herself as an artist, with her limitations and possibility in that time and setting in the South, and with the necessity to embrace her literary patrilineage. Unlike the voice in Welty's story "A Memory," the narrative voice in "The Crop" is satiric, though without the intense ferocity or angularity of the later work. This satiric voice seems the continuation of a practice begun by O'Connor in her first years of creativity, dating at least from the time that she was a student at Peabody School in Milledgeville. In an interview in the *Peabody Palladium* of December 1941, Mary Flannery, then sixteen, is presented as firmly ambitious and decidedly tongue-in-cheek. She announces that her hobby is collecting rejection slips and that she has produced three books, "Mistaken Identity," "Elmo," and "Gertrude," all concerned with a goose and directed to an indeterminate audience: "too old for young children and too young for older people" ("Peabodite Reveals Strange Hobby" 54). Noting that O'Connor "wants to keep right on writing, particularly satires," the author of the article mentions O'Connor's assortment of pets by name: Herman, the gander; Haile Selassie, the rooster; and Winston, a black crow. Haile's roommate, Adolph, another rooster, is deceased; O'Connor reports that before his death Adolph's name had to be changed because of the neighbors' curiosity about the cries of "Here Adolph!" emanating from the O'Connors' backyard.

We see early evidence of O'Connor's self-deprecating wit in her comment that, in addition to the clarinet and accordion, she plays the bull fiddle "because . . . I am the only one who can hold it up." Finally, the article reminds the audience of O'Connor's skill as a cartoonist (she was art editor of the *Palladium*), those cartoons also demonstrating "a keen sense of humor." Further evidence of O'Connor's characteristically irreverent humor and interest in parody and satire may be found among the early manuscripts, presumably written while O'Connor was an undergraduate at Georgia State College for Women: a parody of Proust's *Remembrance of Things Past*, a fragment of a poem with a persona who "lack[s] that certain grace" and has dirty hands and face and "a temper like a turtle" (Collection 3), and an undergraduate writing exercise for English 324 in which O'Connor describes a girl chewing gum to the rhythm of "Missouri Waltz." This exercise is written under the pseudonym of "Jane Shorebanks" and dated March 29, 1943 (Collection 4b). Surely we do not find it difficult to imagine that the dirty girl lacking in the social graces and possessed of what one must assume is a snappish temper is at least partly a self-description and a portent of the child in "A Temple of the Holy Ghost" and Joy/Hulga Hopewell of "Good Country People." As we observed earlier, these characters derive in some measure from O'Connor's rebellion against southern expectations of female propriety.

Furthermore, as a number of commentators have noted, the startling figures of O'Connor's fiction owe a great deal to the acute visual imagination evident in the drawings the writer made during her undergraduate years. In addition to her work as illustrator of the yearbook and as art editor and cartoonist for the *Palladium*, O'Connor decorated the walls of the student lounge with her cartoons. (Much to the dismay of the GC&SU community, the cartoons were covered when the walls were painted many years ago.) I suggest that O'Connor's extant drawings possess the boldness of line and the light satire of human folly to be found in the work of that very talented satirist of the time, James Thurber. In fact, such works of Thurber's as the popular *My Life and Hard Times*, first published in 1933, *My World and Welcome to It* (1942), or *The Thurber Carnival* (1945) are possible sources of inspiration for O'Connor. Like Thurber, the youthful O'Connor seemed interested in the relationship between visual and verbal caricature. Later, of course, although O'Connor disclaimed any talent as a visual artist, she employed those bold strokes and that keen eye for detail in her fiction. The possible influence of Thurber on the early work deserves a closer look.

James Thurber—a writer who, until the last several years, has received little or no academic attention and who has never been regarded very seriously by the academicians who create the anthologies—was quite popular in the 1930s, 1940s, and 1950s. Published primarily by the *New Yorker* during these years, Thurber's cartoons and humorous sketches and stories established the "Thurber style," characterized by its appreciation of the zany, the frivolous, and the foolish in human behavior; its devastating portraits of marriage and the relationship between the sexes in general; and its dislike of pretense and affectation. In an appreciative essay in the *New Yorker*, commentator Alan Gopnik notes that in the early 1950s, when Thurber was on the cover of *Time*, "it was pretty much taken for granted that, as he himself liked to say, he was the greatest American humorist since Mark Twain." Gopnik adds, however, that in 1994, which marked Thurber's centenary, "his work is dead, or dying" (169).

Perhaps because of the brevity of his sketches and the popularity of his cartoons, Thurber was doomed to be dismissed as a minor writer of light fiction, a comic artist whose work was topical and ephemeral. As Gopnik notes, he was "a light stylist of the heavy heart" (171). As the years passed, Thurber became increasingly resentful at being known only for his humor (170). He clearly acknowledged that fact when, in the "Preface to a Life" in *My Life and Hard Times*, he countered that "writers of light pieces" are not carefree and gay; instead, "they sit on the edge of the chair of Literature." Thurber adds, "In the house of Life they have the feeling that they have never taken off their overcoats" (14), concluding, "This type of writing is not a joyous form of self-expression but the manifestation of a twitchiness at once cosmic and mundane" (15). He notes that *humorist* is "a loose-fitting and ugly word" and that to label writers "humorists" is to fail to recognize that the "little wheels of their invention are set in motion by the damp hand of melancholy" (15), a fact that obviously would not be lost on a Charlie Chaplin or a Woody Allen or a young Flannery O'Connor.

Although there is no reference to Thurber in *The Habit of Being*, O'Connor was familiar with the *New Yorker* at least by the time she was an undergraduate. In a 1963 letter to Janet McKane, O'Connor wrote: "I like cartoons. I used to try to do them myself, sent a batch every week to the *New Yorker*, all rejected of course. I just couldn't draw very well. I like the ones that are drawn well better than the situations" (*Habit of Being* 536). O'Connor began publishing cartoons in high school. Sally Fitzgerald affirms that in April 1944 when O'Connor was still an undergraduate, she sent cartoons to the *New Yorker*, but her work was rejected (*O'Connor* 1240). To be sure, O'Connor's familiarity with the *New Yorker* would indicate knowledge of the work of James Thurber, to whose cartoon style O'Connor seems indebted. Her cartoons satirize the vicissitudes of daily life in a woman's college, with a playful emphasis on the drudgery of schoolwork, lack of social life, and anticipation of vacation. O'Connor knew her undergraduate audience well and played to the common understanding of what life is like in a woman's college, and like any good comic, she put aside her own habits and beliefs and deferred to the popular view. As Margaret Meaders, Betty Boyd Love, and others have noted, O'Connor was a serious and talented student, who seemed undaunted by any presumed deprivations in her high school and undergraduate years. As a day student, she was involved in campus life, her energies amazingly focused. Such confirmations of the author's personal deviation from the stereotypes presented in her cartoons underscore O'Connor's sense of her audience and her early grasp of the techniques of humor. Moreover, the cartoons themselves display the wry and mocking wit evident in small doses in the thesis stories and developed fully in the mature fiction. Alan Gopnik writes that Thurber's drawings "depend on a simple animated line to express something about the enclosure of modern life" and that this line "is a yearning, anxious line" (175). Moreover, Thurber's drawings are funny because they "find a suggestion of normality in an impossible situation, which is what modern living demands" (176). If O'Connor did not borrow cartooning technique and style from Thurber, she certainly would have found reinforcement of her approach in his work.

The same assertion can be made about Thurber's fiction; O'Connor likely found support there for her own developing technique and ideas. Without denying the strong influence of other modernist writers, especially male, and without underestimating O'Connor's developing mission as a Christian writer, we can nonetheless argue that Thurber's work is worth considering as we attempt to discern the origin of O'Connor's attitudes.

The current reader of Thurber's "light" fiction might be surprised at the presence of attitudes that today would be called, at best, sexist and perhaps even misogynist. Indeed, Gopnik calls the obvious misogyny in Thurber "relentless," although he repeats Wilfrid Sheed's defense of Thurber in this context by suggesting that Thurber's women are "tough" because "they spend so much time carrying Thurber's men around" (176). However, neither Sheed's defense nor Gopnik's proposal that most women who are given the choice of being presented as either ideal or nasty would choose nastiness obviates the fact of Thurber's misogyny. Surely such popular stories as "The Secret Life of Walter Mitty" and "The Catbird Seat" succeed, in part, because of the negative portraits of women. (The former story, easily the most frequently anthologized of Thurber's fiction, is included in Brooks and Warren's *Understanding Fiction*; the first edition of this text was published in 1943 and was chosen by O'Connor as a supplement in her course in literary criticism at Iowa [*O'Connor* 1241]. A later edition, containing the Thurber story and O'Connor's "A Good Man Is Hard to Find," is among the books in O'Connor's private library.) Walter Mitty, we are led to believe, must flee to dreams of heroic deeds in order to escape constant nagging by his wife; in "The Catbird Seat" the character of Ulgine Barrows, one of the most memorable "castrating bitches" in twentieth-century literature, drives Mr. Martin to forceful and uncharacteristic retaliation. Stereotypical portraits of the selfish, shrewish wife combine with images of woman as dominating, suffocating, and shrill throughout Thurber's fiction and cartoons to indicate the author's deep misogyny. In such pieces as "The Macbeth Murder Mystery," "The Case of Dimity Ann," and "A Couple of Hamburgers," Thurber stresses woman's penchant for driving man to acts of desperation, vengeance, even torture. In fact, in "The Curb in the Sky" the husband is driven insane by a wife who constantly interrupts and corrects him. Of course, Thurber's dependence on the female as the butt of the joke was not an unusual practice in the humor of that time — or of our own time, for that matter. The popularity of Thurber's style, in cartoons and in prose, may indeed have resulted from his use of that most common object of laughter and ridicule, woman — usually presented in her role as wife. After all, women have only recently learned not to laugh at their depiction in sexist jokes.

In several of his essays Thurber also displays unmistakable misogyny. For example, in "Courtship Through the Ages" he describes the difficulty experienced by the male of all species in attracting the female, who is fickle and interested only in being entertained; after all, he notes, the peacock had to learn "to vibrate his quills" to interest the peahen (10). "Death in the Zoo" also uses the animal kingdom to explain human behavior by arguing that the male polar bear's murder of his female partner is the result of her meddlesome, smothering nature. One of the clearest examples of Thurber's misogyny is the essay "After Cato, What?" in which Thurber admires Cato the Elder's treatment of women. Declaring that "all women are plaguey and proud, and that if a man were quit of them he would lead a less godless life" (290), Cato, Thurber notes gleefully, "considered it a lot of damned nonsense and a major mistake on the part of the gods that women were so constituted as to play a necessary part in the perpetuation of the race" (291).

Not surprisingly, the woman who wants to write is satirized in "What's So Funny?" Most of the essay is aimed at proving the ignorance and frivolity of the woman writer. Thurber concludes with this question: "Why don't you become a bacteriologist, or a Red Cross nurse, or a Wave, like all the other girls?" (4), reminding us of Mrs. Hopewell's consternation at having a "philosopher" for a daughter. In this connection we remark that in most of his essays directly concerning literature, Thurber typically assumes that the writer is male. The victorious wife in "The Case of Dimity Ann," for example, is tempted to a triumphant salute to "the invisible wives of all the writers in the world" (119). Furthermore, in a more direct though still decidedly comic discussion of contemporary literature, "The American Literary Scene," Thurber comments that "there has been no woman novelist since Miss Cather's death" (193), revealing a penchant for the easy dismissal of the female and her accomplishments common among male writers and critics of the time.

Beneath the surface of Thurber's laughter is usually an extremely frustrated male persona, often identifying himself as "James Thurber," caught in a repressive and bitter marriage, given to drink, exaggeration, and a cynical self-mockery that covers a deep pessimism. Thurber's vision contains no transcendental solutions; for Thurber, progress is no panacea, but neither is faith the answer. In "Footnote on the Future," a piece that calls to mind O'Connor's adolescent poem "Prehistoric Man," Thurber attacks the cheerfulness by which scientists claim to view the future: "What, I keep saying to myself, is to keep Man [in the future] from becoming four times as ornery, four times as sly and crafty, four times as full of devilishly ingenious devices for the extinction of his species?" (115). Thurber, like Mark Twain, harbored many misgivings about science and technology based on his pessimistic view of human nature, although he was certainly no spokesman for the Christian idea of the fall and original sin. In "*What* Cocktail Party?" Thurber chooses to ignore the obvious Christian content of T. S. Eliot's work; instead, he spoofs its difficulty, suggesting, indeed, that it is pretentious and meaningless. After all, one character in the story insists to another that in order to understand Eliot's play, "You should have read either a great deal more or a great deal less than you have" (222); the narrator, who purports to be Thurber himself, offers as his strategy for understanding Eliot the suggestion that one must ascertain what Eliot "would never not say" (224). What appeals to Thurber is usually the sensible and the down-to-earth. Certainly the young O'Connor would very likely have been drawn to Thurber's attacks on both scientific progress and literary pretension, although, of course, she would later be greatly influenced by Eliot's depiction of the modern world in *The Waste Land* and find herself in strong agreement with Eliot's later Christian vision.

I suggest that in the early years of the exercise of her talents, well before her commitment as a Christian writer was firmly established, O'Connor, as cartoonist and writer, found something of a model in Thurber. Clearly she shared his skepticism about science as the hope of the future. In the spring 1944 issue of the *Corinthian*, the literary magazine of GSCW, M. F. O'Connor's essay entitled "Biologic Endeavor" satirized the "refined" methods of modern medicine that provide "ways and means of relieving any distressing conditions that may arise as a result of [physical] incapacities" (7). Indeed, had he but known of the scientific advances to come, Great-uncle Benedict would not have "stumbled along in his ignorance, treating his faulty digestion by temperance" (7). O'Connor concludes with this cautionary note:

> As time goes on, and more and better methods of preventing indigestion and illness are discovered, something will have to be done about providing natural methods of leaving this world. On the assumption that when the present younger generation takes control of the government, war will be refined to such a degree that it will no longer take the complete life of the individual, a group of representative youth from the progressive high schools of the country has met in Philadelphia to set up research committees for the development of new diseases. Because of the foresight of these young people, we may look forward to the pleasure of dying neither sooner nor later than we would naturally expect.
>
> Great-uncle lived in the dark ages. (18)

It is interesting to note that O'Connor's father had died just three years before this essay was published, a fact suggesting that, although O'Connor had been greatly attached to her father and was devastated by his death, she was able to distance herself from that loss enough to write about death. Satirical technique seems to have afforded the necessary measure of detachment, in this essay and in other O'Connor works. In a similar attack on the "advances" of science in the *Corinthian* of the next year (the last issue in which her work would appear), O'Connor wrote in "Education's Only Hope":

Any faculty living in the twentieth century ought to be able to apply the scientific advantages of the age to the problems of education. Yet not one has shown any initiative whatsoever—while all about lie the machines and gadgets of an age overflowing with electrical possibilities. Why, may we ask, could not the class-room discussion be electrified? It would be relatively simple to wire each chair to a button board on the teacher's desk so that he might plug a student in. Upon being automatically raised from her chair by a slight electric shock, the student would at least have to give evidence of her ignorance before being allowed to sit down again in a chair free from electricity. (14)

The satire here is light, particularly in view of the harshness of later work. However, the satirical impulse is clearly dominant in this early writing. Furthermore, O'Connor would undoubtedly have been delighted by Thurber's popular essay "University Days" in *My Life and Hard Times* in which the narrator/author is presented as the prototypical "nerd": unable to pass botany because of his inability to see a cell through the microscope, confusing botany with economics and doing badly in both, and so physically inept that he must take ROTC for four years rather than two. The essay also attacks the university's emphasis on a winning football team and laughs at the simple-minded "aggie." Anybody attempting to satirize college or university life would have found a model in this Thurber classic.

Sally Fitzgerald notes that in her college years O'Connor wrote "comic depictions of family members and their vagaries," providing illustrations as well (*O'Connor* 1240). In this connection, a number of Thurber selections concerning his own family come to mind, particularly several in *My Life and Hard Times*. There, in "The Car We Had To Push" and "The Night the Ghost Got In," the grandfather is presented as a man quite confused about time. In the former story, he thinks the family's discussion of the "dead" car concerns his long-dead brother Zenas, and he keeps urging his family to proceed with the funeral. Such silly episodes concerning the senile grand-father might anticipate those of O'Connor's "General" Tennessee Flintrock Sash of "A Late Encounter with the Enemy." Moreover, in "The Night the Ghost Got In," Thurber recalls that his grandfather "was going through a phase in which he believed that General Meade's men, under steady hammering by Stonewall Jackson, were beginning to retreat and even desert" so that later, when the police came to investigate the reported burglary, the grandfather, in a wildly comic scene, began to shoot at them, believing they were "deserters from Meade's army, trying to hide in his attic" (64–65). The next day, the grandfather returned to sanity long enough to ask, "What was the idee of all them cops tarryhootin' round the house last night?" (67). The irascible grandfather also appears in "Draft Board Nights," in which he threatens to leave the house without his clothes and insists on talking to General Sherman, shouting, "Git that goddam buggy!" (118). Although Thurber's grandfather and General Sash fought on opposite sides, they are both confused and cantankerous men who speak their minds freely and often fiercely.

J. O. Tate has established O'Connor's use of "General" William J. Bush as her model for General Sash, and O'Connor found the colorful General Bush worthy of "an act of artistic appropriation" ("O'Connor's Confederate General" 53). However, Thurber's grandfather provides another analogue worthy of attention, perhaps especially since O'Connor transforms the real Mrs. Bush—who had received her degree when she was in her sixties and was attended by her uniformed Confederate warrior-husband, then in his nineties—into a granddaughter. Sally Poker Sash, another character who provides a vehicle for O'Connor's satire of southern female propriety, is a foolish woman indulging in family pride, wanting to display on stage "what all was behind her" (*O'Connor* 252). The distancing afforded by satire of the Thurber variety may have provided O'Connor with a model. After all, though General Bush was not "family," the graduation exercise in which his wife was involved did take place on the GSCW campus. It is certainly possible to argue that because much of her material derived from actual local events, O'Connor found satire and its distortion appropriate tools for much of her work. Thurber was extremely popular at the time. (In this connection, we note another parallel. In "The Car We Had to Push," Thurber writes that Zenas went to South America when the Civil War broke out and returned when it was over only to catch "the same disease that was killing off the chestnut trees in those years" (40), and he passed away. Thurber concludes, "It was the only case in history where a tree doctor had to be called in to spray a person, and our family had felt it very keenly" (40). We recall, of course, that O'Connor's Asbury of "The Enduring Chill" contracted undulant fever, or, as Dr. Block observes, "the same as Bang's in a cow" [*O'Connor* 572]).

Furthermore, we might propose that Thurber's deliberate placing of himself as narrator/character in many of these works, his blurring of the distinction between the author and the character of the narrator (and, in the case of those pieces which are primarily narrative in structure, the consequent blurring of story and essay) may have served as an example to O'Connor, even as she, at least unconsciously, absorbed Thurber's technique. Thurber's use, for example, of the "real" Mrs. Thurber in his piece "See No Weevil" suggests the fusion of fact and fiction (here in an essay) rather typical of his style. In this narrative, Thurber imagines that when "Thurber" tells Mrs. Thurber that he is researching the Thurberia plant, she might respond, "If I had it to do over again . . . I wouldn't have married a desert botanist. I don't know why you have to go in for things like mesquite and toadbush, when everybody else's husband is finding such lovely flowers" (256). In this same vein, the publication of *The Habit of Being* allowed O'Connor's readers to discover just how she transformed events and people in her own life into fiction, particularly the pragmatic, socially conservative, unliterary habit of mind of Regina O'Connor.

In a 1956 letter to "A," O'Connor writes, "My mother says, 'You talk just like a nigger and someday you are going to be away from home and do it and people are going to wonder WHERE YOU CAME FROM'" (*Habit of Being* 148), echoes of which statement and the personality who utters it we hear in several of O'Connor's fictional mothers, perhaps most memorably in Julian's mother and in her words in "Everything That Rises Must Converge." This story has as its background the civil rights movement in the South. Julian is convinced that the benighted, bigoted attitudes of his mother will have to change and that he will be the agent of that change. Smug in his own shallow liberalism, Julian sneers at his mother's "graciousness" as she reminds him, as Sally Poker Sash might have put it, of "what all is behind [him]." She declares that the world is a "mess," but "if you know who you are, you can go anywhere" (*O'Connor* 487), suggesting that the fact of his distinguished ancestry will give him identity and direction in times of confusion. Even though O'Connor makes it clear that Julian's foolish mother does not understand what true self-knowledge is—contrary to what she and many southerners believe, it involves more than knowledge of and pride in the family tree— she also treats the mother in this story sympathetically. The mother, after all, has sacrificed herself to fulfill his needs ("Her teeth had gone unfilled so that his could be straightened" [*O'Connor* 491]), and she believes in his future as a writer. She tells the woman on the bus, "He's selling typewriters until he gets started" (491).

Indeed, Julian is the object of O'Connor's fiercest satire. And if we take

Julian to be a surrogate, at least in many respects, for the author herself,[1] we see that the story can be viewed as a kind of self-chastening, not in the strictly theological sense, as Brinkmeyer would have it (Catholic author versus fundamentalist narrator), but in the sense that O'Connor comes to terms with her own mother as a real person, one capable of both bigotry and extraordinary self-sacrifice, just as she also comes to terms with her own arrogance and condescension. The process of self-chastening was not an easy one, and it was surely ongoing. In a 1959 letter to Cecil Dawkins, for example, O'Connor writes, "The other day she [Regina O'Connor] asked me why I didn't try to write something that people liked instead of the kind of thing I do write. Do you think, she said, that you are really using the talent God gave you when you don't write something that a lot, a LOT, of people like? This always leaves me shaking and speechless, raises my blood pressure 140 degrees, etc. All I can ever say is, if you have to ask, you'll never know" (*Habit of Being* 326). In "The Enduring Chill" Asbury, a character in many ways like Julian, is admonished by his mother:

> "When you get well . . . I think it would be nice if you wrote a book about down here. We need another good book like *Gone with the Wind*."
> He could feel the muscles in his stomach begin to tighten.
> "Put the war in it," she advised. "That always makes a long book." (*O'Connor* 560)

Here again the mother is a grave intellectual disappointment to her son, and Asbury considers her totally responsible for his failed life. Yet she is solicitous and kind to her son — to a fault. In fact, we see that her most serious shortcoming is not her intellectual inadequacy but her blindness to her son's selfishness and self-indulgence. Like Julian, Asbury will learn a terrible lesson. O'Connor here might be said to be coping with her own resentment of her mother in the best way she knows how — by dramatizing her own dilemma and allowing that satirical narrator to get the best of Asbury's arrogance.

Unlike Thurber, O'Connor never appears in her own fiction as "Flannery O'Connor," nor would she have ever wanted to do so. Thurber's ability to dramatize his own experience, however, and to do so in often large and startling figures — without regard for how he as narrator/character/author is perceived by the reader — may have served as impetus for O'Connor as she moved toward greater freedom in the use of the narrative voice. Although it is not a story in which Thurber appears as a character, "The Whip-Poor-

Will" concerns a man who is driven to madness and murder by the early morning sound of the whippoorwill. We note the similarity in plot structure to O'Connor's "Greenleaf," with Mrs. May's increasing agitation over the bull's constant presence on her premises and the desperate measures by which she will deal with the problem. In Thurber's story Mr. Kinstrey, in a failing marriage, views his wife with disdain: "The mechanism of her mind was as simple as a cigarette box; it was either open or it was closed, and there was nothing else, nothing else, nothing else" (196). We recall O'Connor's description of Mrs. Freeman's mind in the opening paragraph of "Good Country People": "Besides the neutral expression that she wore when she was alone, Mrs. Freeman had two others, forward and reverse, that she used for all her human dealings. Her forward expression was steady and driving like the advance of a heavy truck" (*O'Connor* 263). We see that it is O'Connor's narrator, in the story's opening lines, who presents Mrs. Freeman in this way, not, as in the case of the Thurber story, a *character* who presents another character. O'Connor appears to have gone beyond Thurber's technique as she allows the narrator to pass judgment on Mrs. Freeman's character, even at the risk of appearing condescending or mean-spirited. This narrator is certainly not the fundamentalist side of Flannery O'Connor, as Brinkmeyer would argue; instead, the narrator is O'Connor's satirical weapon, the means of her distancing, the method of her humor. And forewarned is forearmed: If we as readers aren't able to accept this bold and wickedly satiric narrator, we had better light out for the territory.

A final note on "The Whip-Poor-Will" is in order here. In this story Thurber uses a bit of the indirect discourse that becomes characteristic of his satire and that anticipates what O'Connor will do with indirect discourse in a number of works. In Thurber's story, Mr. Kinstrey seeks consolation from the servants Margaret and Arthur concerning the bird noises after his wife says that she does not hear them:

> Margaret hadn't heard it either, but Arthur had. Kinstrey talked to them in the kitchen while they were clearing up after breakfast. Arthur said that it "wuk" him but he went right back to sleep. He said he slept like a log—must be the air off the ocean. As for Margaret, she always slept like a log; only thing ever kept her awake was people a-hoopin' and a-hollerin'. She was glad she didn't hear the whip-poor-will. Down where she came from, she said, if you heard a whip-poor-will singing near the house, it meant there was going to be a death. Arthur said he had heard about that, too; must have been his grandma told him, or somebody. (194)

In many of her works O'Connor is far more successful than Thurber in her use of indirect discourse, from limited use of the technique in *Wise Blood* through its fullest use in the stories in *Everything That Rises Must Converge*.

Often indirect discourse becomes a major means of O'Connor's satire, particularly as she pokes fun at smugness and ignorance. In the opening chapter of *Wise Blood*, for example, O'Connor writes that "Mrs. Wally Bee Hitchcock, who was facing Motes in the section, said that she thought the early evening like this was the prettiest time of day and she asked him if he didn't think so too," and she immediately follows this sentence with the narrator's vivid description of Mrs. Hitchcock: "She was a fat woman with pink collars and cuffs and pear-shaped legs that slanted off the train seat and didn't reach the floor" (9). Throughout O'Connor's fiction the harsh narrative voice often combines with indirect discourse to effect its sharpest satire. Frequently the characters who receive the most scathing treatment in this manner are female — the smug, narrow-minded, ignorant women for whom O'Connor's writing is famous. Mrs. Hopewell in "Good Country People," for example, emerges clearly in this passage, which combines indirect discourse with the narrator's additions, enriched by dialogue demonstrating O'Connor's ear for the rhythms and idioms of local speech:

> Mrs. Hopewell liked to tell people that Glynese and Carramae were two of the finest girls she knew and that Mrs. Freeman was a *lady* and that she was never ashamed to take her anywhere or introduce her to anybody they might meet. Then she would tell how she had happened to hire the Freemans in the first place and how they were a godsend to her and how she had had them four years. The reason for her keeping them so long was that they were not trash. They were good country people. *She had telephoned the man whose name they had given as a reference and he had told her that Mr. Freeman was a good farmer but that his wife was the nosiest woman ever to walk the earth.* "She's got to be into everything," *the man said.* "If she don't get there before the dust settles, you can bet she's dead, that's all. She'll want to know all your business. I can stand him real good," *he had said,* "but me nor my wife neither could have stood that woman one more minute on this place." *That had put Mrs. Hopewell off for a few days.*
>
> *She had hired them in the end because there were no other applicants but she had made up her mind beforehand exactly how she would handle the woman.* Since she was the type who had to be into everything, then, Mrs. Hopewell had decided, she would not only let her be into everything, she would *see to it* that

she was into everything—she would give her the responsibility of everything, she would put her in charge. *Mrs. Hopewell had no bad qualities of her own but she was able to use other people's in such a constructive way that she never felt the lack. She had hired the Freemans and she had kept them four years.* (O'Connor 264, my italicizing of the narrator's voice)

This passage effectively demonstrates O'Connor's freedom in moving from indirect discourse to interior monologue created by the narrator ("Mrs. Hopewell had decided . . .") and to the narrator's storytelling to produce her stunning irony and consequently her most biting satire. Indeed, in this and other matters, James Thurber may well have been one of the writers whose example gave the young O'Connor a direction, a modus operandi, for the storyteller she would become. Unlike the more "literary" influences on Flannery O'Connor, including that of Nathanael West, Thurber anticipated O'Connor in the satiric vision present in both his cartoons and his prose, his blurring of fact and fiction, his use of exaggeration, and, perhaps most significantly, his creation of a narrative persona/character that allowed him to be a part of the human folly he ridiculed.

O'Connor's fiction also echoes another *New Yorker* writer, Dorothy Parker. Most of Parker's short stories, collected in *Here Lies* (1939), were first published in the *New Yorker* and in tone and technique bear a strong resemblance to those of Thurber. Parker's urbanity, her searing attacks on smugness and superficiality, and frequent use of the outrageous and grotesque would doubtless have appealed to O'Connor. For example, in "The Wonderful Old Gentleman" we find this description of the Bains' living room:

> The opposite wall was devoted to the religious in art; a steel-engraving of the Crucifixion, lavish of ghastly detail; a sepia-print of the martyrdom of St. Sebastian, the cords cutting deep into the arms writhing from the stake, arrows bristling in the thick, soft-looking body; a water-color copy of a "Mother of Sorrows," the agonized eyes raised to a cold heaven, great bitter tears forever on the wan cheeks, paler for the grave-like draperies that wrapped the head. (Parker 21)

Aside from the allusion to St. Sebastian reminiscent of the opening of "Everything That Rises Must Converge," we note the attack on religious sentimentality and bad taste, from the engraving of the Crucifixion "lavish of ghastly details" to St. Sebastian's "thick, soft-looking body." Mrs. Bain, whose questionable taste informs this setting, has not married well, a fact that may help to explain her soft spirituality. She is in marked contrast to her sister,

Mrs. Whittaker, whose affluence allows her to tolerate her sister and other relatives:

> But Mrs. Whittaker's attitude of kindly tolerance was not confined to her less fortunate relatives. It extended to friends of her youth, working people, the arts, politics, the United States in general, and God, Who had always supplied her with the best of service. She could have given Him an excellent reference at any time. (Parker 23)

Many of O'Connor's middle-aged female protagonists resemble Mrs. Whittaker, especially Mrs. Hopewell, Mrs. McIntyre, and Mrs. Turpin. The fierce attacks on ladylike behavior in Parker's story (a theme Parker employs in a good many of her narratives; see "Little Curtis" and "The Custard Heart," for instance) are also clearly present in such O'Connor stories as "A Good Man Is Hard to Find" and "Good Country People." Mrs. Whittaker in Parker's story sounds amazingly like the grandmother in "A Good Man" and Ruby Turpin in "Revelation": "The word 'lady' figured largely in her conversation. Blood, she often predicted, would tell" (Parker 25). She is obviously a woman to whom appearance is everything: "Mrs. Whittaker always stopped things before they got to the stage where they didn't look right" (26).

Parker is also concerned with hypocrisy, particularly in such stories as "Arrangement in Black and White." This story presents a white woman in "pink velvet poppies" (3), who is eager to meet the black musician Walter Williams, performing at the party she is attending. She repeatedly declares how unprejudiced she is, revealing, of course, that she is deeply bigoted. O'Connor parallels are obvious here. In "Horsie," Miss Wilmarth, whose nickname is given to her behind her back by her employer, Mr. Cruger, because of her resemblance to the animal, is a pitiful and pitiable character. Miss Wilmarth, the nurse for Mr. Cruger's wife and new baby, bears a resemblance to Miss Willerton in O'Connor's "The Crop." It is worth noting that in each story a female writer is rather relentlessly attacking the silliness and empty life of a single woman. In fact, in a 1993 essay in the *New Yorker*, Joan Acocella writes that by the early 1930s Parker, a poet, fiction writer, and book reviewer, was established as the wittiest of the Algonquin group and was the most popular *New Yorker* writer, a celebrity, a person followed at cocktail parties in the expectation that she would "say something funny" (76–78). However, success did not by any means bring the tortured Parker happiness.

She came to despise her own work and increasingly turned to alcohol. Eventually she ceased to write.

Acocella notes that the short story was Parker's best genre; it was the form on which she worked the hardest and for which she wanted to be known. Unlike her elliptical poetry, the stories fleshed out Parker's most frequent theme, the relations between men and women. Her choice of story essentially prevented Parker from relying on her wit or on those witty asides for which she is famous. Acocella argues that, possibly because Parker's wit was restrained, "something curious happens to her [familiar] vulnerability-cruelty formula": "Instead of deploying the two forces sequentially — buildup, then letdown — she works them simultaneously. Her heroines are all vulnerability, but from the very start they are observed with a cold precision" (79). In her most famous and perhaps most successful story, "Big Blonde," for example, Parker presents the apparently hedonistic and alcoholic Hazel Morse, who is severely disappointed in her marriage and, perhaps primarily for that reason, goes through a succession of men, all of whom bore her. She attempts suicide and fails, ending up, at the story's conclusion, returning to drink as her solace. The similarity of the name to that of the protagonist of *Wise Blood* is remarkable, as is the fact that Hazel's nickname in Parker's story is "Haze." Moreover, Hazel's pride in her small feet is like the foot-pride of several of O'Connor's female characters (Mrs. Turpin, perhaps most notably): "She prided herself upon her small feet and suffered for her vanity, boxing them in snub-toed, high-heeled slippers of the shortest bearable size" (Parker 213). And like Mrs. Greenleaf of "Greenleaf" and Thomas's mother in "The Comforts of Home," Hazel "would cry long and softly over newspaper accounts of kidnaped babies, deserted wives, unemployed men, strayed cats, heroic dogs. Even when the paper was no longer before her, her mind revolved upon these things and the drops slipped rhythmically over her plump cheeks" (Parker 217).

That these details of character actually influenced O'Connor's work is perhaps, finally, only conjecture. Unlike O'Connor, Parker certainly never had any underlying spiritual theme or motivation. However, the toughness of Parker's style and the "cold precision" (Acocella 79) of her presentation of character are clearly remarkable forerunners of O'Connor's biting portraits.

Perhaps most important, O'Connor's treatment of female vulnerability appears to be directly connected to that of Parker. Acocella cites the aftermath of Hazel's suicide attempt as "an inverted sex scene" (79), stating that "never has female vulnerability been more terribly portrayed" (79–80). Parts of that passage are worth noting:

> Mrs. Morse lay on her back, one flabby, white arm flung up, the wrist against her forehead. Her stiff hair hung untenderly along her face. The bed covers were pushed down, exposing a deep square of soft neck and a pink nightgown, its fabric worn uneven by many launderings; her great breasts, freed from their tight confiner, sagged beneath her arm-pits. Now and then she made knotted, snoring sounds, and from the corner of her opened mouth to the blurred turn of her jaw ran a lane of crusted spittle. . . .
>
> . . . [W]ith one quick movement [the doctor] swept the covers down to the foot of the bed. With another he flung her nightgown back and lifted the thick, white legs, cross-hatched with blocks of tiny, iris-colored veins. He pinched them repeatedly, with long, cruel nips, back of the knees. She did not awaken. (Parker 244–46)

Acocella asserts that what makes the scene compelling is that it takes "Hazel's situation down to its root, the female body," presenting *not* the body in seductive loveliness but "the body . . . fat and tired," an occasion of "cold scrutiny" (79). Thus Parker casts a hard eye on all aspects of female vulnerability: dependence on the male (see "Big Blonde" and "Horsie" as well as such stories as "New York to Detroit"), emotional weakness, limitation of education and sensibility, the horror of faded beauty. Acocella concludes that Dorothy Parker's "unique contribution" was her depiction in her stories of "female dependency":

> This was a central concern of nineteenth-century women writers—Jane Austen, George Eliot, the Brontës—and also of some of the men, notably Thackeray. . . . But in the twentieth century the rules change. With the move to the city and the loosening of ties to family and class, women were thrown into a new situation— one in which they should have been freer, and in which some were (witness Sister Carrie) but in which others found themselves wholly abandoned, both by the system that had formerly hemmed them in and by the new one, which still had no place for them (witness Lily Bart). Even after women began to make their way economically in twentieth-century culture, they were still left with an ages-old inheritance of emotional dependency, the thing that marriage and the family, having created, once ministered to and now did not. If in the old days women were enslaved by men, they nevertheless had legal claims on them. Now [in the twentieth century] they had no legal claims, so all the force of their dependency was shifted to an emotional claim—love, a matter that men viewed, and still

view, differently from women. Hence Parker's heroines, waiting by the phone, weeping, begging, hating themselves for begging. This is a story that is not over yet. Parker was one of the first writers to deal with it, and she addressed it in a new way. Because, it seems, she identified with the man as well as the woman, she saw these women from the outside as well as from within, heard the tiresome repetitiousness of their complaints, saw how their eyelids got pink and sticky when they cried. She did not feel sorry for them. They made her wince, and we wince as we read the stories — for, burning with resentment though they are, they are even more emphatically a record of shame. Female shame is a big subject, and for its sake, Parker should have been bigger, but she is what we have, and it's not nothing. (81)

Parker's tough-mindedness, especially on the subject of female vulnerability, may have influenced the development of O'Connor's satiric detachment, her own boldly unsentimental view of the female. O'Connor may well have found in Parker a woman writer capable of openly attacking female weakness and dependence, attacks usually associated with male writers. The influence of Parker may have combined with that of Thurber to produce the rapier wit that characterizes O'Connor's view of life, especially her trenchant satire of the relationships between the sexes. (O'Connor's mature fiction is, however, decidedly different from that of either Thurber or Parker in that O'Connor's interest in social satire and caricature in her fiction is only a means to an end: to demonstrate humanity's fallen condition and the need for salvation.)

Although the satiric impulse is present in O'Connor's thesis stories in only a limited way, those stories do give evidence of the author's penchant for delighting in human foolishness. "The Crop" and "The Barber" are the most completely satiric in tone, yet the satire in both is mild when we consider the swift and deadly thrusts of the mature work. Obviously indebted to Ring Lardner's "Haircut," "The Barber" presents a racist barber who aids and abets the superficial liberalism of the central character, Rayber, who is himself intellectually kin to the character of the same name in *The Violent Bear It Away*, to Julian in "Everything That Rises Must Converge," and to Sheppard in "The Lame Shall Enter First." No one would quarrel with the assertion of a Lardner connection here, for O'Connor likely knew of Lardner's work as early as her undergraduate years. However, we might add the possibility of Thurber's influence on this story in the matter of Rayber's fantasy life. Rayber's need to assert himself and establish his masculinity is akin to that of Walter Mitty, the most famous of a number of Thurber characters who escape unbearable situations (often those in which their masculinity is threatened by overbearing or suffocating females) through dream or fantasy. O'Connor seems surprisingly interested in the question of manhood in many of the thesis stories; in fact, "The Crop" is the only one of them not concerned with a male protagonist. Certainly "The Geranium" and "The Turkey" are centrally concerned with their protagonists' feelings about themselves as men. In the case of the former, Old Dudley obviously needs reassurance that the standards of manhood that he adhered to in the South still obtain in this northern urban setting. In "The Turkey" Ruller believes that his capture of the turkey will admit him to manhood in the eyes of his family.

Of course, Thurber's cynicism regarding intellectuals and their tendency to a kind of abstract thought having little relevance to reality or to the affairs of everyday life is also present in O'Connor's "Barber" and in many later works as well. O'Connor's character Jacobs, who is Rayber's model of the liberal intellectual, turns out to be a man who is able to take no side in the election debate, having no moral base or standard from which to judge. We seriously question Jacobs's liberalism when we learn that, while lecturing at a black college for a week and being required not to use the terms "Negro — nigger — colored — black," Jacobs returned home every night and "shouted 'NIGGER NIGGER NIGGER' out the back window" (*O'Connor* 715). Although O'Connor obviously does not take the side of the racist barber and his pro-Hawkson group, she raises serious questions about the liberal, integrationist position championed by Rayber, who seems more intent on establishing his own "credentials" with the men in the barbershop than on defending the right of blacks to share classrooms with whites.

Thus the question of moral conviction here is not tied to Christian belief, as it will be in later O'Connor, but instead appears to be a matter of a man's need for intellectual empowerment in male-dominated society. O'Connor clearly satirizes Rayber's foolishness from a very pragmatic, secular vantage point, very much in the manner of Thurber. In the final barbershop scene, Rayber delivers himself of his prepared speech, which begins, "For two reasons, men elect other men to power" (*O'Connor* 720), and thus in its language underscores the power of the patriarchy at the time. O'Connor clearly does not satirize patriarchal power but accepts it without question — the presumably benighted men to whom Rayber addresses his remarks appear to be accepting of him and even attempt to tease him affectionately. However, at this point Rayber is inconsolable, particularly since he has been unable to persuade even the black helper George to vote for the liberal candidate. He strikes the barber and leaves the shop "almost running, lather [beginning] to drop inside his collar and down the barber's bib, dangling to his knees" (O'Connor 724). The story's final words emphasize Rayber's childishness, the image of the dangling bib suggesting that Rayber has just left the infant's high chair and has much to learn. A story like Thurber's "Teacher's Pet," which also questions maleness or manhood, comes to mind here; in this work Thurber presents the middle-aged Kelby, a teacher's pet in his childhood, physically attacking a boy who embodies the same effeminate characteristics that he believes he possessed as a boy.

In the early stories O'Connor's repeated concern with the question of manhood may seem strange to today's readers, but we must remember that in O'Connor's time, and long before, the male power structure virtually dictated that issues of maleness and male coming-of-age dominate culture and literature. If the fact that a female writer chose to present those situations in her fiction is disconcerting to readers today, we must recall Gilbert and Gubar's use of the Freudian model of "normative" female behavior discussed in chapter 1. O'Connor appears to be choosing the subject matter that would best represent the authority and power of the patrilineal inheritance. As Nina Baym has noted, in American literature "melodramas of beset manhood" have dominated our appraisal of what is valuable; she argues that important critics such as Matthiessen, Chase, Trilling, and Fiedler declared directly or indirectly that "the matter of American experience is inherently male" (70). Like many of us educated in the first half of the twentieth century, O'Connor absorbed this idea, as well as its corollary: "In these stories [of beset manhood], the encroaching, constricting, destroying society is represented with particular urgency in the figure of one or more women" (72), who are usually depicted as "entrappers and domesticators" (73). Like the work of his more "serious" contemporaries, Thurber's work is concerned with "beset manhood" and, as we have remarked earlier, the female is usually presented as either weak and empty-headed or repressive, suffocating, often shrewish. In either case, women are inevitably the obstacle to the achievement of men's goals.

The same presentation of women occurs in much of O'Connor's work. In the thesis story "Wildcat," for example, the female is obviously associated in old Gabriel's mind with weakness and failed manhood, and therefore his being left with the women is tantamount to defeat. A story obviously in-debted to Faulkner's "That Evening Sun" in its emphasis on a black's fear of the encroachment of death, "Wildcat" is surely one of the weakest in the thesis collection. Here there are no attacks on cultural foolishness and pre-tentiousness, no vivid descriptions, and no satirical narrative voice; instead, O'Connor tells this story about a black community through old Gabriel's consciousness and in a dialect so clumsy that the narrative nearly breaks with the strain. Yet here again the author presents the *male* dilemma: in this in-stance, the need to possess the courage to face death with equanimity ("It won't gonna hit him like he was a woman" *O'Connor* 729). Ironically, of course, Gabriel, left alone, exhibits no courage at all. When the men return, he lies about the broken shelf to cover his own cowardice, evidently feeling the need to appear in control in the eyes of the male community. Thus, early in her career, O'Connor acknowledges the lengths to which men will go to mask their human frailty, often linked, as it is linked throughout western culture, to the experience of being female or "weak."

As Judith Fetterley and others point out, in a patriarchal culture "the pre-sumed reader is male" ("Reading about Reading" 150); therefore, writers like O'Connor directed their fiction (most likely, unconsciously) to the concerns of a male audience. Conversely, writing that is directed at a female audi-ence is, even today, considered of little significance. We are constantly made aware that such works as *Gone with the Wind* are less than critically satisfying in some measure because they are centrally concerned with women's issues and aimed at a female audience. Although generations of southern women boast about having read *Gone with the Wind* scores of times and some can even recite whole passages by heart, "serious" students of southern literature have not in the past considered the novel a bona fide object of literary anal-ysis. Like Flannery O'Connor, many of us learned this attitude — along with the proper scorn for Edgar Allan Poe and Thomas Wolfe — in the 1940s, 1950s, and 1960s.

Not until recently has Margaret Mitchell been taken seriously in academic circles, a development largely resulting from the impact of the women's move-ment and feminist studies. In this same context, O'Connor's disdain for an-other Georgian, Carson McCullers, may have something to do with her sense that McCullers was concerned primarily with human personality and rela-tionships, typically the fare of "women's" fiction. Certainly O'Connor's ac-knowledged masters — among them, Hawthorne, Conrad, Flaubert, James,

Eliot, Joyce, Faulkner, West — include no women, unless we consider Caroline Gordon, Katherine Anne Porter, and, as indicated earlier, Eudora Welty. Although I would question O'Connor's assertion in the following passage that she had not really read at all until she went to graduate school (course descriptions and the testimony of her peers at GSCW would cast doubt on such deprecation of her undergraduate experience), her statement in this letter to "A" in 1955 is revealing:

> I didn't really start to read until I went to Graduate School and then I began to read and write at the same time. When I went to Iowa I had never heard of Faulkner, Kafka, Joyce, much less read them. Then I began to read everything at once, so much so that I didn't have time I suppose to be influenced by any one writer. I read all the Catholic novelists, Mauriac, Bernanos, Bloy, Greene, Waugh; I read all the nuts like Djuna Barnes and Dorothy Richardson and Va. Woolf (unfair to the dear lady of course); I read the best Southern writers like Faulkner and the Tates, K. A. Porter, Eudora Welty and Peter Taylor; read the Russians, not Tolstoy so much but Dostoevsky, Turgenev, Chekhov and Gogol. I became a great admirer of Conrad and have read almost all his fiction. I have totally skipped such people as Dreiser, Anderson (except for a few stories) and Thomas Wolfe. I have learned something from Hawthorne, Flaubert, Balzac and something from Kafka, though I have never been able to finish one of his novels. I've read almost all of Henry James — from a sense of High Duty and because when I read James I feel something is happening to me, in slow motion but happening nevertheless. I admire Dr. Johnson's *Lives of the Poets*. But always the largest thing that looms up is *The Humerous* [sic] *Tales of Edgar Allan Poe*. I am sure he wrote them all while drunk too. (*Habit of Being* 98–99)

O'Connor relegates most of the modernist women writers to the realm of "the nuts," and except for listing Porter (whom she cites as "K. A.," an interesting touch in light of the name awareness discussed in chapter 1), Welty, and Gordon ("the Tates"), her statement contains no indication that the works of any female writer exerted significant influence. Caroline Gordon served as a sort of literary mentor for O'Connor throughout much of her early career, but O'Connor had probably not read much of Gordon's fiction. In the essays and letters she mentions only *The Malefactors*, "Old Red," and "Summer Dust." *The Malefactors* and the collection *Old Red and Other Stories* are the only fiction by Gordon in O'Connor's private library at Georgia College & State University. (It appears also that O'Connor in some measure "outgrew" Gordon, just as her friend Elizabeth Bishop essentially "outgrew" Marianne Moore, as should be the case with writers and their early mentors.) Although both Gordon and Porter were personal friends and supporters of O'Connor's work, O'Connor does not seem to have ranked their fiction very highly. (In "The Nature and Aim of Fiction," O'Connor does comment at some length on her admiration for Gordon's technique in "Summer Dust," a four-part story in *The Forest of the South*.)

We note also that in O'Connor's statement about her reading she adheres to the academic taste of the time; she has read (only?) "the best Southern writers," and she dismisses Dreiser and Wolfe and most of Anderson summarily, just as these writers generally tended to be considered second-rate by the academic critical establishment. O'Connor's reading of Poe in her early years was a fact of which she was obviously not proud. Asserting that most of what she read in her childhood was "Slop with a capital S," O'Connor adds, "The Slop Period was followed by the Edgar Allan Poe period which lasted for years" and proceeds to describe some of the "humerous" plots. She concludes, "This is an influence I would rather not think about" (*Habit of Being* 98). Until the late 1960s, the place of Poe in academic and critical circles was an ambiguous one; more often than not, Poe's stories of horror and his mellifluous and haunting verse were the subject of ridicule and parody on the academic scene. However, Marion Montgomery, Frederick Asals, and Blanche Farley have effectively argued the influence of Poe on O'Connor's work, Asals asserting that O'Connor owes more to Poe than she would perhaps have liked to admit. Flannery O'Connor was an *educated* writer, and, unlike Faulkner or Welty, neither of whom was formally "schooled" in literature, O'Connor had her taste formed, at least in part, by the predominantly male academic establishment. In this context, Thurber too might have been an influence that a writer might not want to mention in public statements.

We cannot, therefore, be remonstrative that, with the exception of "The Crop," O'Connor's thesis stories are essentially concerned with male protagonists whose manhood is imperiled in one way or another. As we noted in our discussion of Miss Willerton of "The Crop," the woman who wants to write faces serious obstacles, not the least of which are her lack of knowledge of the "larger" world and her need for courage in writing freely about whatever subject she chooses. And if she chooses to write about the domestic matters traditionally associated with the female, she risks being accused of sentimentality, triviality, and insignificance. Perhaps most disastrous for her reputation would be the refusal of the powers-that-be to take her seriously as a professional, and the achievement of widespread popularity (the popularity of a writer like Margaret Mitchell, for example) is a certain way to achieve such a dismissal.

Thus a woman writer's decisions to use satire—a tough, traditionally male strategy—and to concern herself with "strong," "universal" subjects and subject matter (a male facing physical debility, fear, and death; a male seeking respect for his knowledge and opinions among his townsmen) would seem to assist in her being taken seriously in the world of letters. If we add to this mixture the fact that southern writers of either sex had difficulty in the first decades of this century in gaining credibility among the powerful northeastern literary establishment, we have perhaps more indication of why it behooved O'Connor to set herself apart. Moreover, we have not even broached the subject of O'Connor's Catholicism and the requirements it would make of her fictional intent. The "language of extremity," the "insistence on duality, dissociation, splits, paradox, the tension of opposites" that Asals finds in the Christian existentialists and in the Thomist Jacques Maritain (35), were certainly compatible with O'Connor's needs and with her vision. Suffice it to say that, for O'Connor, faced with formidable odds as she undertook her life's work, the development of the fierce narrator seems inevitable.

Essential to our discussion of O'Connor's evolving style is what we might call the transmogrifying of source apparent in "The Geranium," the first version of O'Connor's first published story. With a plot that would occupy the author until the end of her career, "The Geranium" appeared in *Accent* in 1947 and concerned the displacement and loneliness of Old Dudley, an aging white southerner transplanted to a large urban setting in the North by his daughter, who fears that he can no longer manage alone. O'Connor's indebtedness to Caroline Gordon's "Old Red," undoubtedly Gordon's best-known story and one included in Brooks and Warren's classic text *Understanding Fiction*, has been noted by several critics, including Frederick Asals. However, no critic to date has discussed this connection very fully. O'Connor herself, in a 1957 letter to "A," implies the story's importance when she writes that, although she hasn't read "Old Red" for ten years, it did have its impact: "It merely introduced to me what I could be expected to do with a symbol and I sat down and wrote the first story I published" (*Habit of Being* 200). The symbol O'Connor uses most obviously in this story is, of course, the geranium itself, introduced in the first paragraph; clearly Gordon's use of the symbol of the fox showed O'Connor the way. Moreover, I believe that

"The Geranium" resembles "Old Red" in other significant ways that O'Connor does not acknowledge.

Although the tone and thematic concerns of the stories are markedly different, both "Old Red" and "The Geranium" have, as background, father-daughter relationships that leave much to be desired. The widower Aleck Maury, at sixty-one, comes to visit his aged mother-in-law and there encounters a household of female relations, including his own daughter, Sarah, and her new husband, Stephen, all of whom appear to be determined to thwart his desire to fish. For Aleck Maury, an educated man who is much respected and admired, fishing is not merely sport or entertainment; as Brooks and Warren point out in their notes following the story in *Understanding Fiction*, it is the "activity in which body and mind participate harmoniously" (85), clearly an antidote to the dissociated or fragmented modern sensibility. Gordon clearly contrasts Aleck Maury's wholeness with the abstraction of Maury's scholarly son-in-law, who is writing an essay on the poetry of John Skelton, the name itself suggestive of Stephen's own bodiless and abstracted condition. To Maury, the young man's face "was like that of a person submerged," and he thinks of Stephen as "dead to the world" and probably doomed to "be that way the rest of his life" (75). Maury, on the other hand, appears to be almost a Renaissance man, surely a twentieth-century anachronism; he is able to quote classical poetry as well as to converse with the blacks in their own dialect. He is in control, although he is aware that his time is limited. Thematically central to the story, then, are the passage of time and the fact of mortality. In a passage lyrical in its cadence and images, Gordon writes that Maury

> saw time suddenly, a full, leaden colored fabric depending from the old lady's hands, from the hands of all of them, a blanket that they pulled about, now this way, now that, trying to cover up their nakedness. Or they would cast it on the ground and creep in among the folds, finding one day a little more tight rolled than another, but all of it everywhere the same dull gray substance. But time was a banner that whipped before him always in the wind. He stood on tiptoe to catch at the bright folds, to strain them to his bosom. They were bright and glittering. But they whipped by so fast and were skipping always ever faster. The tears came into his eyes. (66–67)

The image that comes to be associated with time's elusiveness in Maury's memory is that of the fox, Old Red, who was always able to elude his pursuers—"A smart fox, Old Red" (73). Indeed, until the close of the story, Maury himself is one of the hunters, ever in pursuit. However, in the story's final lines, Maury, unable to sleep, thinks of hunting the fox, of trying to cut him off, of even getting down from his horse to chase the animal on foot. Yet as he runs with the dogs after the fox, Maury becomes aware that Old Red has already made it to the mountain, and his own gait slows. He proceeds to the place where "the shadow rose and swayed to meet him," that shadow presumably the presence of death. Now Maury becomes the fox, feeling the shadow's "cool touch . . . on his hot tongue, his heaving flanks." Gordon ends the story by describing the powerful transformation by which Maury, the old hunter, becomes the fox, the hunted, and we are brought face to face with the inevitability of death for even the smartest and wiliest: "He was sinking down, panting, in black dark, on moist earth while the hounds' baying filled the bowl of the valley and reverberated from the mountainside" (82).

O'Connor's version of Gordon's plot is revealing. Both writers, as we have noted, use male protagonists who are thwarted by their situations. Yet O'Connor's Old Dudley is a provincial, ignorant, and bigoted old man, who finds himself homesick and displaced in nearly every way. His relationship with his daughter is strained; he feels that she is merely doing her duty by inviting him to live with her, and the two can think of little to say to one another. Like Aleck Maury in his friendships with Ben Hooser and, earlier, Uncle Teague, Old Dudley has enjoyed the daily companionship of a black man, although in both cases the southern white men are decidedly superior to the blacks who, in the southern white tradition, must often be "managed" as though they are less than human, certainly less than adults. Gordon appears to use the black/white relationships in "Old Red," however, simply to demonstrate Maury's ability to communicate on any level and his appreciation for the blacks' knowledge of the natural world, a knowledge that Gordon implies is sorely needed by the likes of Stephen. On the other hand, Old Dudley's relationship to Rabie in O'Connor's story is central to the plot. Much of Old Dudley's anxiety and alienation derives from his sense that he is insignificant in this strange land where "[p]eople boiled out of trains and up steps and over into the streets . . . rolled off the street and down steps and into trains—black and white and yellow all mixed up like vegetables in soup" (*O'Connor* 705). That his daughter is about to have a new black neighbor is at first inconceivable to Old Dudley; he is later horrified that his own flesh and blood could live in such a situation. The only blacks he has known well are Rabie and Lutisha, and they were certainly not his social equals. In the complex system of southern "manners," acknowledged by both Gordon and O'Connor, a "nigger" like Rabie or Ben Hooser could be a white man's best friend and still not be his equal. O'Connor strongly suggests that men like Old Dudley, of little economic or social status in the southern hierarchy, needed to feel superior to blacks to maintain their own rickety self-esteem. Thus, when Old Dudley took apart his gun and Rabie cleaned it, Old Dudley "would explain the mechanism" to Rabie, who "always marveled at the way he could put it together again" (704–5). As Old Dudley considers the terrors of the big city, he, not surprisingly, thinks that "[i]f he could have showed it to Rabie, it wouldn't have been so big—he wouldn't have felt pressed down every time he went out in it" (704). Rabie becomes a kind of alter-ego for the old man, who consoles himself in the city by mentally addressing his black friend: "It ain't so big. . . . Don't let it get you down, Rabie. It's just like any other city and cities ain't all that complicated" (704).

Old Dudley's fear of displacement and his ensuing anxiety mask his real problem, his fear of death. In several passages of vivid and horrifying description, O'Connor presents Old Dudley's dilemma as, on the surface, a fear of enclosure: "They came back to the building and the apartment. The apartment was too tight. There was no place to be where there wasn't somebody else. The kitchen opened into the bathroom and the bathroom opened into everything else and you were always where you started from" (705). These lines are a kind of wry echo of Eliot's reflections on home in "Little Gidding" in the *Four Quartets*: "We shall not cease from exploration / And the end of all our exploring / Will be to arrive where we started / And know the place for the first time." The passage certainly serves as a forecast of the concern with metaphysical themes of home and place that will occupy O'Connor to the end of her career. Furthermore, near the end of the story when Old Dudley is contemplating going downstairs to pick up the fallen geranium, he looks down the steps and sees that "[t]he steps dropped down like a deep wound in the floor. They opened up through a gap like a cavern and went down and down" (712).

In Old Dudley's eyes, the urban world is a waste land, and, indeed, by this time, O'Connor was under the influence of Eliot's poem, particularly as she worked on *Wise Blood*. The urban/rural conflict that pervades much of O'Connor's fiction is present here in its early stages. Relying on timeworn, almost stereotypical associations, O'Connor implies that the rural setting fosters community and communion and, conversely, that the urban is the place of psychic fragmentation, alienation, and fear. Certainly, in this emphasis, at least, O'Connor is a true descendant of the Agrarians, with whom Caroline Gordon was tangentially associated through her marriage to Allen Tate. The value Caroline Gordon places on the wholeness of life lived close to the earth and to its seasonal rhythms was not lost on O'Connor. However, although Aleck Maury seems to have been able to appreciate and learn from the blacks' natural knowledge of the land and the water, Old Dudley has not: "Rabie knew the river up and down for twenty miles. There wasn't another nigger in Coa County that knew it like he did. He loved the river, but it hadn't meant anything to Old Dudley. The fish were what he was after" (702). The voice of the narrator in these sentences suggests that the black man's communion with the natural world is lost on Old Dudley, who is anything but Aleck Maury, Caroline Gordon's Renaissance man. The subject that Gordon had presented seriously — even lyrically — O'Connor distorts, finding refuge from lyricism and even sentiment in her creation of a true provincial. We are clearly observing the evolution of the fierce narrator.

The geranium, the only green living thing in Old Dudley's new setting in the city, becomes symbolic of that lost rural past in which community was consoling, where everybody knew your name. Although the geranium reminds Old Dudley of "the Grisby boy at home who had polio and had to be wheeled out every morning and left in the sun to blink" (701), he is nonetheless dependent on its presence in the window of the apartment across the way. The geraniums at home were certainly treated better and were healthier looking, but this one has become a sort of companion to the old man, initially evocative of the past and its powerful hold and coming to signify, by the story's close, his own life. Like Gordon's transformation of symbol in "Old Red," O'Connor's story concludes with a merging of the fact of Old Dudley's rescue by the kind black stranger, by whose generosity the old man is humiliated, with the fact of the fall of the geranium, to suggest that Old Dudley *is* the fallen geranium. In a penultimate sentence that is resonant of lines from *The Waste Land* ("I think we are in rats' alley / Where the dead men lost their bones"), O'Connor interrupts the rude remarks of the "neighbor" by presenting Old Dudley's perception of the fallen geranium: "It was at the bottom of the alley with its roots in the air" (713). The symbolism of uprootedness is obvious here, perhaps explicit in the way only a young writer can be explicit. O'Connor learned this lesson, and others as well, from Caroline Gordon.

Gordon tells her entire story almost exclusively from the point of view of Aleck Maury, one notable exception being her dipping into the consciousness of the daughter Sarah as she thinks about her father's pretty speaking voice. For the most part, O'Connor follows suit. Her story is told essentially from within the consciousness of Old Dudley; in only a few instances, such as the previously quoted passage describing Old Dudley's indifference to the river, do we feel the intrusion of the narrator. Although both writers use essentially this third-person-limited point of view, there is a decided difference in the tone of the two works.

Unlike the other stories in the thesis collection, the consciousness of Old Dudley is characterized by hints of that narrative fierceness that we are accustomed to seeing in the later works. The old man compares the geranium to the Grisby boy with polio. He visualizes himself in the past as the capable man of the house who suffered at night "when the old girls crabbed and crocheted in the parlor" in their "sparrow-like wars that rasped and twittered intermittently" (703). The old man perceives his new neighborhood (again with Eliotic overtones) as "a row of buildings all alike, all blackened-red and gray with rasp-mouthed people hanging out their windows looking at other windows and other people just like them looking back," the buildings with halls that "stretched like dog runs" (704). Old Dudley notices that people, "all mixed up like vegetables in soup," were "boiling out of trains" and "rolling" off streets and down steps into yet more trains so that "[e]verything was boiling" (705). And, finally, he is aware that his new world is filled primarily with unfamiliar, abrasive, even threatening noises: "Somewhere down the hall a woman shrilled something unintelligible out to the street; a radio was bleating the worn music to a soap serial; and a garbage can crashed down a fire-escape. The door to the next apartment slammed and a sharp footstep clipped down the hall" (705–6). All of these descriptions, with their sharp, vivid images and strong, often monosyllabic verbs, signal the O'Connor style that is to come.

The occasional fierceness of Old Dudley's consciousness may well be another self-excoriation. Several commentators have noted that this story about homesickness was written during O'Connor's first real time away from her own home and may reflect her own experience of loneliness and hunger for the familiar. By this argument, Old Dudley is the displaced O'Connor—transformed, exaggerated, and perhaps pitied. On the other hand, Caroline Gordon's style in "Old Red" is appropriate to the consciousness of an educated, caring man, for there is nothing biting or harsh about it. Gordon leads us to understand that the man whose perception is reflected here is confident, not threatened; whole, not divided or dissociated; at home in the world, not displaced. O'Connor is thus beginning to veer away from the beaten path; she eschews the familiar psychological realism of a story like "Old Red" to stake new territory, to create her own distinctive text. However, both Gordon and O'Connor appropriate the point of view of the male protagonist, as though to embrace his power and authority.

That both writers use male protagonists is not surprising, of course, in light of the climate of the times. Both were southern writers brought up in conservative, white, middle-class households. Gordon was a fervent convert to Roman Catholicism, and O'Connor was a devout "cradle Catholic." Both writers are today associated with the conservative Fugitive Movement at Vanderbilt University in the 1920s, Gordon through her two marriages to Allen Tate, and O'Connor, less directly, through the encouragement and support given her by several figures associated with that movement, namely, Andrew Lytle, Robert Penn Warren, and, of course, Tate and Gordon. Rather predictably, both Gordon and O'Connor have internalized in these works the patriarchal view of women: the male's problems are universal; women are either insignificant or are obstacles in the way of the male's freedom and fulfillment. Maury's dead wife, Mary, did all she could to change him, to thwart his passion for fishing, to make him adhere to society's formulas for success, and Maury feels constrained in his mother-in-law's house by female social obligations. Old Dudley feels no real connection with his daughter, who, having taken him in in his old age, nonetheless talks down to him and functions primarily as his keeper; in fact, Old Dudley's fond thoughts are of Rabie, not of his daughter. Her negative role, we note, is expanded in later versions of the story. Finally, in this same connection, O'Connor suggests that Old Dudley's problem has much to do with his sense of failed manhood in the new situation, a theme that O'Connor will also expand in later versions of the story. Old Dudley's pride in having been the man of the house in the boardinghouse is smashed in the city, where he is fearful and terrified of getting lost. His memories of fishing and hunting with Rabie sustain him for a while, but here he cannot "get out his gun" (703), and in the ultimate affront to his manhood, the only black man around is clearly better educated and more well-to-do than he is.

In the only thesis story with a decided religious dimension, O'Connor presents in "The Turkey" another version of the classic male coming-of-age story. (Furthermore, the narrative continues to haunt O'Connor, as is evident in its later versions, "The Capture" and "An Afternoon in the Woods.")[2] Without the presence of the fierce narrator, "The Turkey" opens with a fantasy worthy of, if not indebted to, Thurber's Walter Mitty: Young Ruller, out in the woods for the afternoon, imagines himself armed and confronting "Mason," evidently an outlaw. His attention is diverted from this heroic task by the sight of the eye of the ungainly, though commanding, wild turkey. His wish for a real gun seems a Freudian anticipation of his need to assert himself to his family and to compete with his brother Hane, who seems headed for a life of crime. Indeed, in the later version of the story, "An Afternoon in the Woods," O'Connor changes "Ruller" to "Manley," clearly suggesting his need for male assertion. (She uses the name Manley Pointer in "Good Country People" to suggest the Bible salesman's sexuality as well as his function in pointing Joy/Hulga's way toward humility and the acknowledgment of dependence, essential prerequisites for salvation.) Intent on impressing his family with his capture, Ruller runs, stumbles, and falls, convinced that he cuts a ridiculous figure: "He sat there looking sullenly at his white ankles sticking out of his trouser legs and into his shoes" (*O'Connor* 744).

This self-consciousness and disgust lead him to experiment with profanity, in one of the truly comic episodes in the thesis stories. His first tentative blasphemy changes to defiance as he recognizes the importance and power of words:

> "Good Father, good God, sweep the chickens out the yard," he said and began
> to giggle. His face was very red. He sat up and looked at his white ankles sticking
> out of his pants legs into his shoes. They looked like they didn't belong to him.
> He gripped a hand around each ankle and bent his knees up and rested his chin
> on a knee. "Our Father Who art in heaven, shoot 'em six and roll 'em seven,"
> he said, giggling again. Boy, she'd smack his head in if she could hear him. God
> dammit, she'd smack his goddam head in. He rolled over in a fit of laughter.
> (*O'Connor* 745)

O'Connor repeats the earlier sentence (744) describing Ruller's sight of his ankles and follows it with a sentence indicating that a kind of dissociation of sensibility has set in as the result of the boy's blasphemy. The "she" referred to in the last several sentences is, of course, Ruller's strictly Christian mother, who, he imagines, would be horrified by his language. The thematic emphasis here on the power of words, the relationships between language and feeling and between language and action, the use of language as a form of rebellion, and the responsible choice involved in the use of words is repeated in other O'Connor works, most notably in *Wise Blood* and *The Violent Bear It Away.*

Furthermore, Ruller's experiments with language and his recognition of its relationship to truth and moral choice — as Ruller imagines what will happen when his parents ask how he tore his clothes and got the knot on his head, he thinks that he will answer that "he fell in a hole. What difference would it make? Yeah, God, what difference would it make?" (*O'Connor* 746) — seem directly relevant to the matter of O'Connor's own style. In a sense, Ruller's consideration of his mother's horrified response to his own bad language echoes Miss Willerton's concern with her family's response to her story dealing with that forbidden subject, passion, in "The Crop." "The Turkey," however, adds to the question of female propriety what is, to O'Connor, the far more significant question of religious propriety. On one level, "The Turkey" is concerned with a boy's coming of age or initiation into the realm of experience, a staple plot in the history of male literature. In this coming-of-age story, Ruller learns that his own "evil" is nothing compared to the very real existence of evil in the world and that the "Something Awful" which seems to be pursuing him at the story's close may be either the reality of evil or, as I shall suggest presently, his own doubts about God's benevolence. Read in this way, the story hints at the fuller development of an idea that will recur in "Good Country People" and "Everything That Rises Must Converge," the last sentences of the latter story very similar to the final words in "The Turkey."

On another level, the story might be read as suggesting the author's own concerns with language and its relationship to belief. Ruller's impulse to shock his fundamentalist grandmother, first by the use of foul language and then by stealing, evolves into a consideration of right attitudes toward God and an even more important recognition: that words give shape to thoughts that, in impetus or intent, are either denial or affirmation of trust in God. Do we believe that God plays dirty tricks or not? In a sense, even the formulation of the question seems to imply lack of trust, a fact that Ruller appears to recognize, and yet such grappling with doubt, with its notable biblical antecedents, is surely a part of faith. Although O'Connor chooses to cast Ruller as the heir to a rigid fundamentalism, his dilemma is that of every thinking believer and certainly that of O'Connor herself. In this story, however, she describes it in male terms:

> He remembered the minister had said young men were going to the devil by the dozens this day and age; forsaking gentle ways; walking in the tracks of Satan. They would rue the day, he said. There would be weeping and gnashing of teeth. "Weeping," Ruller muttered. Men didn't weep.
>
> How do you gnash your teeth? he wondered. He grated his jaws together and made an ugly face. He did it several times.
>
> He bet he could steal.
>
> He thought about chasing the turkey for nothing. It was a dirty trick. He bet he could be a jewel thief. They were smart. He bet he could have all Scotland Yard on his tail. Hell.
>
> He got up. God could go around sticking things in your face and making you chase them all afternoon for nothing.
>
> You shouldn't think that way about God though.
>
> But that was the way he felt. If that was the way he felt, could he help it? He looked around quickly as if someone might be hiding in the bushes. (*O'Connor* 747)

As he explores the relationship between words and reality—gnashing his teeth to connect the sound of the word to the action it describes and recognizing the contradiction between the biblical words and society's teaching that *men* don't weep—Ruller comes to acknowledge the presence of thoughts that are rebellious against God and at the same time to feel guilt about those thoughts and feelings.

This scene involves more than Twain includes in the pivotal episode in *The Adventures of Huckleberry Finn* in which Huck makes the moral decision to go against society's teachings about slavery and lying in order to protect Jim, the runaway slave. O'Connor, though obviously still the apprentice writer, attempts a more subtle point by suggesting that the battle of belief is not necessarily waged in the world in dramatic confrontation (for example, as Huck decides to counter what society says is wrong and risk going to hell) but is inevitably waged most furiously within the individual, who must resist the temptation to believe that "God could go around sticking things in your face and making you chase them all afternoon for nothing." Through the consciousness of a child who has taken literally the words of biblical teaching as his fundamentalist inheritance, O'Connor is able to dramatize in a fresh way the age-old struggle of faith. This conflict is certainly a large and universal (i.e., traditionally male) one, and, not surprisingly, O'Connor places this spiritual burden on a male protagonist. As a writer, she once again and perhaps predictably embraces the power and authority of the patriarchy. The boy's experimentation with language, moreover, may be seen as O'Connor's coming to terms with the possibility of expanding her stylistic boundaries, particularly those associated with female propriety or softness. The fierce narrator is even more essential to the writer with Christian concerns who wants to be taken seriously in a world in which pious cliché dominates much spiritual writing.

O'Connor's fellow Catholic Walker Percy observed in "Notes for a Novel about the End of the World" that the Christian writer in the twentieth century, experiencing the "massive failure of Christendom" (111), recognizes that Christianity's vocabulary is "worn out" and that "the old words of grace are worn smooth as poker chips and a certain devaluation has occurred, like a poker chip after it is cashed in" (116). O'Connor acknowledges the truth of Percy's observation, I believe, as early as her creation of "The Turkey" in which she begins to stake out new territory for the old but essential questions. The temptation to question God's goodness and to believe that God toys with us is, of course, a basic one for thinking Christians, and the matter is not simply resolved for Ruller. Believing that he has been presented the "gift" of the turkey by God and imagining that his family will consider the turkey to be proof that he is "an unusual child," Ruller regrets his earlier thoughts about God and, in pharisaical fashion, thanks Him: "We are certainly much obliged to You" (*O'Connor* 748). He then prays for a beggar to appear so that he can repay God by demonstrating his charity. Although Ruller's prayer is ostensibly answered by the appearance of Hetty Gilman (whose status as a beggar is questionable), he soon loses the turkey, the trophy of his manhood, to the very tenant children whom he had earlier thought, in a fit of magnanimity, he would help. Their treachery is horrifying to Ruller, who must now, presumably, question whether the loss of the turkey was also God's will.

O'Connor implies that Ruller will have to question his grandmother's fundamentalism and the narrow view that everything that happens is the will of God. We suspect that, like Hazel Motes and Francis Marion Tarwater, who also must come to terms with strictly fundamentalist backgrounds, Ruller faces rough days ahead. His experiments with blasphemy, including his important acknowledgment of the capacity of language to name and to damn one in the very act of naming, are central to O'Connor's concerns and to her development of the fierce narrator. Ruller's wrestling with the essential questions here is, of course, only a portent of what is to come in the later, far more startling fiction.

Just as Ruller tests the limits of language and comes to understand its importance as an indicator of the disposition of the soul, so in this story O'Connor begins to move away from the work of her apprentice years, often imitative and tentative, to confront the limits of her own language. If we have not answered the question of the identity of the fierce narrator, we at least know who she is *not*. With largely male models, O'Connor has opted for a tough narrative style that eschews "feminine" lyricism. She has found her fierce voice and the license to use it, for within that monologic vision stands the convicted artist.

The general intelligence is the intelligence of the man of letters: he must not be committed to the illiberal specializations that the nineteenth century has proliferated into the modern world: specializations in which means are divorced from ends, action from sensibility, matter from mind, society from the individual, religion from moral agency, love from lust, poetry from thought, communion from experience, and mankind in the community from men in the crowd.
—Allen Tate, "The Man of Letters in the Modern World"

He decided to go to Delehanty's for a drink. In the speakeasy, he discovered a group of his friends at the bar. They greeted him and went on talking. One of them was complaining about the number of female writers.

"And they've all got three names," he said. "Mary Roberts Wilcox, Ella Wheeler Catheter, Ford Mary Rinehart. . . ."

Then some one started a train of stories by suggesting that what they all needed was a good rape. —Nathanael West, *Miss Lonelyhearts*

3 *Literary Lessons*
The Male Gaze, the Figure Woman

If it may be said that we are what we read, then surely as students of writing and literature, we read much in the way that we have been taught to read, a fact attesting, of course, to the immense power of the academic literary establishment. Surely at no other time in history has so much attention been paid to reading—to the complexity of its habits, to the effects of its choices, to the power it confers on the text itself—than at the present time. As readers, we bring to every new text what we have assimilated from all of our old texts; as writers, we create texts that give body to the world as we have read and experienced it; as critics, we develop and cultivate awareness of the myriad communities of reading that affect any one text. The critic, in fact, has the dubious distinction of and responsibility for a kind of multiple awareness, by which she must now situate author, work, audience, and herself (for she is and is not the audience) in time and place in order to assess the effects of the word and its importance.

In attempting to come to terms with Flannery O'Connor's strange fiction, we must acknowledge, among a number of significant factors, the importance of O'Connor's own reading and the climate of literary education at the time. We must allow ourselves to wander in and about certain literary landmarks; sometimes when we visit one remarkable site, our thoughts may veer elsewhere, causing us to retrace our steps, to reenter a familiar house by a new door. We must also be reminded that to concentrate for a time on O'Connor's early literary environment is not to say that other forces, such as O'Connor's strong Catholicism, had less influence; on the contrary, this discussion will only underscore the connections among the factors that helped shape O'Connor's fiction. After all—if I may be allowed to simplify for a moment a complex series of exchanges—we shape our reading, and our reading shapes us.

When Flannery O'Connor left Milledgeville for graduate school in Iowa, she felt, by her own account, as ill prepared and unread as most of us did when we began graduate school. O'Connor seems especially critical of her undergraduate education at Georgia State College for Women, claiming, among other things, that she had never even heard of Faulkner, Kakfa, and Joyce when she left for graduate school, and that, in fact, she "didn't start to read" until she went to Iowa and "began to read and write at the same time." In fact, her letters suggest that, once away from Milledgeville, she "began to read everything at once," a situation that, she asserts, kept her from being "influenced by any one writer" (*Habit of Being* 98). As we have already noted, however, O'Connor had been quite active as a writer and artist in her undergraduate days, surely as active as any gifted undergraduate of the time. She had presumed to send cartoons to the *New Yorker* and poems and stories to other commercial magazines. She had edited the literary magazine, written a parody of Proust as well as comic pieces about Coleridge and Chaucer, and established a reputation for her talents sufficient to garner the support of one of GSCW's most discerning and influential faculty members, George Beiswanger. Beiswanger evidently saw O'Connor's genius and encouraged her to attend graduate school at the University of Iowa. Viewed in light of this encouragement, O'Connor's deprecation of her undergraduate education may appear at the least ungrateful, and her claim that her literary education began at Iowa is baffling when one views her undergraduate transcripts and the literature courses that she took. O'Connor may simply have been self-conscious at having attended "only" a Georgia teachers' college. Although her letters convey the clear impression that she was less than enthusiastic about her alma mater, she did later accept invitations and awards from the institution and enjoyed friendships with several of its faculty.

In any event, O'Connor's bona fide, systematic literary education began in the Midwest, where, after her transfer from journalism to the writing workshop, she read widely in modern literature and, as we have previously noted, absorbed the tenets of the New Criticism. Indeed, John Crowe Ransom, Robert Penn Warren, and Andrew Lytle, all associated with the American version of the New Criticism, visited the Writers' Workshop and offered encouragement to O'Connor, who, according to Sally Fitzgerald, now introduced herself as Flannery O'Connor.

O'Connor's shy and self-conscious demeanor may well have been drawn to the emphasis in the New Criticism on the necessary impersonality of the work of art and the need for the writer to erase herself from the work. The assumptions of the New Critics that poetic or literary language differs from practical language and that the temperature of the text can be taken by analyzing its linguistic and metaphoric structures may have appealed to O'Connor's disdain for the subjective and sentimental and her established penchant for irony, satire, and caricature. With this approach the author might use her own experience, *transformed*, in any way she liked. What mattered was the end result, the created thing, the work of art. (O'Connor's Milledgeville readers, of course, were unschooled in the New Criticism and thus had no qualms about searching the text for the author!) Such a view of creativity would likely have afforded a great deal of freedom to a young southern woman away from home for the first time and needing to establish her text and territory outside the expectations of her region, her class, her race, and her sex. I believe that O'Connor found a measure of that freedom at Iowa and within her schooling in the New Criticism. Surely she learned to take certain risks as a writer and not to take others. For example, as we noted earlier, the master's thesis stories usually center around male protagonists— "The Crop" is exceptional in its focus on the limitations of the female writer—and they represent genuine attempts on O'Connor's part at getting outside her own experience to write about "universal" matters. "The Turkey" affords the first real insight into the direction O'Connor's writing would take in the years ahead, most notably in *Wise Blood*, on which O'Connor began working in December 1946 in Iowa. "The Train," included among the thesis stories and published in *Sewanee Review* in 1948, was revised to become the first chapter of the novel. Moreover, in 1948 Andrew Lytle, editor of *Sewanee Review*, began to "oversee" O'Connor's work on the novel. We know, furthermore, that Caroline Gordon, certainly at least indirectly associated with the New Criticism through her marriage to Allen Tate, had a strong hand in shaping the work.

Although recent arguments insist that literary modernism has been far too narrowly defined and interpreted, few would question the importance of T. S. Eliot, T. E. Hulme, Ezra Pound, and John Crowe Ransom to the development of the modernist tradition. Hulme's attack in "Romanticism and Classicism" on the romantic fallacy—the idea, popularized in the nineteenth century, that the individual, through his or her own energetic will and power to reason, can overcome any obstacles—is indicative of the modern distrust of the romantic faith in the individual and in the subjective (and hence the emotional). Hulme's argument, of course, influenced Eliot's insistence on the writer's need for humility and restraint before "the tradition" in his landmark essay, "Tradition and the Individual Talent," an essay that O'Connor knew well.[1] Eliot's essay insists on the necessity for the writer's awareness of his place in a tradition that begins with Homer, and it concludes by advocating a retreat from subjectivity: the artistic consciousness must transform the personal into the objective so that in the ensuing work the artist himself is nowhere to be found. Such ideas are congruent with the approach of the American New Critics, among whom were Ransom, Cleanth Brooks, W. K. Wimsatt, Allen Tate, Monroe Beardsley, and R. P. Blackmur.

Strongly aided by the Fugitives at Vanderbilt University in the 1920s, the New Criticism focused upon poetry, arguing that the poem "existed as a self-enclosed object" and that "each of its parts was folded in on the others in a complex organic unity." Furthermore, the poem as object had to be severed "from both author and reader" (Eagleton 47); the author's intentions and the readers' responses were deemed irrelevant to interpretation. (Indeed, is such objectivity possible? After all, as we now recognize, even the choice of tools and angle of approach are dependent on individual preference and response.) For the New Critics, as the poem is transformed "into a self-sufficient object," it must be removed from historical and social context: "The poem must be plucked free of the wreckage of history and hoisted into a sublime space above it" (48). Analysis of the poem is possible only through "the toughest, most hardheaded techniques of critical dissection" (49), the assumption being that in a scientifically oriented society only the most "objective" tools should be employed in any respectable literary analysis.

Although the artist as individual personality is absent from the work, that artist must attempt to follow Pound's dictum to "make it new," that is to say, to strive for freshness of approach "not only in terms of the language used in [his or her] own generation but also against the background of language used in texts perceived as literary in previous generations" (Clark and Holquist 192). The force of the New Criticism, however, was conservative and formalist, considering the literary text itself as "a self-contained object independent of its extraliterary environment" (Clark and Holquist 186). Later critics — including Mikhail Bakhtin, who had serious objections to the formalist school in Russia — would point out that, although technical analysis of any work is valuable,

> such [technical] aspects are only part of a work of art. Technical features have mostly to do with the material out of which a work is crafted, and just as it is important to understand marble in order to analyze a statue, it is also necessary to understand language in order to analyze literature. But what is important about a Praxiletes statue is ultimately the human form, not the stone, and similarly the aesthetic aspect of a literary work of art goes beyond words, at least as they are treated by linguists. (Clark and Holquist 189)

After all, Bakhtin explains, although the sculptor uses a chisel, that chisel does not go into the work of art (Clark and Holquist 189).

Bakhtin argues that, for all their claims of objectivity, the formalists "merely redirected the old-fashioned critical concern for the psychological life of authors and characters to the psychology of readers" (Clark and Holquist 191), perhaps, we might add, preparing the way for today's reader-response criticism. Bakhtin himself believed the literary work to be open-ended, a confluence of many discourses that are in themselves acts of understanding "not yet completely understood" and that "[a]ny attempt to limit art to its brute form treats art as if it were over, as if it were a thing and not a deed" (Clark and Holquist 189). Bakhtin's view, of course, is antithetical to the New Critics' emphasis on the text as verbal icon, an entity that is, in Joyce's terms, static rather than kinetic. Sometimes attacked today for being "a recipe for political inertia" and for its rigidly masculine bias, the New Criticism nevertheless made its mark on graduate education in the 1940s and 1950s, so much so, in fact, that "it seemed the most natural thing in the literary critical world; indeed it was difficult to imagine that there had ever been anything else" (Eagleton 50). Some of O'Connor's earliest teachers of writing were among the New Critics, and they offered real encouragement to her work.

While O'Connor was a graduate student at Iowa in 1945, John Crowe Ransom, then editor of *Kenyon Review,* "chose one of her stories to read aloud during [a] classroom visit and comment[ed] favorably upon it" (*O'Connor* 1241); later Robert Penn Warren and Allen Tate would offer encouraging words. In a course in literary criticism taught by Austin Warren, O'Connor chose James Joyce's *Dubliners* and Brooks and Warren's *Understanding Fiction* as her supplementary texts (*O'Connor* 1241). *Dubliners* was an especially popular object for exploration by the New Critics as their technique expanded to include fictional analysis. Throughout her essays O'Connor alludes to the tenets of the New Criticism. For instance, suggesting Eliot's recommended detachment, she maintains that "the writer's business is to contemplate experience, not to be merged in it" (*Mystery and Manners* 84), and in "The Nature and Aim of Fiction" she offers her own brief history of the novel, explaining that the essential difference between the eighteenth-century novel and today's novel "is the disappearance from it of the author." In the matter of authorial absence, the work of Henry James marked the turning point: "[Henry James] sat behind the scenes, apparently disinterested" so that "[b]y the time we get to James Joyce, the author is nowhere to be found in the book" (*Mystery and Manners* 74). Repeatedly in her essays and letters O'Connor insists on the dramatic integrity of the work of art. In statements such as the following she demonstrates that she has learned well the lessons of the New Critics:

> [A] piece of fiction must be very much a self-contained dramatic unit.
>
>   This means that it must carry its meaning inside it. It means that any abstractly expressed compassion or piety or morality in a piece of fiction is only a statement added to it. It means that you can't make an inadequate dramatic action complete by putting a statement of meaning on the end of it or in the middle of it or at the

beginning of it. It means that when you write fiction you are speaking with character and action, not about character and action. The writer's moral sense must
coincide with his dramatic sense. (*Mystery and Manners* 75–76)

At issue here is not whether O'Connor herself always succeeded in effecting
the desired dramatic effect; the point is that O'Connor, although for a time
geographically displaced from the southern community that provided her
subject matter, found in her graduate education the basis for her aesthetic.
To the end of her life, in her comments on fictional art O'Connor would
argue a curious blend of the tenets of the New Criticism and those of Catholic Christianity.

Wise Blood is a work deeply influenced by O'Connor's reading in the mod-
erns, her assimilation of the New Criticism, and the emergence of a stringent
Catholicism as the bedrock of her fiction. Poe, Nathanael West, and T. S.
Eliot are the three writers most central to O'Connor's version of the modern waste land in *Wise Blood,* a work that demanded seven years for its creation and for the articulation of O'Connor's Christian vision. Even a cur-
sory look at the nearly two thousand pages of typescript drafts of *Wise Blood*
in the O'Connor Collection at Georgia College & State University reveals
the painstaking process of the novel's creation and the author's groping for
subject matter consonant with her Christian vision and with the stylistic
demands of the New Criticism. Within these limitations, these "givens,"
O'Connor would fashion her own text; it would not be a work of the dialogic
imagination, of course, but would speak monologically and unflinchingly
from the patriarchal Church and the patriarchal literary establishment.

Indeed, Allen Tate's important essay "The Man of Letters in the Modern World," a statement from which serves as an epigraph for this chapter,
might be said to summarize quite accurately the ideological or theological
base of O'Connor's first book. Tate presented this essay as the Phi Beta Kappa
Address at the University of Minnesota in 1952, also the year of the publication of *Wise Blood.* Deeply influenced by the work of T. S. Eliot and especially dependent on Eliot's idea of the dissociation of sensibility, Tate argues
that the artist—always referred to as the "man" of letters and described in
terms of his responsibilities to "the image of *man*" and "other *men*" (italics
mine), a gender discordance in our generation though not in Tate's, unfor-
tunately—must do more than "communicate," the word itself suggestive to
Tate of the modern mind's dissociation. The artist must be in communion

with his world: "We use communication; we participate in communion" ("Man of Letters" 9). Like Eliot in his condemnation of the Cartesian split, Tate asserts that Descartes "divided man against himself" and that "the dehumanized society of secularism . . . imitates Descartes' mechanized nature" and seriously threatens "the eternal society of the communion of the human spirit" ("Man of Letters" 4–5). In Tate's view (and using the gender that he inevitably chooses), modern man is separated from himself, without direction, removed from the communion of love:

> Man is a creature that in the long run has got to believe in order to know, and to know in order to do. For doing without knowing is machine behavior, illiberal and servile routine, the secularism with which man's specific destiny has no connection. I take it that we have sufficient evidence, generation after generation, that man will never be completely or permanently enslaved. He will rebel, as he is rebelling now, in a shocking variety of "existential" disorders, all over the world. ("Man of Letters" 7)

In *Wise Blood* the character who "does without knowing" is, of course, Enoch Emery, who follows his instincts backward to the bestial. Hazel Motes, on the other hand, is the man who will never be "enslaved," who must rebel on the most profoundly existential level. In fact, in one of the typescript drafts of the novel, O'Connor has Haze's roommate say, in a remark that could be a description of the dilemma of Haze in the published novel, that he is "caught between articulateness on a small scale and feeling on a grand scale" (Collection 128a, 2).[2] O'Connor is thus very much in accord with the prophetic description of the modern world provided by Allen Tate:

> [A] society which has once been religious cannot, without risk of spiritual death, preceded by the usual agonies, secularize itself. A society of means without ends, in the age of technology, so multiplies the means, in the lack of anything better to do, that it may have to scrap the machines as it makes them; until our descendants will have to dig themselves out of one rubbish heap after another and stand upon it, in order to make more rubbish to make more standing room. The surface of nature will then be literally as well as morally concealed from the eyes of men. ("Man of Letters" 10)

This description calls to mind Slade's used car lot in *Wise Blood*, a setting evocative of O'Connor's outlook on the entire ugly, urban landscape: "full of old cars and broken machinery" (*O'Connor* 68). Further emphasizing the desolation and confinement of the place, O'Connor writes that the lot is closed in on either side by "two old buildings reddish with black empty windows, and behind [it] there was another without any windows" (70). Obviously Slade's son, the boy with the face "like a thin picked eagle's" (69) and a penchant for blasphemy, is one of several doubles for Haze, as the boy mutters repeatedly, "Sweet Jesus, sweet Jesus, sweet Jesus" (73).

O'Connor and Tate write from the point of view of Catholic sacramentalism, and both writers suggest that, when the artist finds himself in a "secularized society of means without ends," that artist "shouts to the public," as Tate puts it.

> When the poet is exhorted to communicate, he is being asked to speak within the orbit of an analogy that assumes that genuine communion is impossible: does not the metaphor hovering in the rear of the word *communication* isolate the poet before he can speak? The poet at a microphone desires to sway, affect, or otherwise influence a crowd (not a community) which is then addressed as if it were permanently over there—not here, where the poet himself would be a member of it; he is not a member, but a mere part. He stimulates his audience—which a few minutes later will be stimulated by a news commentator, who reports the results of a "poll," as the Roman pontifex under Tiberius reported the color of the entrails of birds—the poet thus elicits a response, in the context of the preconditioned "drives" ready to be released in the audience. Something may be said to have been transmitted, or communicated; nothing has been shared, in a new and illuminating intensity of awareness. ("Man of Letters" 12)

Although she apparently does not share Tate's aversion to the word *communication*, O'Connor writes, in "The Regional Writer," that "[u]nless the novelist has gone utterly out of his mind, his aim is still communication, and communication suggests talking inside a community," attributing the success of southern fiction to just such a sense of community (*Mystery and Manners* 53). She continues the point: "The isolated imagination is easily corrupted by theory, but the writer inside his community seldom has such a problem" (54). The community, with its shared values, is therefore central to the effectiveness of the writer's vision. Extending Tate's observations about the modern audience, O'Connor suggests that when a community with shared values cannot be assumed, the writer must use extravagant tactics. In this oft-quoted passage she notes, "When you can assume that your audience holds the same beliefs you do, you can relax a little and use more normal means of talking to it; when you have to assume that it does not, then you have to make your vision apparent by shock—to the hard of hearing you shout, and for the almost-blind you draw large and startling figures" (*Mystery and Manners* 34).

In the context of Tate's remarks, this statement appears to be not only an underscoring of the value of community but also an aid in understanding the value O'Connor placed on region, especially the South, with its Bible belt inheritance: a sense of the meaning of place and time that is largely Christian and conservative. The vision of wholeness is, of course, biblical, and, for O'Connor, in the "Christ-haunted" South that vision was still evident, whereas more secularized parts of the country reflected the fragmentation of the modern psyche. However, the disease of secularism was spreading. The South was not safe. Allen Tate states that the "list of dissociations" has no end, because "there is no end, yet in sight, to the fragmenting of the western mind" ("Man of Letters" 13), a theme reiterated in much of O'Connor's prose and certainly dramatized in her fiction. And, as we have seen, in O'Connor's fiction fragmentation and alienation are frequently associated with the urban; in fact, *Wise Blood* fully develops this theme, anticipated as early as "The Geranium."

Thus, O'Connor's recognition of the need for a community with shared spiritual values, her acknowledgment of the necessity for a dramatic rendering of subject whereby the artist's own personality is erased, and her educated conviction that the work of art is a nonpolemical, discrete entity were significant in determining her approach to *Wise Blood*. Nevertheless, the task of creating this novel was arduous. If we examine the drafts of the novel, we will understand the painstaking process by means of which O'Connor gradually exerted control over her material. Under the aegis of the New Criticism and in the context of the western tradition of the male quest narrative, O'Connor defines her territory.

A number of recent feminist commentators have called our attention to the western tradition of viewing the spiritual journey as a linear one that chronicles the male hero's turning away from the world and its temptations to focus on the end goal, salvation. This pervasive view of spiritual quest is goal-oriented, as the soul proceeds from disbelief, doubt, or spiritual aridity, and moves through and then beyond the world and the flesh to the spiritual. In fact, so ingrained is such a view in our culture that many of us today have difficulty framing the soul's journey in ways other than this traditional male, linear progression — the story of Everyman. Certainly in O'Connor's time this metaphor was long established. In her published fiction O'Connor does not appear to question the paradigm, nor would we really have expected her to do so.

In an insightful book on the subject, *Women and Spirituality*, Carol Ochs posits that when spiritual "maturity" follows a "male developmental model," the goal is "individuation" and requires "separation of the self from its supporting environment." On the other hand, when a "female developmental model" is used, spiritual maturity is defined by the acknowledgment of "interconnectedness," a "coming into relationship with reality" (Ochs 10). The linear view of existence, of course, underlies western theology, which, as Ochs notes, "emphasize[s] an end of days, a final judgment, and an afterlife" (85). Ochs goes on to argue that the otherworldly direction of the male developmental model at the least tends to devalue life in the present, in this world, and, in its more extreme form, to view situations, things, and people as roadsigns or even roadblocks on the way to somewhere else: "Life becomes a journey filled with obstacles and traps over which we scramble and struggle in an effort to reach the release from our tainted fleshly existence" (21).

In such a struggle, of course, one loses one's sense of connection to others; the journey is a solitary one in which the individual soul often must be estranged from experience, constantly forced to reject those aspects of reality that do not in some way serve to move him forward. Ochs's distinction reminds us of the dualism of the Manichaean heresy, the necessity of turning away from the world as tainted and evil, a view that O'Connor decried even as she was charged — and in some corners continues to be charged — with committing the heresy. Over the years conservative readers of O'Connor have risen to her defense, and O'Connor's essays and letters seem to underscore her awareness of the heresy. In this statement, for example, O'Connor clearly associates Manichaeanism with that same dissociation of sensibility that paralyzes and fragments the modern psyche: "The Manichaeans separated spirit and matter. To them all material things were evil. They sought pure spirit and tried to approach the infinite directly without any mediation of matter. This is also pretty much the modern spirit, and for the sensibility infected with it, fiction is hard if not impossible to write because fiction is so very much an incarnational art" (*Mystery and Manners* 68).

O'Connor had read and admired William Lynch's *Christ and Apollo* and its exposition of incarnational art, as well as other theological commentary on aesthetics.[3] Surely her fiction would never have succeeded had she not understood the difference between polemic and art. At the same time, as we have noted earlier, O'Connor's penchant for satire led her to caricature, to the rapier thrust, to the savage put-down, a tendency obviously difficult to reconcile with a determination to be more than one-dimensional. Her aim was always to ground her characters, to make them, at least initially, as real and recognizable as possible, to move away from the one-dimensionality of a Sunday school pamphlet and, I believe, away from art that was thinly allegorical. For a writer with a developing sense of spiritual purpose, the challenge is obvious: how to create respected fiction that is not merely a covering for dogma and, at the same time, fulfill the responsibility one feels toward God-given talent, i.e., to use that talent to shake the shoulders of a spiritually drowsy (if not sleeping) humanity. O'Connor's use of the male spiritual journey in both of her novels certainly suggests her knowledge of the importance of that tradition, even as she stretched and shaped it to her own needs.

As Mary Gordon has observed, "The image of the moving boy has been central in American writing," and she reminds us that this boy "*must* be able to move" and to move "freely" and "quickly" ("Good Boys and Dead Girls" 3). Clearly O'Connor's male heroes in the novels, Hazel Motes and Francis Marion Tarwater, follow this American tradition of the moving boy: "The boy on his strong legs cuts through the world, through time, constricting space, the accidents of birth, class, limitation, law" ("Good Boys and Dead Girls" 3–4). By the time she began working on *Wise Blood*, O'Connor had internalized the male-centered spiritual journey in the tradition of Melville, Hawthorne, and Twain, and even though there is evidence in the drafts that a female character might have had at one time a large role—even a prophetic one—O'Connor demonstrates in the final published version of the novel that Hazel Motes's journey is what matters.

Although Haze might seem an unlikely spiritual hero, he is actually not very different from the western paradigm: Like Oedipus, who gains a terrible wisdom through suffering and finally turns away from the world, Haze appears to move forward only to go backward to the truth: the reality of the Fall and his own sin, guilt, and need for redemption. In the end, he, too, is cast out (through his own free choice). Both Oedipus and Haze, self-blinded, are at last able to see, and what they are able to see is themselves, overwhelmingly repugnant. We now know that O'Connor resolved the problems she was having with the ending of *Wise Blood* when Robert Fitzgerald suggested that she read Sophocles' Oedipus plays. Given O'Connor's literary education, the tradition of southern conservatism of which she was a part, and her fierce Catholicism, her attraction to the story of Oedipus's initiation into tragic humility is not surprising. Thus she follows the classic model of the male journey into spiritual awareness, never raising the questions that Ochs and others today find so central to acceptance of the journey metaphor:

> If the spiritual journey is the journey of the mind to God, is God found only at the end of life? Where is God in childhood, in friendship, "where two or three are gathered in my name"? The notion of stages along a journey is so pervasive that it occurs not only in spiritual writing but in writings on developmental psychology, the stages of moral development, and the "seasons" of people's lives. (Ochs 118)

Many O'Connor readers today complain of the absence throughout her fiction of the plain old milk of human kindness, of love in any human relationship, of simple friendship. Often these readers are not comforted by the disclaimer that O'Connor was not describing the real world, that her satirical technique precluded the presentation of mercy, with its connotation of softness and acquiescence. In many cases these rebellious readers are Christians (often female), who seek their own affirmation of God's love in the world.

To such readers we can offer little consolation. As Carol Ochs warns, if we use another common western metaphor for the spiritual journey, the ascent of the mountain, we should be warned that "[t]he farther up we climb, the more distant we become from our world," the components of which, after a time, "take on the appearance of children's toys," so that "people, their houses, and their enterprises seem diminished, even trivial" (119). Similarly, if we use the metaphor of the journey into the desert or away from civilization, also familiar in western literature, we may come to believe that, because it has turned away from God, "civilized" society is completely corrupt, that human achievement is illusory, and that our best hope is complete dependence on God. Arguing that "a view of radical otherness" is part of the "pronounced dualism" of traditional spirituality, Ochs sees the emphasis on this dualism in all aspects of life: "this world vs. the otherworld; the profane vs. the sacred; civilization vs. the desert; heaven vs. hell." Mary Gordon, a twentieth-century Catholic like O'Connor, writes that the word *spiritual* suggests "the twin dangers of the religious life: dualism and abstraction."

Gordon asserts that abstraction is "the error that results from refusing to admit that one has a body and is an inhabitant of the physical world" and that dualism, abstraction's "first cousin," admits that there is a physical world but "calls it evil and demands that it be shunned" ("Getting Here from There" 160).

Paradoxically enough, this same tendency to polarize is inherent in Tate's description of the nineteenth-century specializing mind presented in the first epigraph of this chapter. Thus the very condemnation of the "dissociation of sensibility" or Cartesian dualism found overtly or implied in such thinkers as Eliot and Tate seems to be presented in language undergirded by that same dualism; these writers use abstraction and polarizing language even to decry abstraction and dissociation. I believe that O'Connor absorbed that mind-set. As a case in point, we might note her tendency to flatten certain characters or character types to create her satire — the liberal intellectual in various guises, for example — a reduction or flattening that is certainly dependent on the power of abstraction. O'Connor herself, therefore, engages in the very habit of abstraction that she clearly satirizes in such characters as Rayber in *The Violent Bear It Away* and Sheppard in "The Lame Shall Enter First."

Perhaps the most obvious evidence of O'Connor's dualism occurs in her treatment of women and male-female relationships. After all, Carol Ochs warns us that we should not be surprised to find "[a]t the *pinnacle* of dualism . . . male vs. female" (122, the author's emphasis).

At this juncture it is imperative to note that O'Connor lived and died before the flourishing of the so-called second wave of feminist revolutionary thought in the twentieth century and that she certainly would not have been aware of the feminists' radical questioning of duality of thought, a questioning that has wide-ranging implications, especially for literary criticism. Furthermore, to observe that a kind of "natural" dualism underlies O'Connor's works — natural, that is, in light of the assumptions of the time and in light of O'Connor's Catholicism — is not to fault O'Connor. The observation simply serves to underline her conformity to certain important intellectual trends of the time. Frederick Asals's admirable 1982 work, *Flannery O'Connor: The Imagination of Extremity,* was among the first critical discussions of O'Connor's dualism as a central tension in all the work. However, Asals does not consider in any depth the matter of O'Connor's treatment of women and her frequent association of the fleshly with the female, nor does he emphasize the relationship between O'Connor's technique and her literary reading and education. Nor do other critics of O'Connor's work. Only recently have scholars begun to examine the negative associations of the female body, especially in western theology. Such recent works as Margaret R. Miles's *Carnal Knowing: Female Nakedness and Religious Meaning in the Christian West*, arguing that throughout western history "women's bodies were dissociated from women as subjects and represented as figures in a male drama" (xv), would likely be the object of O'Connor's satiric scorn. However, such works cannot be ignored as we come to terms with the theological implications of O'Connor's fiction.

When we read O'Connor today, our response may differ radically from our response of five or ten years ago, although we recognize that O'Connor might accuse us of being distracted by the "accidents" of fiction (male protagonist or female protagonist, what's the difference?); she would undoubtedly argue that the substance or "essence" of her vision is genderless, timeless. Her mentors among the New Critics would enthusiastically concur. However, those of us who struggle with the place of woman in the Christian scheme of things believe that ignoring the "woman question" is perilous, if not, at last, impossible. Mary Gordon's account of her Catholic upbringing explains succinctly the stifling atmosphere for women in the Catholic Church:

> I was born into a church shaped and ruled by celibate males who had a history of hatred and fear of the body, which they lived out in their lives and in the rituals they invented. They excluded women from the center of their official and their personal lives. When I tried to think of any rituals that acknowledged the body, except for rituals involving death and in a very oblique way birth, the only one I could think of was what used to be called "the churching of women," which is a blessing for the mother, a kind of purification after the mess of birth. It's a remembrance of the purification of the Virgin Mary; she would have been actually submerged in water, not merely symbolically cleansed, for the re-entry into the legitimate world, where body life could once again be hidden. ("Getting Here from There" 161)

Gordon is obviously struggling with the "woman question," especially as woman is often associated in Catholic theology with the flesh, the body. Gordon thus deals forthrightly with an issue that O'Connor was privately concerned with and that she resolved in perhaps predictable fashion in the published version of *Wise Blood*. I believe that O'Connor's treatment of her female characters in the final published version of *Wise Blood* is deeply relevant to this matter, particularly in light of evidence — in the draft versions — that O'Connor experimented for a time with a female prophet figure.

In the published version of *Wise Blood*, Sabbath Lily Hawks serves as one of the fleshly tests that Hazel Motes sets for himself in proving that sin does not exist. She is, in keeping with Ochs's description, one of the roadblocks on the male hero's quest for salvation. Although Sabbath believes that Haze is "just pure filthy right down to the guts" (*O'Connor* 169), she recognizes also his urge for the holy: "I seen you wouldn't never have no fun or let anybody else because you didn't want nothing but Jesus!" (*O'Connor* 188). In her own way Sabbath reiterates and dramatizes the message her father, Asa, gave to Haze earlier, "I can smell the sin on your breath" (*O'Connor* 49), for she is the first to present Haze with the message "Jesus Calls You" (*O'Connor* 21) on the pamphlet she hands him. Thus, Haze is, in a manner of speaking, the "moving boy" of American literature. As Mary Gordon observes, this moving boy "wriggles out from under the crushing burden of fate," which, in the paradigm, is that "unmoving weight," the female: "She who does not move, who will not move, who cannot move. Who won't allow the boy to move" ("Good Boys and Dead Girls" 4). The final version of Sabbath therefore fits the stereotyped or the paradigmatic female who is an obstacle in the male's spiritual quest. It matters not that Sabbath, presented as a caricature of the femme fatale, exudes no real sensuality or eroticism; O'Connor is nevertheless using the frame of the traditional male spiritual quest.

However, the drafts of *Wise Blood* in the library at Georgia College & State University reveal a startlingly different Sabbath, one who, for a time at least, occupied a central space in the novel and on whom a great visionary burden was laid. Although the approximately two thousand pages of *Wise Blood* typescripts still remain an incomplete record of the novel's progression, sufficient evidence exists that O'Connor was experimenting with a major role for Sabbath in the novel. In an early prospectus of the novel intended for her publishers, O'Connor wrote,

> The principle [sic] character, an illiterate Tennessean, has lost his home through the break down of a country community. Home, in this instance, stands not only for place and family, but for some absolute belief which would give him sanctuary in the modern world. All he has retained of the evangelical religion of his mother is a sense of sin and a need for religion, which eventually torments him

into taking up with a blind man and his wife, members of a small religious sect called in the novel, David's Aspirants. This sense of sin is the only key he has to finding a sanctuary and he begins unconsciously to search for God through sin. The ultimate sin becomes the seduction of the blind man's wife. An explanation of this act and of the realization it brings him to can only be had through the novel itself. (Collection 21, 1–2)

Noteworthy in this statement, of course, are O'Connor's intentions to present the central struggle of the novel as a male struggle, to emphasize the breakdown of the modern world, to focus on the male protagonist's search for belief by which he can find "sanctuary," and to present fleshly (female) temptation as a barrier to that male character's salvation. In fact, "the ultimate sin" is to be adultery. Furthermore, the central character's struggle was to involve his immersion in sin to defy its existence, an obviously absurd proposition but, in O'Connor's view, typical of the secular twentieth century. The obvious difference between the novelist's early intention and the final published version, in which Sabbath is the young daughter of Asa Hawks and not his wife, is striking. In the published version, it is Sabbath who actually seduces Haze, although yielding to that seduction is certainly not his "ultimate" sin.

By no means a child, Sabbath Moats, for so she is known throughout most of the drafts, is a complex character who is utterly lacking in sex appeal, one who is, in some of the drafts at least, an androgynous creature. Page after page of the typescripts depict Sabbath as physically ugly—a large woman, plainly dressed, with oversized and mysteriously shod feet. Several times O'Connor uses this description: "She had on a man's shoes and a washed out dress and a croker sack hung over her shoulder" (Collection 97, 9). In another version O'Connor writes, "[Sabbath] turned and looked at him and her lip curled and Haze thought he had never seen an uglier woman" (71, 12), and in another, "She was like a different kind of woman, like half of her was an animal and half an old man who had been beaten with a whip until his teeth dropped loose" (72, 11). In one version she is described as having "a voice like a boy's after it has changed, like the voice is too heavy for the boy" (71, 7–8). One neighbor describes Sabbath to Haze as having "a face like a garbage truck" (128d, 4), and Haze's sister Ruby remonstrates with Haze for wanting "a mule-faced woman" (121g, 5). With "short no-colored hair" (73, 2) Sabbath is described as walking "like a horse being led, with no particular interest in direction" (75, 5). Animal imagery is repeated in such statements as "Her face was drawn in on its own business and her eyes had a flattened mean look. [*sic*] like a horse's drawn-back ears" (139c, 1) and "She had a boney face, something like a mules [*sic*] but her eyes were glistening like two pieces of sucked green candy" (65, 3). The word *boney* in the last-quoted sentence was substituted for "pan-shaped, impassive," further emphasizing the lack of feminine appeal in Sabbath's expression.

The Sabbath of the typescripts is a compelling figure, however, for the hold she manages over others. Called by the Lord, she is set apart by her vision, often taken in "fits" so violent that Asa has to keep her locked in their room. At one point Asa announces to an assembled group, "This woman has seen God. . . . None of you are fit to be in the same room with her. Liquor in yer glasses and cursing on yer lips, woe to him who . . ." (103, 121). As Sabbath's protector, Asa is obviously subordinate to her in the eyes of the Lord; he is described in one passage as "a little man who looked like a round black boiling pot with limbs and a head, and *he belonged to the woman*" (71, 2, my emphasis). In one draft Asa asserts that the marriage has not been consummated; in answer to Haze's query if they are married, Asa responds affirmatively but adds, "But not for no lecherous purpose. I ain't touched her once ever" (70c, 4), implying that he respects the sanctity of his wife as one chosen by God and therefore one who must remain inviolate. In other drafts, Sabbath and Asa do consummate their marriage, but, not surprisingly perhaps, Sabbath's role is one of mere endurance, of wifely duty. Furthermore, Asa is baffled by Sabbath's refusal to allow him to see her feet:

> He had been married to her three months before he saw her barefooted. That was a fact. The first night he had taken her to bed she had been dutiful as she should, almost with an expression as sweet as—he didn't mean this in any blasphemous way but to show how she was to his heart a part of it; he would not say this aloud outside of his own bosom—Jesus on the cross. But she had kept on her socks. (138, 4)

Asa's curiosity increases, and he comes to believe that the sight of Sabbath's feet is part of his conjugal privilege.

Finally, feeling "the devil" enter him, he fights with her violently, and eventually he does manage to see her feet:

> In the end he had hung over them with his tears; but he had not had the number of tears it would have taken to wash them. That had been the beginning of his

punishment—the Lord had granted him two years by count, and the rest of his remorse had been in pain, dry pain that the Lord had set too deep down even to show on his face. Her feet were twisted like somebody had stomped on them while they were still soft. They looked like old turnip bottoms that had stayed in the ground too long. [*sic*] and overgrown. . . . And she lay, stretched out and shaking like the dead in an earthquake. (138, 5)

Because he has violated Sabbath's sanctity by viewing her feet, Asa is henceforth guilty, believing that every time he takes her in lovemaking he is being made to "pay" for his transgression, a fact suggesting that their sexual relationship continued to leave much to be desired. Asa begins to feel "meanness" growing in him (138, 6). This use of deformity and affliction as an objective correlative for a character's spiritual condition is typical O'Connor; the later characters Joy/Hulga, Tom T. Shiftlet, Lucynell Crater, and Bishop easily come to mind. In the draft versions of Sabbath, however, O'Connor seems intent on establishing Sabbath (who is, incidentally, given few lines of dialogue) as a figure apart; neither her husband nor the reader is allowed too close to her.

Although Asa experiences Sabbath's power in their strange marital relation, Haze Wickers (as he is called in most of the draft versions) experiences most completely the power of her presence. Haze, O'Connor repeatedly implies, is both repelled by and attracted to the woman: "[Asa and Sabbath] turned and the woman stopped halfturned and her eyes caught Haze in the back of the hall. The stare was the same as it had been in the street car and it held him fixed, like a sea current enclosing a bubble" (100a, 8). Sabbath's control of Haze, however, is most assuredly not sexual, except insofar as the stare of Medusa is sexual in its power over men. In fact, Sabbath's power contains much of that punitive quality that O'Connor had Haze associate with his mother's stringent fundamentalism in the published version of the novel. In another draft passage, O'Connor describes Haze as feeling that "[t]he look of her eyes was deep and hard like the cut of leather across the skin" (97, 9); in another, he feels her "staring through him like he was a hollow speck inside her eye" (76, 70–71); and, in still another, "[Haze] felt as if he had to hold on to something to keep from floating out into the darkness" (76, 71). He is a "bubble," "a hollow speck inside her eye," and something which is capable of being both punished by and lost in the "darkness" of her mystery. This association of the female with stasis and death is surely a recurrent one in western—especially American—literature by men. In one analogous context, for example, Joanna Burden in Faulkner's *Light in August* is described in similar language:

> With the corruption which she seemed to gather from the air itself, she began to corrupt him [Joe Christmas]. He began to be afraid. He could not have said of what. But he began to see himself as from a distance, like a man being sucked down into a bottomless morass. (Faulkner qtd. in Gordon "Good Boys and Dead Girls" 14)

As Mary Gordon observes, even the name Burden suggests "the heavy one, the one who slows [the male] down" ("Good Boys and Dead Girls" 13).

Contrary to O'Connor's stated intention in the prospectus cited above — Haze's seduction of Sabbath, Asa's wife, as "the ultimate sin" — in the drafts Sabbath herself wields what appears to be nearly primordial power over Haze Wickers. Across the bottom of one of the draft pages, O'Connor scrawls, "To understand Sabbath will be to understand himself" (143a, 11). Obviously, then, in these early stages of the novel, O'Connor conceived of Sabbath as being of central importance to Haze's salvation. We note, however, that, in the last analysis, the primary focus here is still on *Haze* and his spiritual journey. O'Connor was clearly uncomfortable with a major role for Sabbath. That early ambivalence about Sabbath may in part be traced to a modernist confusion about women, particularly following World War I. As we explore the influence of T. S. Eliot's *Waste Land* and Nathanael West's *Miss Lonelyhearts* on O'Connor, and on *Wise Blood* in particular, our attention will focus on what Sandra Gilbert and Susan Gubar and other commentators describe as the gender confusion of these writers.

The influence of Eliot's *Waste Land* on O'Connor's first novel is unquestioned. In 1984 Sally Fitzgerald argued that, although certainly Poe and West and Sophocles had influenced *Wise Blood*, "it was Eliot and his *Waste Land* who provided for [O'Connor] the first impetus to write such a book as *Wise Blood* at all" ("The Owl and the Nightingale" 55). Fitzgerald follows the lead of J. O. Tate in asserting a number of thematic and even verbal borrowings from *The Waste Land* and other poems, some of which I will comment on presently. O'Connor's private library does indeed contain Eliot's *Collected Poems, 1909–1935*. Fitzgerald believes that in the poetry and critical works of Eliot, O'Connor had "an object of contemplation that was invaluable to her as an artist at the outset and . . . [that] remained so throughout her writing life" ("The Owl and the Nightingale" 57). Certainly, the bleak and sometimes terrifying landscape of *Wise Blood* corresponds to the spiritually arid and chaotic modern world presented thirty years earlier in Eliot's poem.[4] Like Eliot, O'Connor suggests that the alienating urban setting is the objective correlative to the modern spiritual malaise and that this valueless, directionless world is manifested in a banal materialism in which salesmanship is what counts and the traditional Christian emphasis on our fallen condition is discounted. The modern city, after all, is a major character in Eliot's poem, as in this passage in which he presents its death-in-life condition:

> Unreal City,
> Under the brown fog of a winter dawn,
> A crowd flowed over London Bridge, so many,
> I had not thought death had undone so many.
> Sighs, short and infrequent, were exhaled,
> And each man fixed his eyes before his feet.
> (ll. 60–65)

Clearly the modern city represents that total loss of communion later decried by Allen Tate in "The Man of Letters in the Modern World," as "each man fixed his eyes before his feet" and made his way over London Bridge (with the obvious echo: London Bridge is falling down), completely separate from his fellow. Eliot was among the first to suggest the alienating and debilitating effects of urban anonymity, and in the drafts of *Wise Blood* and certainly in the final version we see O'Connor's use of the same idea. Hazel Motes may be seen as just another salesman in Taulkinham, a place of all sorts of "prostitution." The inhabitants of this city, too, have their eyes fixed on their own feet, indifferent to anything but themselves and perhaps their next purchase. In one of the few indications of beauty in the entire novel, O'Connor begins the third chapter with this important description:

> His second night in Taulkinham, Hazel Motes walked along down town close to the store fronts but not looking in them. The black sky was underpinned with long silver streaks that looked like scaffolding and depth on depth behind it were thousands of stars that all seemed to be moving very slowly as if they were about some vast construction work that involved the whole order of the universe and would take all time to complete. No one was paying any attention to the sky. The stores in Taulkinham stayed open on Thursday nights so that people could have an extra opportunity to see what was for sale. (*Wise Blood* 37)

As in Teilhard de Chardin's view, the universe is a place where the good is under construction; nevertheless, the inhabitants of the modern city cannot or will not perceive such a process. Indeed, in the above passage, we seriously doubt that Haze Motes is willing to recognize that "vast construction work" for, although his eyes are not on the merchandise in the store windows, he is intent on proving that sin does not exist and that "Jesus is a trick on niggers" (*Wise Blood* 76).

We are not surprised to find human sexuality degraded in the modern urban environment as it is described by both Eliot and O'Connor. Both writers suggest, for example, that in a society in which the sexual relationship is denied its sacramental value, sexual pleasure is sought for its own sake, and abortion is therefore a popular option. O'Connor's story "A Stroke of Good Fortune," originally intended to be part of *Wise Blood*, presents Ruby Hill as Hazel's sister, who is horrified to learn that she is pregnant; in fact, in the draft versions she contemplates abortion. Part II of *The Waste Land*, "A Game of Chess," is centrally concerned with what Eliot saw as the perversion of human sexuality in the modern secular waste land. The section ends with the conversation between two lower-class women in the pub who comment that their friend Lil has had an abortion. Although the source of the query "What you get married for if you don't want children?" (l. 164) is ambiguous, the question obviously and hauntingly reminds us of the traditional view that marriage and human sexuality exist for the procreation of the species and (as Eliot might later argue) the propagation of the faith. Furthermore, in Part III of *The Waste Land*, Eliot presents the sexual encounter between the clerk and the typist as a brutally mechanical one in which each is using the other for sexual gratification. Here there is no question of real communion or even, at the very least, communication. Told from the bisexual perspective of Tiresias, the episode is characterized by boredom and fatigue:

> The time is now propitious, as he guesses,
> The meal is ended, she is bored and tired,
> Endeavors to engage her in caresses
> Which still are unreproved, if undesired.
> Flushed and decided, he assaults at once;
> Exploring hands encounter no defence;
> His vanity requires no response,
> And makes a welcome of indifference.
>   (ll. 235–42)

The sexual encounter between Hazel Motes and the prostitute Leora Watts in *Wise Blood* is equally mechanical. Haze has found her name and number on a restroom wall and decides that he will use her to prove that sin does not exist. Significantly, when Haze stands outside Leora's window and peeks inside, he finds himself "looking directly at a large white knee" (*Wise Blood* 32); then, entering the hallway, he looks through a crack in the door. His approach is oblique and so is his sight of her; he never sees her in any fully human way. First he sees the knee and then he sees that "Mrs. Watts was sitting alone in a white iron bed, cutting her toenails with a large pair of scissors. She was a big woman with very yellow hair and white skin that glistened with a greasy preparation. She had on a pink nightgown that would better have fit a smaller figure" (*Wise Blood* 33).

To Haze, Leora is a physical presence only. He announces to her that he has "come for the usual business" (*Wise Blood* 34) and, remembering the taxi driver's assumption that Haze is a preacher, he insists to Leora, "I'm no goddam preacher," a fact that makes not a particle of difference to the prostitute. Although we have no indication that Eliot's typist is a prostitute, her attitude toward the sexual encounter is equally dismissive:

> She turns and looks a moment in the glass,
> Hardly aware of her departed lover.
> Her brain allows one half-formed thought to pass:
> "Well now that's done: and I'm glad it's over."
> When lovely woman stoops to folly and
> Paces about her room again, alone,
> She smoothes her hair with automatic hand,
> And puts a record on the gramophone.
> (ll. 249–56)

Haze's encounter with Sabbath Lily Hawks in the published version of the novel is also mechanical. She has pursued him for some time, and although he has appeared to have no real sexual feeling for her—his lack of desire or numbness seems to be a part of the modern malaise—at last he gives in. Timing is everything, however, for Haze's discovery that Asa Hawks has lied about his self-blinding as well as his own encounter with his double, Solace Layfield, has so completely unnerved him that he is ready to allow Sabbath to show him that "he's just pure filthy down to the guts" (*Wise Blood* 169). Perhaps not surprisingly, in sexual intercourse with both Leora Watts and Sabbath Lily, Haze is nearly passive; the women are the aggressors. Nina

Baym, Carol Ochs, and Mary Gordon would surely have us note that the women are merely stops along the way for Haze on his spiritual journey; they have little significance except insofar as they serve Haze's indulgence of the flesh and underscore his spiritual dilemma.

O'Connor's indebtedness to T. S. Eliot is, however, more complex than Sally Fitzgerald, J. O. Tate, and others have posited. Certainly as a Christian writer with a real penchant and talent for satire, O'Connor was drawn to Eliot's memorable evocation of the chaos and ugliness of the modern world. However, she does not seem to question Eliot's ambivalence toward the female, what Gilbert and Gubar call the "anxiety" many male writers experienced about the New Woman and her incursion into the realms of art and culture after World War I. Citing Eliot's early indebtedness to Swinburne's "depiction of the battle between men and women," Gilbert and Gubar maintain that Eliot's early unpublished "The Love Song of St. Sebastian" clearly "associates desire with destruction, sex with violence" and that this "consciousness of sex warfare . . . permeates much of Eliot's work" (*War of the Words* 30–31). In "The Love Song of J. Alfred Prufrock," the self-conscious Prufrock is overwhelmed by a world in which women are now free to "come and go," talking of cultural matters and capable of wielding great power. It is rather obvious that Prufrock's inadequacy is largely related to his encounters with women who, he feels, scorn and deny him (*War of the Words* 32). In the prose poem "Hysteria," included in *Collected Poems, 1909–1935* (the volume O'Connor owned), Eliot presents a male speaker obviously threatened by the power of the female. The short, little-known piece is here quoted in its entirety for its revelation of male terror of the female:

> As she laughed I was aware of becoming involved in her laughter and being part of it, until her teeth were only accidental stars with a talent for squadrill. I was drawn in by short gasps, inhaled at each momentary recovery, lost finally in the dark caverns of her throat, bruised by the ripple of unseen muscles. An elderly waiter with trembling hands was hurriedly spreading a pink and white checked cloth over the rusty green iron table, saying: "If the lady and gentleman wish to take their tea in the garden, if the lady and gentleman wish to take their tea in the garden. . . ." I decided that if the shaking of her breasts could be stopped, some of the fragments of the afternoon might be collected, and I concentrated my attention with careful subtlety to this end. (37)

One wonders, of course, just who the victim of this hysteria is, just who the "hysterical" party is—the title itself obviously female in etymology—the male speaker or the laughing female whose spell the speaker seeks to resist.

Educational advances for women, increased numbers of women in the workforce, the bold achievements of a number of gifted women, many of whom publicly flouted Victorian convention in their sexual lives, appear to have frightened—in some instances, terrified—many male writers and thinkers of the time, including, of course, T. S. Eliot. In fact, Gilbert and Gubar include Ford Madox Ford, James Joyce, William Faulkner, Ernest Hemingway, D. H. Lawrence, and William Carlos Williams among those writers who are preoccupied with "maimed, unmanned, victimized" male characters. "Because until recently the texts in which these characters appear have been privileged as documents in a history of cultural crises, the sexual anxieties they articulate have been seen mainly as metaphors of metaphysical angst. But though they do, of course, express angst, it is significant that these modernist formulations of societal breakdown consistently employed imagery of male impotence and female potency" (*War of the Words* 36).

Gilbert and Gubar trace this imagery back to Rider Haggard's popular *She*, published in 1887, which presented the prototype of primordial female power; this woman's "formal title" is "She-who-must-be-obeyed" (*Sexchanges* 6). The popularity and influence of this novel among male writers of the early modern period largely result from the fact that the woman's "powers allusively evoke the urgency of suffragists unfurling the 'maiden banner' of their rights," thus crystallizing "male anxieties about the New Woman" (*Sexchanges* 6–7). O'Connor's experiments in the drafts of *Wise Blood* with a powerful, sometimes androgynous and often charismatic female seem to reflect the same ambivalence as her male literary models. Gilbert and Gubar assert that although "She" is the New Woman, she is "also an ontological Old Woman—at least figuratively older than the rocks among which she sits—whose serious autonomy brings to the surface everyman's worry about *all* women" (*Sexchanges* 7). The Sabbath of the *Wise Blood* drafts—with her powerful gaze and her mysterious and compelling and sometimes punitive control—seems to partake of that same ontological and autonomous female.

As Gilbert and Gubar observe, Haggard's "She" is also "La Belle Dame sans Merci, Geraldine, Moneta, Venus, La Gioconda, Cleopatra, Faustine,

Delores, Camilla, Lilith, Salome, and Helen," in other words, a being who "is from the first a version of the divine sorceress . . . whose magical powers deprive man of *his* powers" (*Sexchanges* 8). Haggard's *She*, a best-seller at the turn of the century, was an important agent in transforming the Victorian sensibility into the modern. She becomes the femme fatale relocated, as it were, to the modern city. As Gilbert and Gubar note, "The stony waste land She rules is modern in its air of sexual and historical extremity" (*Sexchanges* 22). Among other reasons these critics suggest for the novel's popularity is that it reflected "an obsession not just with the so-called new Woman but with striking new visions and revisions of female power" (*Sexchanges* 26). Joseph Conrad's *Heart of Darkness* at its conclusion presents the figure of She-who-must-be-obeyed "as if she were a silent hieroglyph in the language strange that articulates both her mysterious history and her threatening hystery" (*Sexchanges* 45).

To compare the Sabbath of the drafts with the primordial "She" who exerted such an influence on modernist male writers may seem far-fetched, but I suggest that O'Connor was merely absorbing the prevailing male attitude of the time. After all, one cannot really argue that Eliot, Conrad, and others influenced O'Connor in only one way. It is important to recognize that just as O'Connor, who owned a volume of Eliot's poems and *Heart of Darkness*, learned to see with their eyes the horror and sterility of the modern world, so she also adopted that "male gaze" — with all of its ambivalence — in depicting the female.

The fact that the drafts of *Wise Blood* demonstrate that O'Connor at one time considered a far more central place for Sabbath than the character occupies in the published version of the novel seems to suggest that, at least at one time, O'Connor was very much interested in questions of female power. Moreover, some of the passages suggest that Sabbath at some stages of her development served as a prototype of Francis Marion Tarwater of *The Violent Bear It Away*. In some of the last folders of the *Wise Blood* collection, for example, Sabbath's background is explored: At age ten, Sabbath lives with her Uncle Sedman and Miss Webbie Lee, a guardian figure who hates Jesus and tells Sabbath that her mother and father lived in sin and that the Devil visited her mother often in the disguise of "a red-headed nigger" (Collection 146b, 3) with whom Sabbath's father found her in bed. In his anger the father set fire to the house, and he and the mother were burned to death. The "nigger," unable to be burned, emerged from the flames holding the child Sabbath. In *The Violent Bear It Away* a similarly shameful background is attributed to young Tarwater, whose mother bore the illegitimate child in a car accident, after which she died. Old Tarwater must resist the attempts of the schoolteacher Rayber and the social worker to take young Tarwater from his wilderness training in prophecy and bring the boy to "civilization" and proper schooling. There are other similarities between these prophet figures. In the drafts of *Wise Blood* O'Connor describes the arrival of Miss Peabody and Mr. English, schoolteacher and principal, respectively, at Sedman's home for the purpose of allowing Sabbath to be sent to summer camp, where she can learn to weave and swim (146b, 1–12). Miss Peabody and Mr. English, like their counterparts Rayber and the social worker in *The Violent*, are not successful.

Like young Tarwater, Sabbath at an early age has had her experience with the Devil: "Sabbath never thought much about Jesus until one day when she was twelve years old a voice whispered to her from behind a fence that she was the ugliest white woman in Lithers County and probably in the whole state" (146b, 1). The voice behind the fence, presumably that of the Devil and certainly a forecast of the voice of the stranger in *The Violent Bear It Away*, is described as "a throaty artificial voice, now high and now low" which "began to tell her secret things" (146b, 1). Although she knows that she could look over the fence, Sabbath does not; instead, she continues to walk "by the side of it, listing slightly in the direction, with her face a wild pink color, slick as tin" (146b, 1). This account, which occurs several times in the typescripts, strongly suggests that, from this point forward, Sabbath understands her "call" as a fact that is established and that sets her apart:

> The question had always been in her. It was not a question with words and so she could not ask it. She had not thought any words about it, but it was there — a mystery. It did not concern so much the secret things the voice had told her; she had heard them before; and it did not concern her so much that she was ugly because really she wasn't. The voice behind the fence had been a shock to her because it gave an answer, and the answer was like the question, without words. The voice had said something different to her from what it thought it said. (146b, 1)

The last statement, in particular, suggests that the "secrets" shared by the diabolical voice, as well as its insistence on Sabbath's ugliness (a fact which, as we have seen, O'Connor underscores time and again, though here Sabbath insists to herself that she is not ugly), have the effect of confirming in Sabbath some sense of her specialness.

Later in that same version, O'Connor describes Sabbath as walking through the woods "looking for something." Especially fond of walking in the late fall, Sabbath perceives the woods at one point as "flat . . . as if they were pasted on the bottom of the sky." O'Connor continues, "They [the woods] were hollow then and the something she was looking for seemed to have just passed through them. They were left whipped and bare and the feeling she had was like some strange empty satisfaction, as if she had just missed what she was after; as if she were safe from it for a little while" (146b). Clearly, the paradox of pursuit ("as if she had just missed what she was after") and retreat ("as if she were safe from it for a little while") places Sabbath in the company of many reluctant prophets, including Moses, Jonah, and Paul. Furthermore, Sabbath's very human ambivalence anticipates the resistance of Young Tarwater and, for that matter, the resistance of Hazel Motes in the published version of *Wise Blood*.

That O'Connor initially experimented with a female prophet figure may be surprising, but that indeed appears to be the case. Moreover, in the drafts Sabbath's call to prophecy, her special relationship with Jesus, is acknowledged by many who know her. Asa observes, "She's been drawn to the Lord God. . . . She's felt the touch of God, felt it like she was being drawn into a hurricane" (71, 6). Reminding us of the ontological "old Woman" of Haggard's primordial "She," Sabbath is ageless. Haze, in his confusion, concludes that "she might have been a hundred and she might have been twenty-five" (71, 7), although Asa reports that she had her first "spell" when she was fifteen. She was "struck" after a revival: "Went through the woods straight through the woods for half a mile like she was being drawn on a string and didn't have no weight to her a tall" (71, 7). Having followed her into the woods, Asa secretly watches:

> Then she came to a little clearing was white from the moon and she stopped like she was just waking up or just going to sleep one and she just sunk down like something melting sunk down onto the ground and lay there for about a few seconds and we watched from outside that clearing and all a sudden she sprung up about ten feet in the air and begun to shout and rent her garments and we just stood there like something was seeping into us from her . . . and she sprang and leaped and ripped her clothes and . . . (71, 7)

In the drafts O'Connor experiments with a number of varying accounts of these spells, and on the surface they appear to resemble the visionary spells of Mrs. Shortley in "The Displaced Person" and Mrs. Greenleaf in "Greenleaf." However, the function of these two later characters appears primarily to be an ironic counterpoint to the traits of the central characters: both Mrs. McIntyre and Mrs. May are practical women, proud of their accomplishments and disdainful of the spiritual. Although both Mrs. Shortley and Mrs. Greenleaf seem imbued with the spirit, Mrs. Shortley's "vision" occurs largely because of her fear of being displaced by the Guizacs. Thus her obsessive reading of the Bible and subsequent conviction that she is one of God's chosen lead to her "apocalyptic" revelation and ironic command: "Prophesy!" (*O'Connor* 301) She is anything but a true prophet, and her sense of superiority is a foil to Mrs. McIntyre's conviction that the farm is her place and that all of her employees are "extra," a judgment based on her own Hitlerian superiority. In the case of Mrs. Greenleaf, the visionary impetus seems quite valid, although its manifestation is extreme, bizarre. The excesses of Mrs. Greenleaf's immersion in her God are, of course, repugnant to Mrs. May, who is "a good Christian woman with a large respect for religion, though she [does] not, of course, believe any of it [is] true" (*O'Connor* 506). When she considers the success of the Greenleaf boys, she consoles herself by remembering the figure of their mother "sprawled obscenely on the ground" (*O'Connor* 507).

Although O'Connor suggests that Mrs. May would do well to pay heed to the Christ of Mrs. Greenleaf's frenzy, Mrs. Greenleaf does not have the compelling power of Sabbath in the *Wise Blood* drafts. For example, in one draft passage, Shrike, another Jesus-obsessed character,[5] whispers a warning to Haze about Sabbath's powers: "[L]ook at her, ugly as dead bones but that's not the tempting part. She draws you like night. Don't look at her or you'll get drawn, and then you'll look like Asa" (Collection 70a, 9). As we have previously remarked, Sabbath's strange power, especially the power of her gaze, is repeatedly emphasized in the drafts, and although Haze is drawn to her, the attraction, contrary to O'Connor's stated intention in one prospectus for the novel, is mysterious and compelling—but not erotic. In fact, in one of the rare examples of Sabbath's point of view in the drafts, O'Connor creates an episode presumably centered around Asa's and Sabbath's rescue of Haze to dramatize her struggle with her responsibility to her own calling. When, in his intense pursuit of salvation, Haze has gotten himself drunk and fallen down the stairs of the apartment where Asa and Sabbath are living, neighbors bring him into the apartment and place him on Sabbath's bed. She withdraws into another room and begs Jesus to drive the neighbors away, as He drove the moneychangers from the temple: "Say they couldn't see Him, they could just feel the invisible whip but she would be there and they would know she could see Him and then they'd believe her" (141, 12).[6] Then Sabbath moves outside, where she sees her five roosters in the yard, and begins to pray, first about her own problems and then, ashamed, about the problems of Jesus: "She began to murmur then and to sway slightly, sitting there on the steps, and there were tears in her eyes after a while, real ones, not for her but for Him" (141,14).

Although Sabbath at this point might be accused of sentimental piety, O'Connor makes it clear that Sabbath's faith is a struggling, questioning one: "She saw herself like there were two of her facing eachother [sic], one stern and one slack. She was the slack one and the other one was in front of her, looking so far into her that she felt burnt hollow inside" (141, 14). This honest and rather compelling description of Sabbath's struggles, in this passage and a number of similar ones in the typescripts, certainly provides us with a fuller portrait of a female visionary than we are ever given in Mrs. Greenleaf. In this passage, for example, the prophet struggles with her own spiritual aridity and doubt: "Sometimes she would scream Jesus! Jesus! to herself, but she would still be hollow, there would be nothing to fill her up. There would be nothing anywhere" (141, 14). Further, in a revealing comparison that is later used by O'Connor to describe Haze Motes in the published novel, Sabbath is described in one draft version as walking "with her neck stuck forward like she was trying to smell something that was always being drawn away" (138, 7).[7] She is a new kind of woman, as Asa observes when he compares the dutiful women of his past with his wife, Sabbath:

> They [his grandmother, his aunt Webbie Lee, and others] were content to stay at home and in the country. They were content not to come to town and evangelize and act bold like strange actresses with electric birds sitting on their skulls. They spoke when they were spoken to. He watched her [Sabbath] sullenly from where he was. It looked to him like if the Lord showed Himself to her like she claimed in these spells, He would make the spell full of sweetness; instead he made it black and tight. He had His ways. Still it looked to him like if He was altogether serious, there would be something more happen, there would be some laying on

of hands or some visible wonder. . . . It didn't look like He'd show Himself for just her alone. (139c, 4–5)

What we find in the drafts, therefore, is O'Connor's curious ambivalence toward Sabbath. O'Connor seems to have absorbed the male modernists' awe and even terror of the New Woman and her power and to be simultaneously drawn to the possibility of empowering that woman with spiritual vision and charismatic authority. Perhaps O'Connor's few forays into Sabbath's consciousness in the drafts also indicate her ambivalence about woman-as-object (of the male gaze) and woman-as-subject (an agent with her own gaze).

Certainly O'Connor was experimenting with issues of female power in the drafts of *Wise Blood*, and these experiments are in keeping with the kind of rebellion against "doing pretty" described in chapter 1. As I also noted earlier, the figure of Sabbath who is Asa's wife and singled out by God is not essentially a sexual being. Asa's awe of her power, in fact, prevents him from viewing her deformed feet for some time. O'Connor further emphasizes her lack of traditional femininity by stating that she wears men's shoes and "a washed out dress and a croker sack hung over her shoulder" (97, 9). Something of this same bizarre appearance, of course, will adhere to the child Sabbath of the published version, with the difference that her coyness is obviously sexual — or O'Connor's wry, dark look at the twisted sexuality of the modern world. Most significantly perhaps, the Sabbath who is the child-temptress of the published novel has the ability to recognize the urge for Jesus in others but apparently has no personal experience of that urge.

In the last analysis (and not surprisingly), O'Connor could not follow through with the female prophet figure; she appears unable to reconcile the urge for Jesus with any picture of traditional female behavior. (After all, we might ask, what fictional models of the female spiritual quest were available to her?) It appears that she finally abandoned the draft Sabbath in favor of a protagonist consonant with the dominant model of the spiritual quest in patriarchal society and as O'Connor herself, in keeping with the western Christian tradition, undoubtedly envisioned that quest. O'Connor's ambivalence toward the female in the drafts is apparently resolved as Sabbath is flattened into a nearly allegorical obstacle-figure in the published novel. Sabbath possesses power only inasmuch as she serves as an obstacle to the male pilgrim's progress to salvation.

Of further interest in the drafts, however, is the pervasive association of female flesh with sin and punishment, in a manner consistent with the treatment of the female body throughout much of western literature and art. In addition to her reading of Eliot, O'Connor's reading of Poe and Nathanael West undoubtedly reinforced the association of flesh and the female that continues to pervade our thinking, as we shall see presently.

In the *Wise Blood* drafts, sexuality is a primary concern, and female sexuality is endowed with awesome, indeed frightening, associations. Although the student of these drafts may not be surprised to find that Haze is both drawn to and repelled by the alluring prostitute Leora, that student may be intrigued to learn that Leora is associated in Haze's mind with both his mother and his sister Ruby (the Ruby of "A Stroke of Good Fortune"). As was the case in his encounter with a French prostitute some time before, Haze is horrified by Leora's physicality: "The door opened and he just stood there. She had on a night gown. She was big and real and awful in the door. She was huge and living all over her [*sic*]. He wanted to disappear. He forgot what he had come for. She didn't say anything, she opened the door wider and he went in as if he were pulled in suction. She said, 'I thought you'd come'" (125, 3).

In another version, she is similarly described: "She had on a pink kimono and her hair was hanging down and she was not old; she was huge and living and terrible standing there smiling at him, breathing under the kimono" (124e, 5). Leora's power over Haze is, however exaggeratedly presented, that of the femme fatale. Like Keats's knight in "La Belle Dame sans Merci" and like many other versions of male emasculation in western literature, Haze awakens following his and Leora's night together with terrible feelings of emptiness, numbness, alienation, even momentary loss of identity: "He was cut off. There was no feeling in him or in the arm across him [Leora's]. He tried to remember the pleasure, he remembered it but with no feeling[.] The arm across him might have been a dead arm washed up on a beach. He did not know who he was" (107a, 1). Leora, too, seems to partake of the power of the primordial "She," as presented and popularized by Haggard's novel, although without the spiritual element. Furthermore, Haze confuses Leora with his sister Ruby, who is about to have an abortion — to Haze's horror. He thinks of Ruby's (and woman's) power to "shrivel up" children (140, 2), and in one passage in which he imagines that Ruby has thrown him out of her apartment, the ejection is obviously emblematic of a kind of abortion. Haze himself becomes the aborted fetus:

He saw her fierce, flinging his things out the door and he looked at the mess of it lying in the hall and there was something mashed down in it and it was him, shriveled up like something half made or something a million years old with a building coming down on top of it. He went on crazy, full of awful pictures of half-mashed things jetting out of sewers and flying out of doors and he began to run, trying to clear his head of them. He fell down exhausted on some steps and the pictures stopped and there was nothing he could think of but the selfishness that weighed on his neck. (Collection 125, 2)

He is Ruby's fetus, about to be aborted, and he is also, in his frenzied fantasy, her lover: "He pushed [Ruby] out of his mind and locked it shut, but she would come suddenly, out of nowhere, bloated and wailing at him as if he had done something to her. In her sleep she swam out like a great beaten fish with ax marks in her head. 'I didn't do nothing to you,' he said, 'I did it to Leora'" (144g, 3).

Indeed, when Haze first visits Leora's apartment in the middle of the night, he enters the apartment calling her Ruby several times, even after he has begun to make love to her. She responds, "'I ain't Ruby. . . . Do you know who I am?" (123b, 1). In a similar passage, Haze recognizes, "There was nothing about her but the hair to remind him of Ruby," although at this point he is caught by a "terrible dizzyness in his head": "He thought for an instant that he had killed Ruby and then he thought no he had killed Bill Hill [Ruby's husband]. Then he remembered that he had only slept with Leora" (137h, 2).

Haze's guilt seems to know no bounds. In other typescript passages and in the manner of the published novel, he associates his mother with forbidden sexuality. Like the punishing mother of the novel, the mother in the drafts seems to Haze to be omniscient: "He saw her like a single buzzard, high in a dead tree, watching nothing and seeing everything. He saw her squat and lump heavily into the air, gliding low" (116, 12). Rigidly fundamentalist, she has warned him about women: "[S]he said to watch out for women and sin she said sin rode on your back and grew bigger and bigger until it grew all over you and you shriveled into it" (89a, 1–2). Thus, a man can be "shriveled" by woman into sin, and she can then "shrivel" or destroy his progeny (and thus destroy him) by aborting the fetus. Woman's power appears to be endless and terrible. Further blurring the distinctions that Haze makes among women, he remembers his mother's beating him with a broom when he openly speaks rebelliously against Christianity (92a, 2), and he associates that beating with Leora's sexual attractiveness: "[Leora's] hand stayed heavy on his knee and he felt all over as if he were in Eastrod and his ma was beating him and the beats fell down like shafts of water and he was asleep and burning hot. When he had gone upstairs and she had been in the hall, he had seen the face was a big cat's face, full of wisenesses, and the Eastrod went out of the feeling and it was just the feeling by itself" (82a, 5).

As is the case in a number of the draft versions, the "she" of the last sentence above is ambiguous. O'Connor appears in some instances to have intended a deliberate blurring of Leora and the mother, making the Oedipal association even more emphatic. The incestuous content of the following passage is also obvious: "He knew how others got them [whores] and he had never done it but had thought about it, thought how it would be; (it would be like in bed with his mother when she would let him get in she would let him get in and through the flannel of her nightgown she would be up against him not through it and she would hold him there and when they did that her face was always strange like it was naked and she was having a pain that gave her pleasure" (88, 97). The confusion of mother/sister/lover in Haze's mind is, of course, rather typical of the literature of the patriarchal tradition, clearly underscoring the fact that O'Connor is learning to adopt "the male gaze" in her depiction of Haze's sexual confusion. In any case, throughout the draft versions of the sexual scenes involving Haze, the women are presented as fleshly danger, inviting but perilous in their capacity to annihilate the male. Each of them reflects some aspect of the primordial "She" popularized by Haggard and pervasive in the literature of the modernist male writers. Only the draft versions of Sabbath, however, display O'Connor's consideration of female spiritual power, as I have earlier demonstrated.

O'Connor's ambivalence about female power is to a great extent a clear response to a tradition in which the male quest dominates. Mary Gordon's assertion that American literature is concerned with the "moving boy" echoes Nina Baym's idea that in the literature created by male American writers, the male protagonist places woman in the role of "a character whose mission in life seems to be to ensnare him and deflect him from life's important purposes of self-discovery and self-assertion," adding parenthetically, "A Puritan would have said: from communion with Divinity" (Baym 73).

Baym's observation certainly seems to obtain when we consider *Wise Blood* in its final form. Haze Motes's story is in large measure a matter of his casting off the female, "the unmoving weight" associated with the flesh —

Mrs. Wally Bee Hitchcock, Leora Watts, Sabbath Lily Hawks, Mrs. Flood. The matter of Haze's relationship with his mother is, of course, a bit more complicated. In many respects O'Connor's depiction of the mother is an extension of the Sabbath of the drafts; she is a harsh and forbidding woman whose stringent fundamentalism marks Haze forever. She is largely responsible for teaching Haze to "pay" for his sexual guilt by punishing the flesh, the role of the threatening and punishing mother being a staple of much western male literature. A number of O'Connor critics have noted Haze's obviously Freudian association of his mother with the forbidden flesh of the woman in the "coffin" at the fair. Clearly O'Connor is here having her way with Freudian theory by suggesting that although the world of secular psychology asserts that it is "normal" for Haze to seek to reject his Oedipal attachment to his mother, Haze's salvation will depend on his not being able to rid himself of his mother's teaching, of his fundamentalist legacy, of the "ragged figure who moves from tree to tree in the back of his mind" ("Author's Note to the Second Edition" *O'Connor* 1265).

Thus, although Haze may symbolically reject the mother's teaching (which is in essence the grandfather's teaching) through attempting to prove that fornication and blasphemy are not sins and although he may destroy the glasses with which his mother read the Bible, he cannot escape the guilt that his mother's teaching causes him to associate with indulgence of the flesh. In this respect his mother serves as the vessel through which the family values pass. Haze's grandfather, after all, "had been a circuit preacher, a waspish old man who had ridden over three counties with Jesus hidden in his head like a stinger" (*O'Connor* 20). (We note again the fierce image of Christ associated with bodily pain.) Haze therefore ends up espousing the very fleshly punishment that his mother, as the purveyor of the family's teaching, inculcated in him. Although O'Connor's Catholicism would undoubtedly have prohibited approval of Haze's self-prescribed and self-inflicted penance, O'Connor clearly presented his desire for atonement as genuine. Yet the success of this male hero's journey depends on his punishing or denying his flesh and human connections, very much as Ochs describes the paradigm of the male spiritual quest.

As though in direct rebuttal of the ideas of such feminists as Gordon and Baym, Brian Abel Ragen's *Wreck on the Road to Damascus* maintains that *Wise Blood* is O'Connor's very deliberate use of the male quest in order to *attack* the pervasive myth of the American Adam. He argues that O'Connor employs her incarnational art to subvert the myth of the male hero with his ideas (from Emerson on) of complete freedom and self-sufficiency. However, like Gordon and Baym, Ragen argues that this myth has little room for women:

> The only role women can play in this myth is that of entrapper and domesticator, the representative of the things that it is the glory of our hero to escape. Women represent the ties and responsibilities of society, and they represent history. If they become important to the story, the American myth is spoiled. The solitary male's freedom will be lost in the duties of marriage and family. . . . Our ever-moving hero can only use women or escape them. If they become too important, his story is over. (6)

Ragen believes that, because O'Connor was a devout Catholic and a woman, the model for expression of her grave misgivings about the American Adam was Hawthorne, whose own daughter was a Catholic nun. Ragen reminds us that *The Scarlet Letter* represents Hawthorne's own serious questioning of the myth of the American Adam in its presentation of the powerful Hester Prynne. Because the novel give us "a sexually mature woman" in the central role, Ragen argues, the book is unique among "the classic American novels" (6).

It is easy to concede that O'Connor was drawn to Hawthorne's powers of blackness, just as she was drawn to his work as an antidote to the unbounded optimism of writers like Emerson. However, as we are all too aware, Hawthorne's attitude toward his female protagonist is not very easily ascertained. Indeed, if Hawthorne approved of Hester Prynne's rebellion against Puritan morality, he would seem to be in the camp of just those romantics who maintain that morality is a matter of situation and emotional commitment, not a matter for society or the Church to prescribe. Moreover, the figure representing traditional Christian morality, Dimmesdale, the secret sinner, appears the most pitiable and the weakest of the characters, a man locked in his own guilt and unable to make public profession of sin.

If there are similarities between this novel and O'Connor's work, we might note some obvious ones: In both novels, attitudes toward the flesh are central, the female is associated with fleshly temptation, and both Arthur Dimmesdale and Hazel Motes inflict their own fleshly mortification. At the time of Dimmesdale's death, witnesses claimed to see a scarlet A carved into his flesh. Certainly this self-mortification explains Dimmesdale's growing physical weakness, a debility that Chillingworth exacerbates in his obsessive need to destroy the minister. If Chillingworth is a diabolical figure, he succeeds only insofar as Dimmesdale continues to keep his terrible secret.

Thus, it is quite possible to argue that *The Scarlet Letter* is not the clear antidote to romantic notions of male freedom and autonomy that Ragen posits. And if the novel presents that rarity, a woman-centered journey, just what indeed are we to make of it? Do we applaud Hester Prynne's defiance of convention? Do we lament Arthur Dimmesdale's hypocrisy and fear? Or do we conclude that Hawthorne approved of the adulterous relationship, that he disapproved of only the rigidity of Puritan morality whereby the "sin" of love is punished? I believe that, as much as some of us would like to applaud Hawthorne's creation of a strong female character, we must nevertheless conclude that he had great difficulty deciding exactly what he felt about Hester's defiance. Furthermore, some readers argue that the story is really Dimmesdale's, not Hester's, concluding that Hawthorne was, at least in some measure, writing another version of the male spiritual quest. Moreover, Nina Baym posits that *The Scarlet Letter* becomes a part of the western canon only because critics perform "strenuous critical revisions of the text that remove Hester Prynne from the center of the novel and make her subordinate to Arthur Dimmesdale" (73).

His comments on Hawthorne to the contrary notwithstanding, Ragen writes with real conviction that O'Connor was influenced in the rewriting of the novel after 1949 both by her reading of Sophocles' Oedipus plays and by the story of the conversion and blinding of Saul of Tarsus (Paul). He notes that O'Connor's immersion in the works of her southern contemporaries such as Faulkner and Robert Penn Warren also influenced her idea that there is no escaping the past, "no perfectly fresh start" (6). Even as we acknowledge these influences, however, we see that O'Connor is still relying on the male version of the spiritual quest and that in that version women are largely irrelevant. Furthermore, I find no textual basis for Ragen's argument that O'Connor is attacking the fact that in the American Adam's journey women are deemed irrelevant or, at most, merely encumbrances along the way. As much as I would like to argue that O'Connor rebelled against the pervasive view of women in male literature, I believe that O'Connor adopted those male models, a fact most evident in her two novels.

Writing recently of his own history as a novelist, O'Connor's friend John Hawkes asserts that a "special sympathy for decay, deterioration, destruction (and for the maimed, the victimized), is one of the essential qualities of the imagination" ("Dark Landscapes" 142). He states that his own career as a writer was given impetus when he yielded to the dark side of his imagination, stating that his own "dark landscapes" have included a number of actual places but that "the landscape of the imagination is darkest of all" ("Dark Landscapes" 147). If we acknowledge the truth in Hawkes's assertion, I think that we will find in such writers as Poe, Graham Greene, and Nathanael West landscapes dark enough for O'Connor's interest and for reinforcement of her own technique. Moreover, each of these writers (not surprisingly) associates the flesh with the female, in many instances punishing that flesh violently. Furthermore, although I would concur with Ragen, Brinkmeyer, and others (following Lynch and Bakhtin) that O'Connor espoused an incarnational view of art theoretically consonant with her Christian belief and her aesthetic sensibility, I have concerns about O'Connor's attitude toward the value of life on this earth. Her repeated use of punishment of the flesh, which she appears to associate with the earthly and often with the female, is disturbing in what it seems to reveal about O'Connor's attitude toward the value of female experience.

It is commonly acknowledged that O'Connor's focus on the dark side of our human nature places her in the American "camp" of Hawthorne, Melville, and Poe. Surely John Hawkes would be hard-pressed to find a writer more obsessed with "decay, deterioration, and destruction" than Poe. Although Asals reminds us that O'Connor "never spoke of Poe without a note of deprecation" (25), he goes on to speculate that "Poe's practice of treating his horrific materials humorously may have contributed to that blend of nightmare and ironic comedy which is characteristic of *Wise Blood*" (25–26). Poe's use of "entrapment, suffocation, premature burial, and paralyzing rift in personality" also influenced O'Connor's first novel. Moreover, Asals develops a convincing parallel between the use of doubling in Poe's "William Wilson" and *Wise Blood*, as Haze is doubled several times at least—by Asa Hawks, Hoover Shoats, and, in a most savage way, Solace Layfield. Haze's visit to the sleeping Asa Hawks, to determine whether he is what he says he is, is anticipated by William Wilson's secret visit to the bedside of his sleeping double, and Wilson's violent murder of that double is the antecedent to Haze's murder of Solace Layfield. Sally Fitzgerald notes that O'Connor developed her interest in Poe at Peabody High School in 1941 and that she was especially fond of *The Narrative of Arthur Gordon Pym* and a collection of stories including "The Man That Was Used Up," "The Spectacles," and "The System of Doctor Tarr and Professor Fether" (*O'Connor* 1239). Although these narratives probably influenced O'Connor, I believe that Poe's influence is perhaps more profound than either Sally Fitzgerald or Frederick Asals has acknowledged. Let me say a few words, however, about the three Poe stories alluded to by Fitzgerald.

As if anticipating O'Connor's stories, these three tales are a curious blend of the humorous and the grotesque, and all three emphasize the difficulty of penetrating appearances to determine the real and the true. In "The Man That Was Used Up," Poe presents a fine figure of a man, Brevet Brigadier-General John A. B. C. Smith, apparently perfect in stature and physique. However, after much inquiry, the curious narrator discovers that the General is completely mechanical, having been scalped and mutilated in the late Bugaboo and Kickapoo campaign. The revelation elicits in the reader both laughter and horror, a response typical of the strategy of a Poe or O'Connor story. Surely this use of distortion and the grotesque — the "nondescript" actually moves and speaks, as the narrator observes it "[p]erforming upon the floor some inexplicable evolution, very analogous to the drawing on of a stocking" (Poe 411) — suggests O'Connor's fictional technique, especially her suggestion of man as automaton and her use of the mechanical as a surrogate body or body part (the Essex in *Wise Blood*, Joy/Hulga's artificial leg in "Good Country People," the resurrected automobile in "The Life You Save May Be Your Own," the clubfoot's shoe in "The Lame Shall Enter First," for example).

The truth of appearances is also the center of "The Spectacles," in which the narrator's vanity causes him to refuse to wear glasses. Falling in love with an older woman whom he has seen at the opera, he proposes to her, only to discover after their marriage that he has wed his own grandmother. She has tricked him into this bogus marriage to prove his own foolish vanity; now he must acknowledge his weakness of vision and begin to wear glasses. Spectacles are important in several O'Connor works, certainly in *Wise Blood*. As we have seen, Haze keeps his fundamentalist mother's glasses, along with her Bible, until Enoch Emery brings him the new jesus, at which point Haze destroys the mummy and then the glasses in his obsessive belief that he has "seen" the truth. When he put on the glasses earlier, he experienced a terrible distortion of his vision and then "[h]e saw his mother's face in his, looking at the face in the mirror" (187). In this curious shock of recognition,

Haze seems to recognize his mother's legacy and once again to rebel against it. He casts aside her glasses and, in so doing, casts aside her view of things, the stringency of his fundamentalist upbringing, in the frantic hope that he needs no aid to truth. In both stories, of course, the protagonists must recognize their need for "glasses," whether actual or spiritual, as each comes to terms with his mortal limitations.

Furthermore, the fact of our human mortality and limitation is reflected in both stories through grotesque images. In "The Spectacles" Poe presents the narrator's revelation of the fleshly deterioration of the "bride": she has false teeth, wears a wig, and uses heavy makeup, much to the horror of the groom/grandson. In *Wise Blood* Haze smashes the new jesus, presented to him in a perverse parody of the Nativity with Sabbath Lily as the Madonna and described tellingly as a "shriveled body," by throwing it "against the wall," where its "head popped and the trash inside sprayed out in a little cloud of dust." Sabbath is horrified at his destruction of her "baby," and when she lambastes Haze for his meanness, he nearly hits her, "rais[ing] his arm in a vicious gesture" (*O'Connor* 188). The mummy is a clear reminder of the fact of mortality, of flesh that once lived (the "baby") and its deterioration, of the cord that binds us all in a common humanity. We recall that when Enoch first introduced Haze to the mummy in the museum, he announced, "See theter notice . . . it says he was once as tall as you or me," a statement calling to mind Eliot's "Consider Phlebas, who was once handsome and tall as you" (l. 321) in Part IV of *The Waste Land*, "Death by Water." Eliot surely intends a reminder of our mortal connection. Before she "delivers" the new jesus to Haze, Sabbath herself recognizes something "familiar" about him. She thinks, "There was something in him of everyone she had ever known, as if they had all been rolled into one person and killed and shrunk and dried" (*O'Connor* 185). Ironically, the mummy epitomizes the very "religion" that Haze has been preaching, a kind of atheistic existentialism that places the value of human experience solely on this earth. If human life is all we have, then dust is all we are. Haze's action in destroying the mummy foreshadows his actual murder of Solace Layfield and his infliction of pain on his own body; in each instance, he believes that he is destroying what is "not true." The flesh must be punished.

One of the most bizarre and intensely satirical of Poe's tales is "The System of Doctor Tarr and Professor Fether," in which the narrator visits an insane asylum to observe the "soothing" method of treatment of M. Maillard. At dinner that evening with a large crowd of oddly dressed people, the narrator hears wild tales of various forms of insanity — of people who believed they were chickens, cheese, donkeys, teapots, frogs, pumpkins, and pinches of snuff. One young lady, it is reported, "wished to dress herself, always, by getting outside instead of inside of her clothes" (315). Of course, the narrator discovers that these dinner guests are describing their own maladies and that M. Maillard was driven mad and imprisoned. When he escaped, he freed the other inmates, who have established control over the asylum. Just as the dinner ends, however, the imprisoned "keepers" escape and reestablish control. O'Connor would have undoubtedly delighted in the situation presented in this story and been especially amused by the patients' maladies. Perhaps more significant for O'Connor's use, however, is the "soothing" method of treating the mentally ill, a process whereby the doctor humored the patient in his or her psychosis: for example, if the patient thought himself or herself a chicken, that patient was given chicken food. The "soothing" method of coddling the patient leads to disaster, as the patients eventually drive M. Maillard mad and take control of the institution.

Because Milledgeville, Georgia, is the home of Central State Hospital, at one time the largest mental institution in the world, and because O'Connor repeatedly takes to task those who will not look depravity and insanity in the eye, Poe's story would have been especially appealing to her. Moreover, the idea of a little world in which the lunatics gain control through beating the experts at their own game would have been congruent with O'Connor's vision of a world at the mercy of the "experts" and their theories. We are reminded of O'Connor's story "The Partridge Festival," in which Calhoun and Mary Elizabeth, on their visit to the asylum to visit the "scapegoat" Singleton, learn a dreadful lesson about human depravity and experience a recognition of their own frailty. In *Wise Blood* Hazel Motes may seem the "mad" character in the secular world of Taulkinham, but O'Connor would have us recognize that in this city and in our society the inmates have taken over the asylum. At least Hazel Motes, for all of his aberration, is, in Walker Percy's phrase, "on to something."

Repeatedly in Poe's work the flesh is violently punished; to be sure, such punishment is one of the distinctive and compelling features of Poe's writing.

Not surprisingly, flesh is most frequently associated with the figure of the female. As Poe asserts in "The Philosophy of Composition," there is no more poetic subject than the death of a beautiful woman. Hence such haunting poems as "Annabel Lee," "To Helen," and "Ulalume," to say nothing of such popular tales as "Ligeia," "The Fall of the House of Usher," and "The Black Cat," depend for their success on violence and even death inflicted on the female. In "The Black Cat," for example, after the narrator has murdered his wife, he decides "to wall [the cat] up in the cellar, as the monks of the Middle Ages are recorded to have walled up their victims" (228). This statement is surely directly responsible for the words of Mrs. Flood to Haze when she discovers his secret mortification of the flesh: "It's not normal. It's like one of them gory stories, it's something that people have quit doing—like boiling in oil or being a saint or walling up cats" (*O'Connor* 224). The walled-up cat, of course, is the means by which the narrator/killer in Poe's story is discovered. Hearing the cat's cry, the investigators tear down the wall and find the female corpse, "already greatly decayed and clotted with gore," standing before their eyes. The narrator recalls, "Upon its head, with red extended mouth and solitary eyes of fire, sat the hideous beast whose craft had seduced me into murder, and whose informing voice had consigned me to the hangman" (230). Traditionally associated with the female, the cat is inextricably linked to the wife in the narrator's mind; we are led to believe that he kills his wife because of his anger at the cat. Asals observes that in another Poe story, "The Premature Burial," the narrator's obsession with being buried alive anticipates Haze's association of the train berth with a coffin. Unlike the narrator of Poe's story, however, Haze will not easily overcome his terror of death.

Haze's obsession with the coffinlike berth is associated in his mind with the figure of his mother. He recalls stealing into the sideshow tent as a boy and seeing the scantily clad woman writhing in the coffin, and, upon returning home, trying to avoid his fundamentalist mother's intense, all-seeing eyes. In fact, the figure of the woman in the coffin becomes his mother:

> His mother was standing by the washpot in the yard, looking at him, when he got home. She wore black all the time and her dresses were longer than other women's. She was standing there straight, looking at him. He moved behind a tree and got out of her view, but in a few minutes, he could feel her watching him through the tree. He saw the lower place and the casket again and a thin

woman in the casket who was too long for it. Her head stuck up at one end and her knees were raised to make her fit. She had a cross-shaped face and hair pulled close to her head. He stood flat against the tree, waiting. She left the washpot and came toward him with a stick. She said, "What you seen?" (*O'Connor* 62–63)

Exacerbated by the rigidity of the mother and her horror of fleshly indulgence, the young Haze's guilt over his sexual "sin" causes him to punish his own body by placing rocks in his shoes to "satisfy" God (*O'Connor* 63), clearly a foreshadowing of his later penance for the murder of Solace Layfield. In *Wise Blood* the association of sin and guilt with flesh that is female is undeniable, although perhaps not very surprising when we consider O'Connor's indebtedness to the male tradition. She has adopted the male gaze and views the female accordingly.

Still more emphasis in Poe on fleshly tribulation and the horror of being buried alive occurs in *The Narrative of Arthur Gordon Pym*, considered by Asals as one in a tradition of "short, intense, symbolic works" (161) of which *Wise Blood* is also a part. Once again, the journey is the linear, male one, and the narrator is a stowaway, nearly buried alive on a ship. The story is an adventure, through which the narrator moves from one life-threatening episode to another—mutiny, cannibalism, shipwreck, "ghost ships" full of dead people, and scenes in which images of devouring and desiccation abound. As the story progresses, its dimensions become increasingly fantastic, larger than life, so that we come to recognize that the savage the narrator encounters is the beast within his own human breast. The story ends with Pym's death, after he has recorded in a last journal entry his descent into a cataract where "a shrouded human figure . . . larger by far than any average man, arose, with skin the perfect whiteness of the snow" (882). This strange image of purity, even its shroud, surely suggests the figure of Christ, a mysterious presence in the context of this episodic adventure story and surely a baffling component of any Poe story. Thus beyond the horrors of fleshly tribulation and beyond that worst fear of all, the fear of "living inhumation" (862), Pym finds the vision of Christ, awesome in the purity of his flesh. Similarly, Hazel Motes moves beyond the vicissitudes of this mortal coil to find his peace and to become, for Mrs. Flood, the pinpoint of light. That Asals sees both *Wise Blood* and *The Violent Bear It Away* as continuing this American tradition of the symbolic narrative is significant, for all of the works Asals mentions in this context, with the exception of *The Scarlet Letter*, are linear, male-dominated journeys: Poe's *Narrative of Arthur Gordon Pym,* Crane's *Red Badge of Courage,* Fitzgerald's *The Great Gatsby,* and Nathanael West's *Miss Lonelyhearts.*

Miss Lonelyhearts, concerned with spiritual quest, is a curious narrative, filled with the grotesque and the bizarre in a modern waste land in which individuals search for the meaning of their suffering. The advice columnist, Miss Lonelyhearts, a male using this nom de plume, is keenly sensitive to the world's misery, for some time having received epistolary testimony of the pitiful and the horrible. In an apparently godless universe, Miss Lonely-hearts seeks Christ and the message He would give to each of these suffer-ers. Taunted by the cynical (even diabolical) Shrike, his superior at the newspaper, Miss Lonelyhearts nonetheless attempts to provide comfort to the crippled Mr. Doyle, whose miserable life consists of hobbling up and down stairs to read meters and enduring the insults of his adulterous wife. Miss Lonelyhearts, who is fighting his own darkness and seeks humility, is finally vouchsafed a vision of God's grace, only to be killed by the angry Doyle, who has discovered Miss Lonelyhearts's infidelity with Mrs. Doyle. As Miss Lonelyhearts, mortally wounded, falls down the stairs, he drags Doyle with him. In this strange coupling we recognize that Doyle and Miss Lonelyhearts are similarly afflicted and that Doyle's crippled leg is only the physical manifestation of the misery shared by both men.

West's use of a male character as the advice columnist is important; after all, Miss Lonelyhearts's readers assume, as we do, that names are true indi-cators and (as we consider Abigail Van Buren and Ann Landers) that most advice-to-the-lovelorn writers are female. Moreover, Miss Lonelyhearts has become so much involved in his work that he has *become* Miss Lonelyhearts and has no other identity. Readers of the novel must quickly engage in a willing suspension of disbelief in order to match the female signifier with the male signified, and at the outset we may find ourselves giggling at West's apparent lunacy. Soon, however, we are sobered by the magnitude of Miss Lonelyhearts's burden. West's choice of what we might call a bisexual sensi-bility for his protagonist echoes Eliot's suggestion in the Notes to *The Waste Land* that Tiresias, "although a mere spectator and not indeed a 'character,' is yet the most important personage in the poem uniting all the rest," for Tiresias had lived as both man and woman. Thus, for Eliot in *The Waste Land,* "all the women are one woman, and the two sexes meet in Tiresias. What Tiresias sees, in fact, is the substance of the poem" (III, n. 218, 52).

In similar fashion, what Miss Lonelyhearts sees is the substance of West's narrative and that had "she" been Mr. Lonelyhearts she/he undoubtedly would not have had knowledge of so much suffering and would not have evoked response from her readers. In at least one striking instance, Miss Lonelyhearts demonstrates his capacity to feel a kind of female compassion. Reading Doyle's pathetic letter describing the loneliness and misery of his life, Miss Lonelyhearts finds his hand brushing Doyle's under the table. His immediate impulse is to jerk his hand away, but he forces himself to grasp the crippled man's hand, not letting go but "press[ing] it firmly with all the love he [can] manage." The cripple, initially embarrassed, pretends at first that they are shaking hands but soon gives in "and they [sit] silently hand in hand" (47). Later in the Doyles' apartment, Doyle again takes Miss Lonelyhearts's hand, and as they stand "smiling and holding hands," Mrs. Doyle enters the room. "'What a sweet pair of fairies you guys are,' she said" (49). West clearly suggests that, in the eyes of some, Miss Lonelyhearts's attempt to reach out in human solidarity to Doyle compromises his masculinity.

Miss Lonelyhearts and Hazel Motes are similar in their driving search for meaning and in their inability to find lasting solace in any pleasure of the here and now. Although he will attempt to escape the horrors of urban life with his weekend in the country with the wholesome Betty, Miss Lonelyhearts cannot escape his calling, his obsessive awareness of suffering, his need to find meaning—for himself and others. Both characters have embarked on what Ochs would call the male search for spiritual truth, and thus, to paraphrase Ochs's theory, the arrival—not the journey—matters. However, because Haze's search does not involve any compassion for, indeed even any awareness of, the sufferings of others but is instead focused solely on his own need to have the matter of salvation settled once and for all, the progression of his search seems more nearly to fit Ochs's paradigm than Miss Lonelyhearts's journey. Perhaps the idea that Miss Lonelyhearts has a kind of feminine sensibility or female compassion by virtue of his/her occupation accounts for the difference. To be sure, West suggests that Miss Lonelyhearts's empathy is the primary source of his misery. He is not so much tormented by his own sense of sinfulness as he is tormented by his conviction of the weakness of all humanity and his solidarity with that humanity.

Miss Lonelyhearts's fixation on Christ appears to center on Christ's experience of mortality. Because Christ lived as a suffering man, Miss Lonelyhearts seems to take courage in his own mortality and kinship with his fellow sufferers. Moreover, Miss Lonelyhearts does not pass judgment on these companions in suffering; he suffers with them. Hazel Motes has no such empathy. When he is confronted by anything approaching a positive human emotion, he lashes out in defiance. He is particularly contemptuous of women—from Mrs. Wally Bee Hitchcock to Leora Watts to Sabbath Lily Hawks and Mrs. Flood. Women are ancillary to the quest. On the other hand, in *Miss Lonelyhearts*, Betty is perhaps the character who is most nearly whole. She is, however, depicted as completely lacking in the burden of consciousness or experience of angst. She can respond to Miss Lonelyhearts's riven sensibility only by offering a mundane solution or suggestion. When the two return from the country, Miss Lonelyhearts realizes that "Betty had failed to cure him and that he had been right when he had said that he could never forget the letters" (38). He feels a kind of integrity in knowing this: "Crowds of people moved through the street with a dream-like violence. As he looked at their broken hands and torn mouths he was overwhelmed by the desire to help them, and because this desire was sincere, he was happy despite the feeling of guilt which accompanied it" (38–39). Like Hazel Motes, Miss Lonelyhearts feels that "[i]f he would only believe in Christ, then adultery would be a sin, then everything would be simple and the letters extremely easy to answer" (26). Of course, he does believe in Christ. He is simply tormented by his sexual desire and by his inability to reconcile a loving God with the facts of the world's cruelty and misery. His guilt and torment resulting from his adulterous night with Mrs. Doyle are suggested by his physical illness following the episode.

In similar fashion, O'Connor demonstrates that Hazel Motes, who attempts to immerse himself fully in the sins of the flesh, is increasingly tormented and, after his murder of Solace Layfield, inflicts his own penance to "pay" for his deeds. Yet this similarity is superficial, for Hazel Motes's torment and his eventual release occur within his own soul. Even when he preaches his Church Without Christ on the streets of Taulkinham, we know that Haze is not the least concerned with making converts; he is witnessing to himself. On the other hand, when Miss Lonelyhearts at last receives his vision that "Christ is life and light," he accepts God's plan and, believing that God has sent Doyle "so that [he can] perform a miracle and be certain of conversion," he rushes to "embrace the cripple" so that "the cripple would be made whole again, even as he, a spiritual cripple, had been made whole"

(57). Ironically and tragically, in his gesture of reaching out, Miss Lonely-hearts is killed. Here O'Connor readers are reminded not of Hazel Motes in *Wise Blood* but of the grandmother in "A Good Man Is Hard to Find." She reaches out to the Misfit in an apparent gesture of acceptance and is shot three times. Haze Motes does not reach out; he seems incapable of it. Miss Lonelyhearts, on the other hand, believes himself to be a kind of messenger or vessel through whom God's message moves, and he dies seeking to live that belief. The guilty Hazel Motes punishes his flesh, withdrawing from all human contact to the point that he leaves Mrs. Flood's protection and wanders off to die.

Sexuality is indeed a major concern in West's novel, and questions of adultery and abortion arise here as they do in both the drafts and the final published version of *Wise Blood*. With the exception of Betty, who, as we have noted, is a rather simple, earthy woman suggesting the importance of the natural, the women in *Miss Lonelyhearts* are primarily sexual beings whose sufferings (as expressed in their letters) are for the most part the result of the facts of their biology; they are not seeking souls of the likes of Miss Lonelyhearts or Hazel Motes. When Betty asks Miss Lonelyhearts if he is sick, he responds, "What a kind bitch you are. As soon as any one acts viciously, you say he's sick. Wife-torturers, rapers of small children, according to you they're all sick. No morality, only medicine. Well, I'm not sick. I don't need any of your damned aspirin. I've got a Christ complex. Humanity . . . I'm a humanity lover. All the broken bastards" (12–13). Although Miss Lonelyhearts's problem is not physical or physiological in origin, it often erupts in violence and rage, frequently against women.

In fact, in this novel the physical abuse of women is commonplace. Shrike and Doyle beat their wives, and Miss Lonelyhearts strikes Mrs. Doyle "again and again" (50) to fend off her advances. Only a few moments after Miss Lonelyhearts's words to Betty concerning his "Christ complex," he "pat[s] her shoulder threateningly" and asks her if she doesn't "like the performance" (13). When she "raise[s] her arm as though to ward off a blow," she is described, presumably as she is seen by Miss Lonelyhearts, as "like a kitten whose soft helplessness makes one ache to hurt it" (13). This analogy, clearly underscoring the fleshly vulnerability of the female, is indicative of the pervasive attitude toward women in western male literature, an attitude that has been more than adequately underscored by recent feminist critics.

Although O'Connor struggled in the preliminary drafts of *Wise Blood* with the issue of empowering Sabbath, I believe that even in those drafts we can see the influence of the male modernist view. O'Connor adopts the male gaze; she sees the figure woman. Like many of us who were educated at this time, O'Connor learned this literary lesson well. Indeed, the male gaze was the ideal; no self-respecting woman writer wanted to be thought tender or sentimental or less than aggressive in her pursuit of the truth. To be told that one "wrote like a man" was, in those days, a high compliment. Certainly O'Connor's prodigious talent, her instincts as a satirist, her keen visual imagination, and her training in the New Criticism would seem to have pointed her fiction in one rather inevitable direction. She was, after all, determined to counter the cult of southern white womanhood with its emphasis on "doing pretty" and to prove herself as tough-minded, capable, and dedicated to her craft as any man. Thus, Eliot's dictum of the necessary impersonality of the artist was bound to be appealing to her.

O'Connor indeed learned her literary lessons well. And yet, and yet . . . as a scrupulous and thoughtful Christian, O'Connor had another responsibility: without a suggestion of didacticism or "the Pious Style," she must assert God's continuing love for creation and His presence in it. How, then, to justify the satirist's harsh look at the world? How to explain her repeated emphasis on the ugly, the horrible, the sordid? If the Word came to dwell among us, is not the realm of flesh forever changed? I believe that the intensity of O'Connor's vision and its great success are the result of the sometimes torturous, always difficult struggle of her own words to embrace the flesh, to affirm the very physicality that her background, her education, and her church often asked her to deny.

The act of Christ, His assumption and penetration of all the full and complicated actuality and stages of the human finite, must be taken as the fundamental model for the literary imagination, for aesthetics in general, and for the ordinary act of the human imagination. —William F. Lynch, "Theology and the Imagination"

The problem for . . . [the] novelist will be to know how far he can distort without destroying, and in order not to destroy, he will have to descend far enough into himself to reach those underground springs that give life to his work. This descent into himself will, at the same time, be a descent into his region. It will be a descent through the darkness of the familiar into a world where, like the blind man cured in the gospels, he sees men as if they were trees, but walking. This is the beginning of vision. —Flannery O'Connor, "The Grotesque in Southern Fiction," *Mystery and Manners*

I often ask myself what makes a story work, and what makes it hold up as a story, and I have decided that it is probably some action, some gesture of a character that is unlike any other in the story, one which indicates where the real heart of the story lies. This would have to be an action or a gesture which was both totally right and totally unexpected; it would have to be one that was both in character and beyond character; it would have to suggest both the world and eternity. The action or gesture I'm talking about would have to be on the anagogical level, that is, the level which has to do with the Divine life and our participation in it. It would be a gesture that transcended any neat allegory that might have been intended or any pat moral categories a reader could make. It would be a gesture which somehow made contact with mystery. —Flannery O'Connor, "On Her Own Work"

4 The Gentleman Caller and the Anagogical Imagination

If O'Connor learned her literary lessons well, those lessons were strengthened as the years passed by the author's deepening religious faith. The literary lessons of the modern writers and the New Critics' emphasis on the work of art as icon were perfectly consonant with O'Connor's idea of the responsibility of the writer who is Catholic. In 1955, when O'Connor was thirty years old, she wrote to John Lynch, "I feel that if I were not a Catholic, I would have no reason to write, no reason to see, no reason ever to feel horrified or even to enjoy anything," adding that she had "never left or wanted to leave the church" (*Habit of Being* 114). In a 1956 letter to "A," O'Connor insisted, "I write from the standpoint of Christian orthodoxy . . . with a solid belief in *all* the Christian dogmas" (*Habit of Being* 147), and maintained, as she did on a number of occasions, that orthodoxy did not inhibit her freedom as an artist. As a devout believer, O'Connor considered her talent a gift from God, one to be used wisely and responsibly, and although she decried message-laden fiction, she obviously felt compelled to dramatize humanity's fallen condition in fresh and startling ways to jolt her readers to awareness.

Like T. S. Eliot, Walker Percy, and other Christian writers, O'Connor probed the possibilities of language and its relationship to reality and to ultimate reality, repeatedly reminding the reader (and perhaps herself) that though words "strain, crack, and break under the burden," as Eliot observed in the *Four Quartets*, they are all we have to proclaim "the mystery of existence" (*Habit of Being* 143). Thus the writer with Christian concerns has the responsibility of using words wisely and creating a world of concrete reality, the shadows of which suggest the divine. As has been previously noted, O'Connor found the grounding for her art in the incarnational theory of thinkers like William Lynch. Just as Christ entered the temporal world and redeemed that world, so the incarnational artist uses the here and now, the concrete, as a means of effecting a transcendent vision. The flesh is the medium through which redemption comes. Similarly, words, broken and humanly fallible, are the medium through which the Christian artist recalls readers to transcendent reality.

Beginning with an examination of O'Connor's keen interest in language and its capacity to convey the most profound truths of our experience, I will demonstrate the presence of a persistent fictional pattern — that of the gentleman caller — around which O'Connor, whether consciously or not, organized much of her best fiction. As we shall see, that pattern of the gentleman caller becomes an important metaphor for the soul's call to salvation. We note, first of all, that O'Connor's association of the female with the flesh conjoins the fallenness of humanity with images of woman. However, O'Connor also espouses an incarnational idea of art. By this Christian aesthetic, as Lynch and others point out, the concrete world (the flesh) is penetrated by the artist's vision (the divine) — very much in the way that Christ as God/man entered or penetrated the temporal and offered the fallen world the possibility of salvation. Furthermore, the structure of many of O'Connor's stories may be seen as rather a gloss on the incarnational view of art in that the central female sensibility is approached by the "gentleman caller" — the messenger who brings the Word from Christ the "suitor" — and is thereby afforded the opportunity for salvation. The female sensibility is thus, in one metaphoric pattern, penetrated — or, at the very least, she is entreated or "courted" by God through Christ.

To demonstrate this complex of ideas, we will look again at O'Connor's use of language, undergirded as her practice is with the idea of "the word made flesh," that is to say, the idea of art as incarnational. Through word play and irony O'Connor consistently tests the limits of our abused and fallen discourse as though to distinguish between the Word and our words. She turns our mortal language inside out — with the view to making us *see*. In so doing, she practices an incarnational art, which, as we have suggested, is an essentially masculinist aesthetic, calling for an essentially male perspective or gaze. Not surprisingly, O'Connor adopted the anagogical vision, espoused by the patriarchal Church, and embodied that belief in her art.

Most of O'Connor's fiction alludes in some way to the philosophical relationship between language and the reality it signifies. Sometimes the subject is presented directly, such as in "A Late Encounter with the Enemy" in which the dying General Sash, unable to cope with history on any level, is assaulted by battalions of words that he obviously sees as the enemy; or in "Good Country People," in which Joy/Hulga learns that words, the tools of her own arrogant thinking, can mask the most fearful of deeds: "[A]ren't you just *good country people?*" she asks Manley Pointer as he escapes with her artificial leg (*O'Connor* 282, my emphasis). Not to be outdone and quite sensitive to the pejorative adverb in her question, the Bible salesman retorts, "Yeah . . . but it ain't held me back none. I'm as good as you any day in the week" (*O'Connor* 282). Harry/Bevel in "The River" demonstrates a child's innocent belief in the literal truth of the words he has heard when he returns to the place where he has been told he "counted," only to drown in the river of his baptism. In "The Displaced Person" the ignorant and frightened Mrs. Shortley, baffled by the fact of languages other than English and attempting to puzzle out the difference between "them" and "us," imagines a "war of words" between Polish and English (*O'Connor* 300), providing a kind of perverse actualization of "the word made flesh." In "A Good Man Is Hard to Find" and "The Artificial Nigger," O'Connor is concerned with language as naming. In the first story, the grandmother's fatuous insistence on maintaining the appearance of a "lady" and her desperate plea to the

Misfit that he wouldn't shoot a lady and that he is a "good" man from a nice family heavily underscore the fact that language labels often have little to do with reality. In the second story, Mr. Head's lesson for Nelson that a "nigger" is not a "man" is turned inside out when the two are mysteriously reunited by the sight of the chipped and distorted "artificial nigger," whose humanity is their own. Standing before the statue, this "great mystery," this "monument to another's victory that brought them together in their common defeat," they feel their differences "dissolving . . . like an action of mercy" (*O'Connor* 230).

In the stories in *Everything That Rises Must Converge*, the concern with language continues. The title story concerns the difference between verbalized liberal sentiment and the heart's true disposition. "Greenleaf" and "A View of the Woods" suggest a frequent theme in O'Connor, the power of words to wound. "The Enduring Chill" centers on naming just what it is that "ails" Asbury. "The Comforts of Home" and "The Lame Shall Enter First" also emphasize the power of words to wound and suggest that the way we choose to name things is indicative of our attitude toward earthly creation. In "Judgment Day" and "Revelation," the protagonists struggle to associate the name with the thing; Old Tanner cannot fit the reality of the man in the apartment next door with his idea of what a "nigger" is, and Mrs. Turpin asks, "How am I a hog and me both?" (*O'Connor* 652). Even the titles of many of these stories echo the focus on the important relationship between word and reality. "A Good Man Is Hard to Find," for example, with its obvious indebtedness to the Bessie Smith blues song, takes both the cliché expression and the sultry song and gives them new meaning: Goodness is rare on this earth, the only true and complete goodness, of course, having been provided for us for all time by the example of Christ. The titles of "The Displaced Person" and "Good Country People" signal the thematic concerns of each story, and "The Life You Save May Be Your Own," "The Comforts of Home," "A Temple of the Holy Ghost," and "Judgment Day" also give fresh meaning to familiar statements or phrases, causing the reader to rethink even the most ordinary use of language.

Obviously, then, the often tricky relationship between word and thing was frequently on O'Connor's mind, as it was on the minds of earlier twentieth-century writers, including Eliot and Joyce, both of whom were influential on O'Connor. However, O'Connor rarely allows discursive or hypothetical musings to enter the story proper; as we briefly noted, the focus on the power of language is usually woven into the story line. Furthermore, the responsibility of the writer with Christian concerns to anchor her fiction in reality rather than in ideology was constantly on O'Connor's mind, as her essays and letters testify. In accord with the New Criticism, the public statements that we find in *Mystery and Manners* often emphasize that a story must stand on its own merit, that it must first of all be a good story, and that it must pay "the strictest attention to the real" (*Mystery and Manners* 96). In a shrewd attack on literary message-seekers of all stripes, O'Connor writes, "People talk about the theme of a story as if the theme were like the string that a sack of chicken feed is tied with. They think that if you can pick out the theme, the way you pick the right thread in the chicken-feed sack, you can rip the story open and feed the chickens. But this is not the way meaning works in fiction." On the contrary, she argues, "When anybody asks what a story is about, the only proper thing is to tell him to read the story," for the essence of fiction is "not abstract meaning but experienced meaning" (96), assertions common among the New Critics. The writer's duty is to anchor herself in the real world, finding there the raw material for her work. She must "never be ashamed of staring," for "[t]here is nothing that doesn't require [her] attention." In keeping with Eliot's emphasis on objectivity, O'Connor places on the writer one primary caveat: She must only "contemplate experience, not . . . be merged in it," and, echoing Henry James's idea in "The Art of Fiction" that the work of art is only as fine as the mind that creates it (James 1485), O'Connor writes that cheap thought results in "cheapness" in the writing (*Mystery and Manners* 84).

As we demonstrated in the previous chapter, O'Connor's position is completely in accord with her education in the popular critical thought of her day; her standards for the artist are high, requiring tough-mindedness, self-discipline, and a rigorous refusal to settle for less than immersion in the real. Moreover, for O'Connor the idea of art as incarnation appears to have offered the solution to the knotty set of questions surrounding the responsibility of the Catholic artist. Again and again, by means of her espousal of an incarnational art O'Connor settles matters of artistic freedom and integrity, the obligation of fiction to dogma, and even the responses of disgruntled or disappointed readers.

Perhaps nowhere among the essays does O'Connor make more clear her concern with the artist's relationship to the material world than in "The Nature and Aim of Fiction," in which she combines the tenets of the New

Critics with those of Catholic aesthetic thought to produce her own philosophy of composition. In this essay (actually a combination of excerpts from several of O'Connor's talks) such apparently diverse influences as St. Thomas, the New Critics, Caroline Gordon, Henry James, and Joseph Conrad all have in common their emphasis on the importance of the thing made, "the good of the written work" (*Mystery and Manners* 66). Arguing that the writer begins at the level of sensory perception, O'Connor posits that "the world of the fiction writer is full of matter," a fact that young writers do not want to see because of their concern "with unfleshed ideas and emotions" (67). Because the terrain of the writer is here and now, the Christian writer must necessarily come to terms with her attitude toward this world, actually a matter to be considered by every writer regardless of religious orientation. For O'Connor as a Catholic writer, however, the question is particularly crucial. Dante, for example, clearly viewed this world as preparation for the next, a kind of testing ground whereby all human decisions are viewed *sub specie aeternitatis.* Eliot's position in his overtly Christian poetry appears to be similar; the *Four Quartets* presents a world in which the timeless moment, "the moment in the rose-garden," impinges upon the world of time in such a way that the disciplined soul may achieve illumination, perceiving "the still point of the turning world" ("Burnt Norton," II, 119, 121).

Graham Greene, on the other hand, has seemed to his Catholic readers in particular to be far less than orthodox, suggesting a kind of decadence labeled by one critic as Manichaean. Elizabeth Sewell, with whose work O'Connor was familiar and whose essay "The Imagination of Graham Greene" O'Connor read in 1955, writes that Greene's work is "a literature of decadence" (55), in which the flesh is treated with "revulsion" (54); that whenever Greene "images Evil, he does so in bodily terms" (55); and that "joy and hope" as well as "laughter" are singularly lacking in Greene's fiction (59). Sewell concludes,

> The promiscuous and passionate pity is pity for the self, just as the revulsion is revulsion at the self. One concludes from these books that the writer hates the body—he is himself one; he detests the English and the middle class—he is himself English and middle class; he abhors the Public Schools—he was at one; he rebels at much of Catholicism—he is himself a Catholic. I believe a great many of my generation with a similar background have suffered from this, but it has to be transmuted, for the hatred is self-hatred and the pity is self-pity, and their end is the sterility one sees in Mr. Greene's work, the self-love and preoccupation

not of the poet who moves outward from loving himself to all created things, but the terrible consuming passion which springs from the conviction of one's own worthlessness. (60)

O'Connor was evidently much impressed with Sewell's denunciation of Greene, although she was clearly sympathetic with Greene's dilemma. Sending along the article to "A" in November 1955, O'Connor acknowledged the work of Sewell and William F. Lynch, both of whom became significant to her evolving aesthetic:

> I admire her [Sewell] but all through the piece, my sympathy goes out to Mr. Greene, or his carcus [*sic*], which has to suffer this lady-like vulture dining off him. What I feel I suppose is that she is right without much effort but that he is the one sweating to bring something to birth. A much better piece is the one following by Fr. Lynch, one of the most learned priests in this country I think. I haven't read Greene lately enough to know what I think of him. I don't know whether pity is the beginning of love or the corruption of it, or whether it is harder to love something perfect or something feeble. (*Habit of Being* 119)

However, in spite of this evidence of O'Connor's identification with Greene (whose creative efforts, interestingly enough, O'Connor likens to childbirth), she was certainly impressed by the power of Sewell's intellect. She chided "A" in 1956, "What do you call her little Sewell for? I bet that old girl wears a number-nine boot and could blow us both down with one exhale" (*Habit of Being* 167). Furthermore, two years later O'Connor wrote to Maryat Lee that Sewell's piece was the "best thing I ever read on Greene," concluding, "What he [Greene] does . . . is try to make religion respectable to the modern unbeliever by making it seedy. He succeeds so well in making it seedy that then he has to save it by the miracle" (*Habit of Being* 201). From Sewell O'Connor gets the phrase "neo-romantic decadent," which she uses to describe Greene on several later occasions, for O'Connor seems to have taken Sewell's condemnation of Greene as something of an object lesson in her early acknowledgment of the problems of the flesh for the Catholic writer. This writer who strongly believed that her writing was God's gift was also keenly aware that in God's service that gift could not be allowed to treat the material world as unimportant or, worse, as evil in itself. If the writer considers matter, which is, after all, the raw material with which she works, evil, she is guilty of the Manichaean heresy. In one of the most revealing passages in her nonfictional writing, O'Connor confronts that heresy head on:

The Manicheans separated spirit and matter. To them all material things were evil. They sought pure spirit and tried to approach the infinite directly without any mediation of matter. This is also pretty much the modern spirit, and for the sensibility infected with it, fiction is hard if not impossible to write because fiction is so very much an incarnational art.

One of the most common and saddest spectacles is that of a person of really fine sensibility and acute psychological perception trying to write fiction by using these qualities alone. This type of writer will put down one intensely emotional or keenly perceptive sentence after the other, and the result will be complete dullness. The fact is that the materials of the fiction writer are the humblest. Fiction is about everything human and we are made out of dust, and if you scorn getting yourself dusty, then you shouldn't try to write fiction. It's not a grand enough job for you. (*Mystery and Manners* 68)

O'Connor's insistence on an incarnational art echoes the thinking of William F. Lynch, a marked copy of whose 1954 essay, "Theology and the Imagination," is in the same issue of *Thought* as the Sewell piece and is among the papers in the O'Connor Collection at Georgia College & State University. In this essay, Lynch—like Eliot, Tate, and other New Critics, as well as the Catholic apologist Jacques Maritain—is concerned with the dissociation of sensibility, or (in a passage marked by O'Connor) the separation of "the act of the body and the act of the spirit" that in literature has "produced vast waves of new and pure sensibility and sheer experience" (70). Lynch is obviously intent on finding a way for the emergence of a "reassociated" sensibility, a means by which the artist may know how to use the real, the finite. He maintains, "All manichaean [*sic*] flights into the pure mind or into a pure infinite will always be into a desert" (71). O'Connor underlined this sentence in Lynch's article: "Christianity has from the beginning demanded that the search for redemption and the infinite be through the finite, through the limited, through the human" (71), as though to be reminded of the importance of the here and now to the writer's purpose.

Lynch's next assertion is extremely important: Christ is "the second Adam" who serves as the "athlete" of the "New Law" in "the confrontation of the finite" (72). By analogy, the Christian writer must also confront the finite, the temporal, the historical in order to present most effectively the soul's ascent to the divine. The writer, in other words, must not eschew matter; she must use it. In several later passages in the essay (including the statement that serves as the first epigraph to this chapter), Lynch uses the noun *penetra-*

tion to describe both the activity of Christ in moving down through the material realm and the activity of the writer in descending through the finite, finally to achieve the goal of ascent. Clearly underlying this idea of the necessity for *penetration* of the material realm is the familiar assumption of a kind of sexual possession, with matter, female, "penetrated" by the imagination or mind that is male. Sandra Gilbert and Susan Gubar would doubtless aver that the female writer reading these words would be likely to experience, at least subconsciously, a genuine confusion of roles. Because the assumption that intellect and creativity are largely the province of the male was commonplace in O'Connor's time (if not in our own), a woman who wanted to write would simply have had to ignore the implications of the language or, by some leap of the unconscious, to imagine herself (and/or her ability) as male to effect the proposed result.

In "Theology and the Imagination," Lynch begins to develop the ideas that will occupy him at much greater length in his well-known *Christ and Apollo: The Dimensions of the Literary Imagination,* published in 1963. Although *Christ and Apollo* is not in O'Connor's private library, she announced in a letter to Janet McKane in 1963 that she agreed with "W. Lynch's general theory" and that the writer "need[s] to go through the concrete situation to some experience of mystery" (*Habit of Being* 520). O'Connor's personal library contains a number of Lynch's other works, including "Theology and the Imagination." Moreover, O'Connor's enthusiasm for *Christ and Apollo* was clearly evident in her review of it in the *Bulletin,* a diocesan newspaper for which, from 1956 on, she regularly provided book reviews. Her brief review notes Lynch's separation of the Hebraic imagination, "always concrete," and the agnostic imagination, which she describes as "dreamlike." Much of this review is worth noting:

> In genuine tragedy and comedy, the definite is explored to its extremity and man is shown to be the limited creature he is, and it is at this point of greatest penetration of the limited that the artist finds insight. Much modern so-called tragedy avoids this penetration and makes a leap toward transcendence, resulting in an unearned and spacious resolution of the work. The principle of this thorough penetration of the limited is best exemplified in medieval scriptural exegesis, in which three kinds of meaning were found in the literal level of the sacred text: the moral, the allegorical, and the anagogical. This is the Catholic way of reading nature as well as scripture, and it is a way which leaves open the most possibilities to be found in the actual.

> If Fr. Lynch's book could have a wide Catholic audience in this country, par-
> ticularly in the colleges, it might ultimately help in the formidable task of raising
> our level of literary appreciation. (*Presence of Grace* 94)

In addition to O'Connor's enthusiasm for this book, we note the use of Lynch's word *penetration* several times in her short review. O'Connor obviously did not hesitate to echo a word that seems to us now to denote a significantly male image of creation.

Lynch's emphasis on "the generative finite" is developed in far greater detail in *Christ and Apollo*, in which he argues that "the way up is the way down" (27–28). "Christ's *penetrating* life" (30, my emphasis) becomes the model for the imagination, as it learns not to resist the world of time, "the power of the actual" (100). For Lynch, the *Spiritual Exercises* of St. Ignatius, the Apostles' Creed, and the liturgy of the Church are important means of individual attainment of "composition of place," whereby the soul, contemplating the life of Christ "step by step" (66), learns "to enter, on the divine and the human planes, into an historical, actual, and eventful set of facts which *penetrate* reality to the hilt" (69, my emphasis).

In extensive commentary on both tragedy and comedy, Lynch argues that the tools of both genres necessitate a descent into the particulars of human finitude, so that in tragedy, for example, "the spectator is brought to the experience of a deep beauty and exaltation, *but not by way of beauty and exaltation*" (77). In other words, to ensure the audience's experience of deep beauty and even exaltation, the artist's means may be unbeautiful, even ugly, even harsh. Both tragedy and comedy celebrate the potential for transcendence *through* or within the life of "the beastie man" (102). *Oedipus the King* and *A Midsummer Night's Dream*, Lynch argues, demonstrate in their respective genres that "the mud in man, the lowermost point in the subway, is nothing to be ashamed of. It can produce (St. Thomas would call it *potentia obedientialis*) the face of God" (115). Lynch continues by way of demonstrating the fallacies of what he calls the "univocal imagination" and the "equivocal imagination." The fallacy of the "univocal imagination," exemplified by a thinker like Parmenides, is that it attempts to eradicate all difference or diversity, reducing the many to the one, whereas the "equivocal" imagination errs in the opposite way, by acknowledging difference to the point that the one is subsumed by the many, "only difference . . . reigns everywhere," and thus "[e]verything is a private world; everything is a solipsism. All is absurd, lonely, a private hell" (134). Not surprisingly, Lynch cites the modern writers Albert Camus and André Gide as representative of equivocal thought. The univocal imagination is reductionist and life-denying, whereas the equivocal imagination is without focus or center and, ultimately, without meaning. Bakhtin's dialogic imagination, heralded as the source of true genius, would likely have been described by Lynch as the equivocal imagination, which, as we have indicated, he held in low regard. (For his part, Bakhtin would undoubtedly claim that what Lynch proposes as the anagogical imagination is another version of the monologic. The analogical and the anagogical visions should be clearly delineated, as will, I hope, be evident in what follows.)

Against the univocal and equivocal imaginations Lynch places the *analogical*, that habit of mind anticipated by Plato's later works which argue that the many participate in the one and that, therefore, the one and the many are essentially the same. Similarly, in a literary work, all levels of meaning (or levels of "penetration" of the finite) coexist at the literal level: "A truly analogical idea crackles with light and makes other things crackle with the same and yet with their own light." Thus Oedipus's revelation brings revelation to every other character in the play, and "one vision re-enforces another" (*Christ and Apollo* 157). For Lynch and O'Connor, the true analogical model, however, is always Christ, whose plumbing the depths of human experience both reinforces and inspires all life and art. As Lynch writes,

> It is no small wonder that it is in Christ we come to the fullest possible understanding of what analogy means in the fullest concrete, the facing relentlessly into the two poles of the same and the different and the interpenetrating reconciliation of the two contraries. He who is the Lord of all things is the lord of the imagination. As a good artist, and not an aesthete, he therefore knew what he was talking about when he said: If I be lifted up on the cross (in complete isolation and differentiated uniqueness, without anonymity, without friends), I shall draw all things to me (in sameness, in love, in a universal Church). It is the universal teaching of the Church that it was itself born, not out of the Greeks, not out of the anonymous mind, not out of the chameleon imagination, but out of His blood, at a set hour, in a set place. (158)

Just as the Church was born out of the reality of the blood of the incarnate God, so the Christian artist's imagination is born from that same blood. And just as the descent of Christ into history and time redeems both history and time and provides the analogical model for the artist, the artist must of necessity be immersed in the particulars of place and time in order to ascend to vision. By way of explanation, Lynch uses the metaphor of the fish (metaphor, of course, being one mode of analogy): "[I]t must breathe its air (the infinite) through the water (the finite); if it should pursue its goal more directly, the process of abandoning the water to get the air would end in agony and death" (86). Immersion in the finite is the only means by which art will live. Surely O'Connor found this view supportive of her resistance to the Pious Style and congenial to her propensity for satire and dark comedy.

Most important, however, O'Connor found in Lynch's ideas a strong theological defense of the tenets of the New Criticism. After all, Lynch, who cites Allen Tate with frequency and respect, argues, with both Tate and Eliot, that the dissociated sensibility is the most crucial problem of the modern era. Most of Lynch's work was, in fact, devoted to reuniting that sensibility. Basing his assertions on an analogical model, Lynch places the text itself in the center of the spotlight, going so far as to end his book with a reiteration of the four levels of meaning—literal, allegorical, tropological or moral, and anagogical—common to medieval scriptural exegesis. (Early commentators frequently grouped all levels under the general heading of allegorical—the reading that is "alien" to the historical; similarities to Bakhtin's *monologic* vision seem obvious here.) O'Connor's own knowledge of medieval exegesis is clear in "The Nature and Aim of Fiction," surely her most complete defense of art as incarnation. In this essay O'Connor affirms that what is needed by the fiction writer is "*anagogical* vision," which enables the writer "to see different levels of reality in one image or one situation" and which concerns "the Divine life and our participation in it" (*Mystery and Manners* 72, my emphasis). For his part, Lynch calls the anagogical sense "the world of complete insight, the world of eternity and Christ in glory" (*Christ and Apollo* 189). Following Lynch, O'Connor distinguishes between the anagogical imagination and the Manichaean. For both of these Catholic thinkers, the literary work is centered in the here and now in order to suggest a transcendent reality. The *analogical* vision provides the model by which the Christian writer proceeds and is the basis for our understanding of incarnational art; the *anagogical* vision imbues the work with Christian mystery and is also involved in our perception of this mystery.

In "On Her Own Work," O'Connor expands the anagogical intent of her work by suggesting that the heart of her stories is centered around "some action, some gesture of a character that is unlike any other in the story" that would "be on the anagogical level" and "somehow [make] contact with mystery" (*Mystery and Manners* 111). We note, of course, that the gesture is a *human* one, revealing and unique. It must, however, convey the mysterious or the numinous, serving as concrete pointer away from itself. We might consider the function of the statue of the artificial nigger in "The Artificial Nigger" as just such a pointer or, at least, as affording Mr. Head and Nelson the opportunity to make "contact with mystery." The statue is certainly not an action or a gesture, but it is the catalyst for the gesture of reconciliation that Mr. Head makes to Nelson. If we take the ending of the story at face value, we conclude that the chipped and battered figure suggests the mystery of human suffering and thereby summons Mr. Head to a recognition of his own weakness and dependence on God. In this way the story moves to the anagogical level.

Time and again in the essays and letters O'Connor alludes to the anagogical vision as the basis for her fiction, even as she chides her fellow Catholics for their tendency toward Manichaeanism. For example, in "The Church and the Fiction Writer," O'Connor accuses "the average Catholic reader" of "separating nature and grace as much as possible" and thereby limiting "his conception of the supernatural to pious cliché." As a result, she maintains, this reader is able to recognize literature in two forms only: "the sentimental and the obscene" (*Mystery and Manners* 147). Sounding a great deal like William Lynch, O'Connor in this passage suggests the view of art as incarnation:

> We lost our innocence in the Fall, and our return to it is through the Redemption which was brought about by Christ's death and by our slow participation in it. Sentimentality is a skipping of this process in its concrete reality and an early arrival at a mock state of innocence, which strongly suggests its opposite. Pornography, on the other hand, is essentially sentimental, for it leaves out the connection of sex with its hard purpose, and so far disconnects it from its meaning in life as to make it simply an experience for its own sake. (*Mystery and Manners* 148)

Sentimentality, as O'Connor defines it, would therefore be an example of Lynch's univocal imagination in its denial of reality; pornography, as defined by O'Connor, would be an example of Lynch's equivocal imagination in its denial of focus and purpose. Our participation in redemption, O'Connor suggests, is possible only through our experience of the real and, she might have added in echo of St. Ignatius, by understanding that for us, as for Christ, there is no shortcut to salvation. We must proceed, as Christ did, step by step. Fiction "should reinforce our sense of the supernatural by grounding it in concrete, observable reality" (148). For the Catholic writer, "To look at the worst will be . . . no more than an act of trust in God," although O'Connor concedes, "What leads the writer to his salvation may lead the reader into sin, and the Catholic writer who looks at this possibility directly looks the Medusa in the face and is turned to stone" (148–49).[1] The writer who faces the responsibility of the consequences of his art, as Dante and Chaucer did in their day, recognizes the wisdom of Mauriac's admonition, repeated by O'Connor: Purify the source" (149).

Thus the Catholic writer must never turn away from reality, the world and the flesh, although she must be constantly vigilant in examination of conscience to ensure purity of intent. O'Connor's public utterances on the subject of the uses to which the world may be put would suggest, therefore, conformity with the thinking of the Church. In keeping with Lynch's analogical imagination by which the one and the many are the same (hence there is no real dissociation of sensibility), fiction is concerned with the world of apparent differences, duly presenting the details, the "whatness" of each thing, only in order to convey the essential oneness of all creation in God. In Lynch's theory and the poetry of Gerard Manley Hopkins, O'Connor clearly found support for her own aesthetic, an aesthetic undergirded by the essentially male view of the earthly and of the flesh. Although O'Connor wholeheartedly supported the view of art as incarnational, her view of the flesh was, as we have already begun to discover, rather complicated. As we continue to explore this subject (matter), we will examine those instances in which the incarnational view of art—a rather orthodox Catholic position—is clearly present in O'Connor's fiction and, from there, move to present the aesthetic issue in a bit more complexity. We will thus set aside some of the threads of our tapestry, with the intent of returning to them later in this chapter.

In the midst of acrimony and peevishness among the family members on vacation in "A Good Man Is Hard to Find," a story in which there seems to be little beauty or joy, O'Connor writes, "The trees were full of silver-white sunlight and the meanest of them sparkled" (*O'Connor* 139). The story's narrator makes it fairly plain that neither the grandmother nor the other members of the family notice this beauty, although the grandmother, in spite of her selfishness and pride, would undoubtedly come closest to seeing the trees; she is, after all, the one who seems the most alive and the most appreciative of the sights along the way. Similarly, as we noted in chapter 3, O'Connor begins the third chapter of *Wise Blood* with a lyrical description of the night sky in Taulkinham, with the stars moving slowly "as if they were about some vast construction work that involved the whole order of the universe and would take all time to complete" (*O'Connor* 37). Nobody notices the sky, however. Most of us, with our eyes on our feet or directed at the store windows, will not see the sparkling trees or the black sky in whose depths the stars seem to move mysteriously. We will be looking elsewhere, failing to exhibit the passionate attention essential for experiencing the divine incarnate. The word may become flesh, but our gaze will be elsewhere, or, to use Eliot's words in the *Four Quartets*, we will be "distracted from distraction by distraction" ("Burnt Norton," III, 120).

In this context, Lynch reminds us that Duns Scotus's concept of *haecceitas*, meaning "the pure *thisness*-and-not-thatness . . . in all things," underlies Gerard Manley Hopkins's notion of the "inscape" of all things. In Hopkins's world, "charged with the grandeur of God" (128, l. 1), "[t]here lives the dearest freshness deep down things" (128, l. 10). The divine has penetrated (to use Lynch's term) and continues to penetrate the temporal, although we are oblivious ("nor can foot feel, being shod" l. 8). Yet God is present in the least of creation and certainly in its endless diversity, as Hopkins tells us in "Pied Beauty," perhaps the poem most illustrative of his idea of inscape. I quote the poem in its entirety because of the insight it affords into O'Connor's work and because of its influence on her:

Pied Beauty

> Glory be to God for dappled things—
> > For skies of couple-colour as a brinded cow;
> > > For rose-moles all in stipple upon trout that swim;
> > Fresh-firecoal chestnut-falls; finches' wings;
> > > Landscape plotted and pieced—fold, fallow, and plough;
> > > > And all trades, their gear and tackle and trim.

> All things counter, original, spare, strange;
>   Whatever is fickle, freckled (who knows how?)
>   With swift, slow; sweet, sour, adazzle, dim;
>   He fathers-forth whose beauty is past change:
>   Praise him.
>
> (132–33)

This poem is more than the expression of simple delight in the particularity of God's creation or a celebration of God's plenitude; it is an intense acknowledgment of divine presence at the heart of the diversity of matter: the One is there, inevitably and certainly, in every cast, every color, every contradiction of the many. The poem's strong alliteration, surprising and concentrated use of language, and tight lines enable it to convey in its very form the inscape it seeks to express, as it affirms the sacramental view of the created world. The least of created matter "sparkles" with the grandeur of God. Clearly indebted to Hopkins, O'Connor's story "The River" also embodies the idea of God's mysterious presence here on earth.

The journey of Harry/Bevel in "The River" is that of the boy-child back to the place where he has been told, in no uncertain terms, that he "counted." With little attention or love from his parents, Harry naturally attempts to return to the river, where he has been baptized and from whence, the revival minister has assured him, he will "go to the Kingdom of Christ . . . by the deep river of life" (*O'Connor* 165). The tragedy of the boy's drowning is countered by our certainty that his faith has led him to God, just as surely as the faithless and cynical Mr. Paradise, in pursuit of the child, emerges from the river of life "empty-handed" (171). Throughout the narrative, O'Connor suggests the fact of God's presence, especially in her descriptions of the natural world, in which moments of intense natural beauty contrast with the dreary, gray city where marriages fail and children are neglected. In fact, in describing the journey from Mrs. Connin's house to the river, O'Connor uses rather obvious symbolism. The motley procession — Mrs. Connin with Harry/Bevel in front, followed by the three boys and then by the tall Sarah Mildred — is described as looking "like the skeleton of an old boat with two pointed ends, sailing slowly on the edge of the highway" (159), a comic image suggesting both the mythic journey, age-old, to the river of life and truth and the many New Testament images of the sea, perhaps most especially Jesus' calling his disciples to be "fishers of men." The incongruity of the "skeleton" of a boat on the highway underscores the timelessness of the sacred journey; furthermore, at least three times in the story Mrs. Connin is referred to as a skeleton. In the opening paragraphs, she is described, presumably as she is viewed by Harry's father, as "a speckled skeleton in a long pea-green coat and felt helmet" (155), the word *speckled* suggesting Hopkins's inscape and stressing Mrs. Connin's uniqueness. That which is speckled is marked, singled out, distinctive. We are not far, of course, from Hopkins's "fickle" and "freckled" reality, and indeed O'Connor describes Mrs. Connin's boys paradoxically as possessing "identical speckled faces" (*O'Connor* 157), as if to insist on both unity and particularity. As the boys stare over the head of Harry/Bevel, he is afraid to look behind him, and as O'Connor has him observe, the boys' "speckles were pale and their eyes were still and gray as glass" (159) and "their ears twitched slightly" (158).

Although obviously well instructed in right and wrong by their fundamentalist mother, the boys are nonetheless tempted to frighten Harry/Bevel with the pigs, and they do so. The pig that chases the boy is "long-legged and hump-backed and part of one of his ears had been bitten off." Moreover, according to Mrs. Connin, he "favors Mr. Paradise that has the gas station" and "the cancer over his ear" (159). Horrified and hysterical, the child is calmed by Mrs. Connin, who reads him Bible stories, one of which is, significantly, the story of Christ's "driving a crowd of pigs out of a man" (160). The connection between the pigs—evil—and Mr. Paradise is clear. The story O'Connor alludes to here concerns Christ's expulsion of an unclean spirit from a tormented man. When Christ summons the spirit and asks its name, it responds, "My name is Legion: for we are many" (Mark 5:9). The devils then receive from Christ permission to enter a herd of swine, only to meet their doom: "The herd ran violently down a steep place into the sea . . . and were choked in the sea" (Mark 5:13). The picture in Mrs. Connin's treasured Bible storybook of "the carpenter driving a crowd of pigs out of a man" (160) is especially appealing to Harry/Bevel, for prior to his encounter with the real pigs in Mrs. Connin's yard, he has seen them only in books in which they were "small fat pink animals with curly tails and round grinning faces and bow ties" (158). In Mrs. Connin's book, however, the pigs "were real pigs, gray and sour-looking" (160), and Mrs. Connin tells the boy that "Jesus had driven them all out of this one man" (161).

Perhaps because of his recent horrifying experience with the real pig and perhaps because Mrs. Connin has declared that every word in this book is "the gospel truth" (160)—restoring the meaning to that timeworn phrase—

Harry/Bevel is evidently much moved by the pig story, so much so that he steals the book. Later, O'Connor emphasizes Mr. Paradise's association with the pig by reminding us of their physical similarity, earlier noted by Mrs. Connin: He is "a huge old man who sat like a humped stone on the bumper of a long ancient gray automobile," wearing "a gray hat that was turned down over one ear and up over the other to expose a purple bulge on his left temple" (163). At the story's conclusion, when the boy has reentered the river to find the Kingdom of Christ, Mr. Paradise's shout causes him to turn his head to see "something like a giant pig bounding after him, shaking a red and white club and shouting." On one level, the boy is reliving the pursuit of the pig of the day before; on the most significant level, however, O'Connor suggests that he instinctively flees the devil. The story ends with a description of Mr. Paradise rising from the water "like some ancient water monster" standing "empty-handed, staring with his dull eyes as far down the river line as he could see" (171). The boy has successfully eluded the devil.

The boy believes as only a child can believe, literally and unhesitatingly. As though in accordance with Christ's words — "Suffer the little children to come unto me, and forbid them not; for of such is the kingdom of God" (Mark 10:14) — Harry/Bevel has taken Mrs. Connin at her word, and after she has read from the stories of the life of Jesus and the group is on the way to the river, the boy appears to be transformed. As he begins "to make wild leaps and pull forward on [Mrs. Connin's] hand," it is as though "he wanted to dash off and snatch the sun which was rolling away ahead of them now" (160–61). In creating a narrative that works on the anagogical level, O'Connor here uses the familiar sun/son play on words to suggest the boy's eagerness for Christ, the Son, and for the divine presence in the world.

On the journey to the river O'Connor devotes what is for her uncharacteristic time to the beauty of the natural world, in language reminiscent of Hopkins. The group crosses "a field *stippled* with purple weeds" (161, my emphasis; see "Pied Beauty," line 3 above), and because the boy has never been in the woods before, he walks "carefully, looking from side to side as if he were entering a strange country." In fact, he is entering a strange country, for he is about to be baptized. The paragraph ends with this revealing sentence: "At the bottom of the hill, the woods opened suddenly onto a pasture dotted here and there with black and white cows and sloping down, tier after tier, to a broad orange stream where the reflection of the sun was set like a diamond" (161). This last image seems almost an echo of the line from "A

Good Man" discussed earlier—"The trees were full of silver-white sunlight and the meanest of them sparkled" (*O'Connor* 139)—suggesting God's immanence, the fact that the world is indeed "charged" with God's glory.

The particularity of the black-and-white cows echoes the "brinded cows" of "Pied Beauty" (l. 2) and also testifies to a world where all "[l]andscape plotted and pieced" (l. 5) is God's handiwork. The river, evidently red/orange as many rivers in Georgia clay country are after a rain, is described by the Reverend Summers as "blood red," reflecting Christ's sacrifice: "The same blood that makes this River red, made that leper clean, made that blind man stare, made that dead man leap!" The mind of Harry/Bevel might have added that the same blood drove the pigs out of a man possessed, for such is the certainty of his belief. In any event, as he listens to the preacher, the boy's eyes follow "drowsily the slow circles of two silent birds revolving high in the air" (162), and we are told that beyond the river "there was a low red and gold grove of sassafras with hills of dark blue trees behind it and an occasional pine jutting over the skyline." Never mind that "[b]ehind, in the distance, the city rose like a cluster of warts on the side of the mountain," for the boy is far from that place now. Here, as "[t]he birds revolved downward and dropped lightly in the top of the highest pine and sat hunch-shouldered as if they were supporting the sky" (162), we cannot fail to be reminded of Christ's own baptism and of the descent of the dove of the Holy Spirit. And just before the boy's baptism, he looks over the preacher's shoulder "at the pieces of the white sun scattered in the river" (165), an image of Christ's sacrifice and God's immanence that recurs just after the boy has announced that his mother's problem is a hangover: "The air was so quiet he could hear the broken pieces of the sun knocking in the water" (165). This image is clearly evocative of the idea of Christ's body broken for all of us, a fact that, O'Connor implies, the boy knows at some profound level beyond his years.

If I have seemed to spend an undue amount of time on this story, I have done so because it seems to exemplify, as perhaps no other story does quite as clearly, O'Connor's belief in the incarnation. Simultaneously, it dramatizes that belief in lyrical passages that may go unnoticed because of their scarcity in the totality of O'Connor's work. "The River" demonstrates the unmistakable influence of Hopkins on O'Connor. Furthermore, in Hopkins's poem "That Nature Is a Heraclitean Fire and of the Comfort of the Resurrection," the poet concludes

> Enough! the Resurrection,
> A heart's clarion! Away grief's gasping, / joyless days, dejection.
> Across my foundering deck shone
> A beacon, an eternal beam. / Flesh fade, and mortal trash
> Fall to the residuary worm; / world's wildfire, leave but ash:
> In a flash, at a trumpet crash,
> I am all at once what Christ is, / since he was what I am, and
> This Jack, joke, poor potsherd, / patch, matchwood, immortal diamond,
> Is immortal diamond.
>   (180, ll. 16–24)

This anticipates O'Connor's "sun set like a diamond," an image also suggestive of Christ's radiant presence in the world. Like Hopkins, O'Connor in
"The River" emphasizes the reality of the incarnate God. If she seems reluctant to praise God in the manner of Hopkins's extravagance, she nonetheless implies God's presence in intense images that even borrow Hopkins's
language.

O'Connor's familiarity with Hopkins is evident in several key passages in
her letters. In 1955 O'Connor wrote to "A" on the matter of insomnia: "I
have come to think of sleep as metaphorically connected with the mother of
God. Hopkins said she was the air we breathe, but I have come to realize her
most in the gift of going to sleep. Life without her would be equivalent to
me to life without sleep and as she contained Christ for a time, she seems to
contain our life in sleep for a time so that we are able to wake up in peace"
(*O'Connor* 112). O'Connor here obviously makes reference to Hopkins's
"The Blessed Virgin Compared to the Air We Breathe," a lovely poem suggesting that the "[w]ild air, world-mothering air" is nothing less than the
Virgin, of whose flesh Christ "took flesh: / He does take fresh and fresh, /
Though much the mystery how, / Not flesh but spirit now / And makes, O
marvellous!" (ll. 55–59). O'Connor clearly knows Hopkins's work with its
steady emphasis on the incarnate God, most often depicted by the poet in
images from nature or the natural world. In a 1956 letter, O'Connor mentioned the correspondence between Hopkins and the atheist Robert Bridges
(*O'Connor* 164), and in 1963 O'Connor wrote Sr. Mariella Gable, "I'll be
glad when Catholic critics start looking at what they've got to criticize for
what it is in itself, for its sort of 'inscape' as Hopkins would have had it"
(*O'Connor* 517). On a more biographical note, we recall that in June 1964
O'Connor expressed admiration for Hopkins's poignant "Spring and Fall," as

though its emphasis on mortality—the "goldengrove unleaving"—were a forecast of her own death less than two months later (*Habit of Being* 586).

For a number of Christian writers, Hopkins has provided a model for reconciling the fact of a fallen world with the immensity of God's love. Any number of his poems might be adduced to emphasize Hopkins's near obsession with the incarnation and to demonstrate his influence on writers like O'Connor. The ending of the dazzling sonnet "As Kingfishers Catch Fire," for example, which stresses the importance of the fact that Christ took on our flesh, suggests a technique for the Christian incarnational artist:

> I say more: the just man justices;
>   Keeps grace: that keeps all his goings graces;
> Acts in God's eye what in God's eye he is—
>   Christ. For Christ plays in ten thousand places,
> Lovely in limbs, and lovely in eyes not his
>   To the Father through the features of men's faces.
>   (129, ll. 9–14)

Now Hopkins, who had real difficulty reconciling his own creative talent with his vocation as a Jesuit, was not writing theology here. If we put aside the matter of the plentiful allusions to maleness in these lines, we may observe that the statement that the just man *is* Christ "in God's eye" is, after all, to risk heresy, as it is heretical in the view of the Church to argue that we are Christ. Yet Hopkins's idea of inscape ran that risk. For example, in his journals, which contain the fullest exposition of inscape, Hopkins maintains:

All the world is full of inscape and chance left free to act falls into an order as well as purpose: looking out of my window I caught in the random clods and broken heaps of snow made by the cast of a broom. The same of the path trenched by footsteps in ankledeep snow across the fields leading to Hodder wood through which we went to see the river. The sun was bright, the broken brambles and all boughs and banks limed and cloyed with white, the brook down the clough pulling its way by drops and by bubbles in turn under a shell of ice. (215)

One might even propose that O'Connor had read this very passage, so similar to it is her own description of Harry/Bevel's journey through the woods to the river. In words and in sketches, Hopkins's journal entries refuse to retreat from his belief that God is present in the thingness of things and that "[w]hat you look hard at seems to look hard at you" (204). For example, as he gazes at the clouds one day in March 1871, he writes: "I looked long up at it till the tall height and the beauty of the scaping — regularly curled knots spring if I remember from fine stems, like foliation in wood or stone — had strongly grown on me. It changed beautiful changes, growing more into ribs and one stretch of running into branching like coral. Unless you refresh the mind from time to time you cannot always remember or believe how deep the inscape in things is" (204).[2]

However, there is clear evidence that O'Connor was wary of the dangers of assuming that the Creation *is* God, for in a 1955 letter to "A," she wrote, "Remember that I am not a pantheist and do not think of the creation as God, but as made and sustained by God" (*Habit of Being* 126). We might even hazard the suggestion that O'Connor's own fear of being called a pantheist combined with her proclivity for satire and her wish to be tough-minded and resistant to pious platitude to create an overwhelmingly ugly world and a real scarcity of lyricism in her fiction. In any event, the lovely moment is hard to find. There is surely no O'Connor story quite as lyrical (and lacking in her characteristic humor) as "The River." It is as though O'Connor had to be on guard lest she yield to the lyrical impulse, to the hymn of praise — for all sorts of reasons, not the least of which was to be taken seriously as a writer who was a woman and a southerner.

Perhaps in no other work does O'Connor so clearly delineate the matter of the Christian's right attitude toward the physical than "A Temple of the Holy Ghost," which some call O'Connor's own coming-of-age story, a masterful blend of a young girl's entry into physical maturity and her acknowledgment of her spiritual identity. This story raises serious questions concerning O'Connor's assumptions about female adolescence and sexuality, especially in determining the difference, if any, between male and female flesh as "temples" of the spirit. If indeed the many participate in the one, can we say that they participate equally, in the same measure? The question may seem more pertinent to the debates about sexuality and religion in our own time than it does to a consideration of O'Connor, but I am convinced that the issue is central to the complicated response many of us as Christians and women have to O'Connor's work.

"A Temple of the Holy Ghost" has, at its center, the body. Even those critics who differ markedly on the story's meaning concede that interpretation hinges on the meaning attached to the physical awakening of the young female protagonist. The fact that the story has a young girl at its center

is extremely significant, for O'Connor's narratives involving male protagonists — from *Wise Blood* to "The River" through "The Partridge Festival" and
"The Enduring Chill" and "Parker's Back" — do not concern themselves
with the matter of sexual purity or even with sexual identity as a spiritual issue to the extent that this story does. Louise Westling, pointing out O'Connor's indebtedness to Carson McCullers's *Member of the Wedding*, views "A
Temple of the Holy Ghost" as a manifestation of the author's sexual ambivalence, particularly her ambivalence toward adolescence (142–43). Unlike
McCullers, Westling continues, O'Connor presents a child who "preserves
her fierce individuality with the assurance that it is God-given," thus assuring
us that she will maintain her independence, although that independence
"may be freakish in the eyes of the world" (143). Westling concludes that if
the "religious solution to the problem of feminine identity were fully satisfactory to O'Connor," her exploration of the subject would have ended with
this early story (143). However, such was not the case. Because O'Connor
continued to probe the matter in later stories, we can conclude, according
to Westling, that she continued to be troubled by the question of female
sexuality. Surely there is evidence supporting Westling's assertion, although
we note that after the publication of *A Good Man Is Hard to Find* O'Connor
does not deal with the matter at all directly. In fact, in *Everything That Rises
Must Converge* only two of the nine stories are even concerned with female
protagonists, and Mrs. May of "Greenleaf" and Mrs. Turpin of "Revelation" have long since passed the age of sexual activity. Like the less effective
"Circle in the Fire," O'Connor's "Temple of the Holy Ghost" explores the
dilemma of the smart, sensitive, and rebellious adolescent girl, who wants
some measure of control over her life. Both stories, furthermore, present a
daughter who rebels against the prescribed behavior for young girls, and both
are considered among O'Connor's most clearly autobiographical works.

Even the title of "A Temple of the Holy Ghost" emphasizes the concern
of the story with the physical body, although the use of the familiar religious
phrase suggests O'Connor's particular focus. Sister Perpetua has informed
the child's cousins at the convent that just as Christ took on human flesh, so
the body is God's temple and must be treated accordingly. O'Connor gives
texture and depth to this idea in every episode of the story — from the account of Miss Kirby's courtship and the visit of Wendell and Cory to the
cousins' account of the hermaphrodite at the fair. Finally, the child's epiphany at benediction consolidates all of the "bodies" into the one body, that

of Christ in the Host. The story would therefore appear to be read on one level as simply the story of a girl's (perhaps O'Connor's) acceptance of the sacredness of the flesh, in however lowly or exalted a form. Religious and secular meanings coalesce in such a reading, and the suggestion of an autobiographical impulse only adds to the story's richness.

Nevertheless, critics such as Claire Kahane have resisted this traditional approach and found within the story elements of the "modern Gothic" in which truth is given "grotesque visual form" (343). Centering her discussion on the figure of the hermaphrodite, Kahane contradicts Ellen Moers's notion that the hermaphrodite is "a grotesque image of self-hatred" by arguing that the meaning of the hermaphrodite is ambivalent:

> Especially in a time when the traditional boundaries of sexual identity are in flux, the hermaphrodite, challenging those boundaries by its existence, mirrors both the infantile wish to destroy distinction and limitation and be both sexes — a power originally attributed to the primal mother — and the fear of that wish when it is physiologically realized as freakishness. Leslie Fiedler speaks to this response when he says that "no category of Freaks is regarded with such ferocious ambivalence as the hermaphrodites, for none creates in us a greater tension between physical repulsion and spiritual attraction." (347)

Thus, in Kahane's view, "A Temple of the Holy Ghost" embodies "the transcendent, unseen possibilities of hermaphroditic power" (348). Although the words of the hermaphrodite suggest to the child that "she should submit to her fate as a woman" (349), the fact that O'Connor never shows the double sex of the hermaphrodite directly to either the girl or the reader suggests to Kahane that "the girl's identification with the hermaphrodite is made not through a mirroring physical image but through the symbolic medium of language" (349). Only through the girl's imagined dialogue with the hermaphrodite does she identify with him/her.

Through her use of the "unseen," therefore, O'Connor is able to present an idea of sexual androgyny that becomes, for women, "a symbolic means of transcending the limitations placed on feminine identity" (350). Kahane's idea is certainly in keeping with the argument of Gilbert and Gubar that sexual anxiety caused modernist male writers to use repeated images of female potency and male impotence — presenting what was to them a frightening upheaval of order and values, "since the ultimate reality was in their view the truth of gender" (*Sexchanges* 331). For their part, female writers such as Virginia Woolf, Gertrude Stein, and Djuna Barnes were led to question gender categories. Beginning with the assumption that clothing is merely costume, "many twentieth-century women struggled to define a gender-free reality behind or beneath myth, an ontological essence so pure, so free that 'it' can 'inhabit' any self, any costume" (*Sexchanges* 332). By this argument, O'Connor through the figure of the hermaphrodite would seem to challenge the limits of gender-restricted roles and to present a model for the modern female's heroism in keeping with the self-sacrificial activities of the saints and martyrs.

J. Ramsey Michaels notes that O'Connor's choice of the name Perpetua for the nun who instructs the cousins in the sacredness of the body is significant in that the story of Perpetua, "one of the earliest of the Christian Acts of the Martyrs, probably originating in Africa in the second century" (80–81), contains the account of Perpetua's being turned into a man and "given a man's strength" (82) by which she is able to overcome her adversary. Michaels reminds us that the child in O'Connor's story has imagined herself a doctor and an engineer, two traditionally male roles, and has then decided that she must be more than either a doctor or an engineer: "She would have to be a saint because that was the occupation that included everything you could know; and yet she knew she would never be a saint." She concludes by thinking that "she could be a martyr if they killed her quick," and she imagines herself in the arena converting the lions one by one: "The lions liked her so much she even slept with them and finally the Romans were obliged to burn her but to their astonishment she would not burn down and finding she was so hard to kill, they finally cut off her head very quickly with a sword and she went immediately to heaven. She rehearsed this several times, returning each time at the entrance of Paradise to the lions" (*O'Connor* 204). Michaels also points out that when the child is asked by one of her cousins how she knows so much about the "men" Wendell and Cory, she imagines saying "to someone" that she "know[s] them all right," that she "fought in the world war" with Wendell and Cory: "They were under me and I saved them five times from Japanese suicide divers and Wendell said I am going to marry that kid and the other said oh no you ain't I am and I said neither one of you is because I will court marshall you all before you can bat an eye." What she actually says is "I've seen them around is all" (201). Thus

Perpetua's transformation into a strong male appears to be echoed in the child's Walter Mitty–like dreams of male heroism, in activities that defy the appropriate behavior for females, especially in the South.

As recently as ten years ago, we might have been content to see the hermaphrodite as an ambivalent figure signaling a blurring of gender whereby the female author at least unconsciously exceeds gender limitation and presents an image of androgynous power. In that light, the association of the hermaphrodite with Christ at the story's conclusion would seem to recall images of an androgynous savior. Such images have recently become popular and are based on certain biblical texts, such as Galatians 3:28: "There is neither Jew nor Greek, there is neither slave nor free, there is neither male nor female; for you are all one in Christ Jesus." We might have easily conceded that the child in this story is concerned with power, especially as she attempts to gain control of her own life by accepting the limitations of the flesh, and that the fantasies of power in which she behaves as a male simply indicate the limited potential of women in that time. By this reading, O'Connor might be seen as offering the androgynous Christ as a panacea to the spirited rebellion of the girl-child and as an antidote to the frivolity of female concerns as they are depicted in the story.

However, to read the story in such a way, albeit satisfying in some measure, would be to disregard the body of O'Connor's work and to deny its grounding in Catholic orthodoxy. Furthermore, Margaret Miles's *Carnal Knowing: Female Nakedness and Religious Meaning in the Christian West* presents fresh observations on Perpetua and her "physical gender reversal" that cause us to reconsider O'Connor's story. Positing that the female martyr's body is used as a "textual device" by the editor of Perpetua's journals (probably Tertullian), Miles argues that, although Perpetua sees herself as male, the male editor of the journals sees her as female and is thereby able to provide examples of "modesty for future female readers" (61). This editor supplies reasons for Perpetua's behavior, such as her binding up her dishevelled hair, in keeping with notions of female decorum and propriety of the time. Thus, Miles emphasizes that the female body in western religious art is capable of "alternative and even conflicting interpretations"; in this case, for example, "Perpetua's body could represent 'male' heroism, commitment, and courage even while it remained an object for the male gaze" (61). Moreover, Perpetua's own diary, which presents her dreams of martyrdom, is a curious mixture of her own socialization "even as it narrates her resistance": "Her exclusive attention to men and male dream figures discloses her assumption that her spirituality, like her social identity, will take form in relation to a male-defined reality" (62). In this connection, can we not argue that the child in "A Temple of the Holy Ghost," whose dreams, as we have seen, are essentially male, assumes a spirituality that exists "in relation to a male-defined reality"?

Surely it is possible to read "A Temple" as a Christian coming-of-age story that is permeated with evidence of O'Connor's own assimilation of the Church's teaching, particularly the assumption that the girl-child's spirituality will develop in a male-dominated world. O'Connor's questioning of such an arrangement, if indeed O'Connor can be said to question, occurs in only oblique ways, a fact that may even suggest that the author herself was unaware of the import of such details. For example, the fact that the child and her mother are driven both to and from the convent suggests a kind of female helplessness especially associated with the situation of privileged white women in the South in the 1940s and 1950s. We must assume that because the mother relies on the foul-smelling Alonzo to act as chauffeur, she does not know how to drive. There is no mention of a husband/father, and his absence (as is so frequently the case in O'Connor's stories, the author mirrors her own situation) may in part account for the child's dreams of obtaining power and control. Furthermore, O'Connor shows that traditionally a large part of the life of girls and women is taken up with thinking about and waiting for men; Miss Kirby has only the visits of Mr. Cheatam to ward off her loneliness, and the "boy-crazy" Joanne and Susan are constantly giggling and whispering about the mysteries of sex. The child's disgust at her cousins' behavior is rivaled only by her curiosity to know what it is they know. Knowledge of the facts of life means a certain degree of power and control. The girls trade their experience with the hermaphrodite for the child's story about the birth of the rabbits. When the cousins fail to question the child's version of rabbit birth, we conclude that they know as little as she does.

The child's identification with the hermaphrodite is therefore understandable, although not solely in terms of her perplexity over her changing body, as several commentators have asserted. She is, after all, a girl whose dreams of power and heroism cast her in traditionally male roles. The confusion she feels between the dependence on men that women in her society accept as a matter of course and her own rebellion against that mindless dependence are mirrored in the double sex of the freak at the fair. The lesson she receives from the hermaphrodite involves the necessary acceptance of her own flesh as the gift of God: "God made me thisaway and if you laugh He may strike you the same way. This is the way He wanted me to be and I ain't disputing His way. I'm showing you because I got to make the best of it. I expect you to act like ladies and gentlemen" (*O'Connor* 206). In her dream-dialogue with the freak, the child hears the hermaphrodite call the body, in Sister Perpetua's words, a "temple of God," "a holy thing" (207), and warn against its desecration, a desecration that usually meant, for the female, loss of virginity. Are we to conclude, then, that the child must come to accept herself, rebelliousness and all, as part of God's plan, as the way God wanted her to be? Is the admonition against defiling the body tantamount to a requirement of virginity? Is there any reason for us to believe that the child is in any danger of losing her virginity, or is O'Connor simply using the Church's traditional expectation of virginity as the vehicle for her story of spiritual initiation?

Clearly this child's sensitivity and spiritual integrity (she knows her sins, even recognizes her pride, as O'Connor establishes early in the story) set her apart from her cousins and others, for she seems to possess a profound urge for the holy. We are led to believe that the child's dream of the hermaphrodite will mark the beginning of the consecration of her life to the teachings of God's "temple" on earth, the Church, often figured, we recall, as the body of Christ. I think that what follows the child's dream-revelation is indicative of O'Connor's own acceptance, at the most profound level, of the male-dominated Church and, consequently, her acknowledgment of the necessity for bringing one's vision into complete accord with the vision of the Church. We are therefore not surprised at the story's conclusion.

On the way to return the cousins to Mount St. Scholastica the next day, the child sits in the front of the car with Alonzo yet with her head out the window to avoid his smell. She can look straight at "the ivory sun" (208) as long as her blowing hair covers her face, as if in proof of Eliot's assertion that "humankind cannot bear very much reality." We recall that, the night before, the child stood gazing out her window toward the fair, "looking out over the dark slopes, past where the pond glinted silver, past the wall of woods to the speckled sky where a long finger of light was revolving up and around and away, searching the air as if it were hunting for the lost sun." With her typical irony and, incidentally, with a passing allusion to Hopkins's inscape ("speckled sky"), O'Connor suggests that the light may well have been looking for the lost "son" (Christ), for the child realizes "[i]t was the beacon of light from the fair" (203). Once again playing on the medieval sun/Son idea, O'Connor makes quite plain the connection between the literal sun and the Host, the Son of God, in the monstrance at benediction: the elevated Host is described as "shining ivory-colored" in the center of the monstrance. The final sentence of the story makes that identification complete, with its emphasis on the very real and very bloody sacrifice of the Crucifixion: "The sun was a huge red ball like an elevated Host drenched in blood and when it sank out of sight, it left a line in the sky like a red clay road hanging over the trees" (209). The image of the red clay road created by the trail of the sun in the sky returns us to the early description of Mr. Cheatam, Miss Kirby's "admirer" who "arrived every Saturday afternoon in a fifteen-year-old baby-blue Pontiac powdered with red clay dust and black inside with Negroes that he charged ten cents apiece to bring into town on Saturday afternoons." Furthermore, Mr. Cheatam "was bald-headed except for a little fringe of rust-colored hair and his face was nearly the same color as the unpaved roads and washed like them with ruts and gulleys" (198).

If we recall the centuries-old image of Christ as the lover come to woo the soul of the sinner—an image with which O'Connor was familiar, as I shall demonstrate later—we should not be surprised at the connection here between the red clay roads, Christ, and Mr. Cheatam, Miss Kirby's "gentleman caller." Moreover, O'Connor's indirect allusion in the last words of the story to the deep lines in Mr. Cheatam's face evokes every other image of fleshly reality in the story, from the spots on Joanne's face (remarked in the story's first sentence) to Susan's "pretty pointed face and red hair" (197) to the 250-pound Alonzo Meyers with his "round sweaty chest" (198), the "three folds of fat in the back of his neck," and his ears "pointed almost like a pig's" (209) to the "red faces and high cheekbones" of Wendell and Cory (201) to the "thin blue-gummed cook" (202). In these descriptions O'Connor suggests that all things "fickle, freckled (who knows how?) / With swift, slow; sweet, sour; adazzle, dim" are sanctified by Christ's taking on human flesh and allowing that flesh to be sacrificed for us. This is the vision of the child at the conclusion of "A Temple of the Holy Ghost." The proper posture of the soul is that of anticipation and readiness for the suitor who is Christ, come to woo the soul from sin. Although this eagerness and preparedness is *like* that of the young girl readying herself for her suitor, the necessity for the soul's openness is a matter of the utmost seriousness. We might even speculate that

O'Connor is writing her own parable of the wise and foolish virgins (Matthew 25:1–13), for in this story, which can be said to concern, on one level at least, the matter of female modesty and propriety, she uses gender to transcend gender. Woman's dependence on the male and her readiness for her suitor are analogous to the soul's dependence on God, her readiness for the Suitor.

At the story's conclusion, as the group approaches the convent, "a big moonfaced nun" comes "bustling" to the door and would have embraced the child except that she "stuck out her hand and preserved a frigid frown." The child's acknowledgment that the nuns "had a tendency to kiss even homely children" indicates that she considers herself vulnerable, but she manages to escape such effusive demonstrations. The group is rushed to the chapel where, in a totally female congregation, they will participate in benediction. In the chapel, which smells of incense, the nuns kneel on one side and the girls in brown uniforms kneel on the other side. At the altar "the priest [is] kneeling in front of the monstrance, bowed low" and is assisted by a "small boy in a surplice . . . standing behind him, swinging the censer." In this scene O'Connor inadvertently reminds us of the powerful hierarchy of the Church, a hierarchy that is based in large measure on gender, with the males at the altar and the females constituting the congregation, looking on, waiting, as seems to be their lot.

Well into the service the child is absorbed by "her ugly thoughts" until she realizes that she is "in the presence of God" and begins to pray for help with her sins. Then, just as her mind "[begins] to get quiet and then empty" and the priest elevates the monstrance containing the body of Christ, she is distracted, "thinking of the tent at the fair that had the freak in it" (208). She hears the words of the hermaphrodite: "I don't dispute hit. This is the way He wanted me to be" (209). The child who has identified with the freak is now thereby mysteriously identified with the crucified Christ; the uniqueness, the "whatness" of her own body, indeed her own life, have been given her by God: "This is the way He wanted me to be." Now we understand the full meaning of her instinctive response, early in the story, to the news that she is a temple of the Holy Ghost: "It made her feel as if somebody had given her a present" (199).

Therefore, it is altogether appropriate that the child is at last captured by the large nun who "swoop[s] down on her mischievously and nearly smother[s] her in the black habit, mashing the side of her face into the crucifix hitched onto her belt and then holding her off and looking at her with little periwinkle eyes" (209). In essence, she has been captured by the Church and given its imprint. Marked, changed by her experience of the incarnate Christ, she will now attempt to see everything from the Church's vantage point, as the Church would have her see. Sally Fitzgerald has often remarked that this story represents O'Connor's acceptance of her own life, particularly the restraints her illness forced upon her and her vocation as a Christian writer. I would not contradict that view. I would add only that O'Connor appears to subscribe completely to male-dominated orthodoxy whereby the female is relegated to a position outside the altar and urged to value herself as the Church values her. For O'Connor this is as it should be. We might even suggest that she adopts what we and Margaret Miles call "the male gaze" — in this case, the male gaze of the Church — in seeing the girl-child's dilemma as instructive, useful in providing a metaphoric model in a "male-defined reality." As we have previously noted, even O'Connor's own toughness of style reflects her intention to avoid the softening or compromise traditionally associated with the female.

Scholars like Margaret Miles have added much to our understanding of the religious meaning given the female body in western culture. As Miles points out, not only are female bodies not "the site of heroic spiritual struggle" in western art (144) but they are usually associated with sin. From at least the time of Augustine, the idea that woman's sin comes from her body prevails, unlike man's sin, which is essentially a sin of the spirit. This idea was widely disseminated, particularly in visual representation in the form of Church art that did much to educate an unread populace: "Eve's culpable flesh, the flesh of every woman, was sculptured in stone on cathedral facades, painted in illustrated gospel books, on church walls and ceilings, and set in delicate mosaic tesserae" (117). Miles reminds us that the "first theological meaning of nakedness in Christian tradition was the innocence, fragility, and vulnerability of human bodies in their initial creation," that the wages of sin were physical punishments, and that Eve took the "initiative in sin" (xi). Such a view of Eve obviously pervades western literature and art as well as western theology. Even though thinkers like Hildegard of Bingen, abbess of a Benedictine monastery in the late twelfth century, suggested that Eve, not Adam, was the representative human being because of the combination of frailty and power she possessed — even proposing a kind of mutuality in the sexual relationship between Adam and Eve — the dominant male view prevailed. At the other extreme from Eve who "*is* body" is the Virgin, the ideal, usually depicted as a disembodied figure or, if not disembodied, at least "placed in a heavenly setting, with only enough body to protect and nourish the infant Christ" (Miles 141).

Most significantly, women have over the centuries been educated to see the world "from the perspective of the collective male voice" (116) as that voice has sounded from written texts, works of art, and theological doctrine. For example, Miles shows that Renaissance painters like Rembrandt and Tintoretto, who painted the biblical story of Susanna and the Elders, had no success in creating innocence in the naked female figure of Susanna; such a figure does not seem to be able to "communicate innocence," although "it easily communicates sin, sex, and evil" (125). Rembrandt's and Tintoretto's paintings depict the scene of the elders' spying on Susanna's bath through "the eyes of an assumed male viewer" and suggest "the Elders' intense erotic attraction, projected and displayed on Susanna's flesh." Furthermore, "[v]iewers are directed — trained — by the management of light and shadow and by the central position of Susanna's body to see Susanna as object, even as cause, of male desire" (123). Thus, viewing Susanna's body as innocent was prevented "by repeatedly reiterated and reinforced associations of female nakedness with Eve and original sin" (124). The pervasiveness of the male gaze over the centuries is, in fact, so profound that until recently most women simply accepted it. Even now any genuine attempt to determine the extent to which women's education and social conditioning determine how we women look and think about ourselves resembles the proverbial peeling of the onion. Among the first to attack the pervasive male view of woman as object in centuries of western literature, Virginia Woolf in *A Room of One's Own* demonstrated the difficulty of a woman's daring to counter that male gaze with an alternative vision, one that would allow for a full dimensional portrait of female experience, a subjective view. However, even Woolf did not begin to take on the power of the Church.

The cosmic order established by Augustine, whereby the male is dominant, has undergirded the Church's teaching, as Miles explains:

> From Augustine forward, Christian authors insisted that "inasmuch as woman was a human being, she certainly had a mind, and a rational mind, and therefore she was also made to the image of God." . . . Between men and women "there is no difference except in relation to the body." But this difference was a large one. As Augustine's statement suggests, women's "nature" was determined by their

physical difference from men, that is, by their bodies. Although women possess rationality, men's "nature" was determined by it. Thus, it seemed "reasonable" that human beings defined by mind should rule those defined by body. The "order of creation" — man first, woman second — was understood to reflect cosmic order and to stipulate social order; female subordination was the linchpin of social order. (17)

There is surely little need to belabor a point that has received detailed exposition in recent years. I am simply reminding the reader of another side of O'Connor's conditioning and education: O'Connor came to accept, as most of us did, that flesh is primarily associated with the female, that woman's spiritual journey did not have the significance of the man's journey, and that female experience could best be used in a figurative or metaphoric way to suggest the necessity for the soul's complete subjection to the Church as the body of Christ on earth.

The ending of "A Temple of the Holy Ghost" seems a case in point, for here O'Connor assigns value to the girl's coming of age, both a comic and traumatic experience, as the Church would assign that value. The meaning and significance of her body and, for that matter, the hermaphrodite's body are assigned by the Church. Louise Westling argues that the ending of the story involves O'Connor's shifting of the story's concern with "adolescent sexual confusion" to "a theological plane which previous references to the Temple of the Holy Ghost and the child's religious musings have anticipated" (140). Although I do not see that the story really shifts, I would agree with Westling that O'Connor leaves "dangling" a theme that is "central" and "troubling": The child "remains a *girl* who will grow into a woman" (142). As we noted earlier, Westling attributes O'Connor's evasion of sexuality and her transformation of potentially sexual material into spiritual edification to her own difficulties with adolescence and feminine identity. However, I would suggest that, although O'Connor may have had her difficulties with the common burdens of female adolescence, a primary factor underlying the shape of this story is O'Connor's assumption of the Church's male outlook on a female's coming of age. In the story the presence of the nuns — certainly the embodiment of the Church's emphasis on the importance of female virginity to the point of a kind of sexual neutrality — is simply another reminder that O'Connor, like the Church, views female sexuality as a force to be subordinated to "higher" values that are cerebral or spiritual and usually associated with the male.

Margaret Miles maintains that the "analysis of gender constructions" necessitates readings that are "disobedient" in that they "attempt to reveal the ways in which gender constructions are embedded in communications so naturalistically that the author can count on them to move an argument, to persuade, or to seduce" (xiv). Although I believe that O'Connor's work can be read as subversive of accepted behavior for southern females—as I have already demonstrated and will demonstrate again shortly—and that as a Christian writer O'Connor used exaggeration and comedy to dramatize her beliefs, I also believe that her fiction depends for its very success on embedded gender constructions that appeal generally to an audience educated in the male way of seeing. One does not have to agree completely with Judith Fetterley that in patriarchal cultures "the presumed reader is male" ("Reading about Reading" 150) to accept the premise that most readers have been trained to look and to read from the male perspective. Perhaps it is revealing that the critics of O'Connor's work who seem to have had the most trouble with her vision—from Josephine Hendin to Martha Stephens to Carol Shloss, Claire Kahane, and Louise Westling—have been predominantly women who have resisted the "orthodox" readings and sought through various approaches (psychoanalytic, deconstructionist, feminist) to find in the texts something about the writer's own life and her position as a woman in southern society in the twentieth century. Of course, what these commentators are hard-pressed to accept is the essentially patriarchal view that pervades O'Connor's writings, both fiction and nonfiction. I believe that most of these commentators, as women, want more for their spiritual lives than O'Connor appears to give, and thus they are dissatisfied and sometimes angry in taking her to task.

Therefore, even as O'Connor agreed with Lynch that art is incarnational and even as she was influenced by Hopkins's emphasis on inscape—the divine "whatness" of each created thing—she also seems to have associated the body and fleshly weakness with the female, as social, literary, and religious institutions had trained her to do. Like many of us, she did not overtly challenge these assumptions. However, in much of her fiction we find a subterranean current of rebellion that appears to be finally checked by or channeled into a dogmatically acceptable position.

As is the case in "A Temple of the Holy Ghost," the perils of female adolescence are also center stage in "A Circle in the Fire." This story sounds an even stronger note of warning about our human vulnerability—symbolized by the link between the female body and the land itself—than is found in "A Temple." From its opening lines in which Mrs. Pritchard broaches the subject of the woman who "had that baby in that iron lung" (*O'Connor* 232), the vicissitudes of our mortal bodies are presented in largely female terms. Mrs. Cope must manage by herself both the farm and her twelve-year-old daughter, Sally Virginia, who is full of resentment of her mother because the mother is domineering and smug and because Sally Virginia, like the child in "A Temple," rebels against the code of ladylike behavior that is being forced upon her. Although Sally Virginia was at first amused and even intrigued by the boys' resistance to her mother's attempts at superficial hospitality (in all likelihood because such hostility mirrors her own), she comes to despise the boys' staying power, their disruption of her and her mother's lives, and finally, perhaps most important, their success in rendering her mother powerless. Sally Virginia is on the verge of puberty, and regardless of her bravado in pulling on overalls over her dress and strapping on the pistols by which she means to roust the interlopers, what she learns is her own helplessness as a female. When the boys set the farm on fire, she stands nearby, transfixed, for a time unable to move even to warn her mother. In fact, she appears momentarily paralyzed by the boys' power and exaltation as they dance and shriek their insurrection: "They began to whoop and holler and beat their hands over their mouths and in a few seconds there was a narrow line of fire widening between her and them" (250).

The fire is not all that separates her from them, for they have been able to *cause to happen* what she has only imagined. The following passage early in the story establishes the emphasis on vulnerability and makes a connection between the vulnerable land and the female fear of physical harm that is central to the rest of the story. Indeed, even its opening sentence implies a mythic suggestion of sexual intercourse whereby the sky (male) penetrates the female earth:

> The child thought the blank sky looked as if it were pushing against the fortress
> wall [of trees], trying to break through. The trees across the near field were a
> patchwork of gray and yellow greens. Mrs. Cope was always worrying about fires
> in her woods. When the nights were very windy, she would say to the child, "Oh
> Lord, do pray there won't be any fires, it's so windy," and the child would grunt
> from behind her book or not answer at all because she heard it so often. In the

> evenings in the summer when they sat on the porch, Mrs. Cope would say to the child who was reading fast to catch the last light, "Get up and look at the sunset, it's gorgeous. You ought to get up and look at it," and the child would scowl and not answer or glare up once across the lawn and two front pastures to the gray-blue sentinel line of trees and then begin to read again with no change of expression, sometimes muttering for meanness, "It looks like a fire. You better get up and smell around and see if the woods ain't on fire." (232–33)

O'Connor suggests that the child might even be said to have willed the fire that is finally set by the boys (just as, in another context, Julian might be said to have willed his mother's death in "Everything That Rises Must Converge"), so strong is her resentment of her mother. And yet the child is initiated into the reality of fear and helplessness, as the boys' stay on the farm continues and as their presence demonstrates her mother's helplessness. Through repeated images of female vulnerability, images that depend for their success on our common acceptance of female weakness, we are provided a lesson about our common mortality. Just before the boys' arrival, in fact, Mrs. Cope, like the Pharisee, has been recounting her own daily prayers of thanksgiving, denying Mrs. Pritchard's fear that trouble might "all come at oncet sometime." Mrs. Pritchard seems to know better, however, as she "[folds] her arms and [gazes] down the road as if she could easily enough see all these fine hills flattened to nothing" (235). Immediately the three boys appear. They are sullen and refractory, and Powell, the obvious leader, is twice described (presumably as the child sees him) as looking "as if he were trying to enclose the whole place in one encircling stare." When Mrs. Pritchard, pointing out that the boys are carrying a suitcase, suggests that they may plan to spend the night, Mrs. Cope gives "a slight shriek" and responds, "I can't have three boys in here with only me and Sally Virginia" (238). Here, of course, O'Connor relies on the familiar female fear (especially widespread in the South) that women alone are at risk. As Westling and others have noted, behind Mrs. Cope's words is her fear of rape, of violation.

O'Connor reiterates the link between the land, usually seen as female in myth and metaphor, and the vulnerable female body. Mrs. Cope fears violation, and the boys come to represent the prospect of that violation. The fact that they release the bull reinforces their association with threatening male power, and indeed, they cause all of Mrs. Cope's troubles to "come at oncet." The boys are not the "gentlemen" Mrs. Cope has urged them to be, and Sally Virginia does not behave like a lady when she threatens to "beat the daylight out of Powell." Her mother admonishes her: "Ladies don't beat the daylight out of people" (242). Something beyond gentlemanly or ladylike behavior is at stake here, however, as O'Connor clearly indicates by the images of fire at the story's conclusion. We are obviously intended to see that the boys serve a prophetic function in presenting Mrs. Cope and Sally Virginia with the need to recognize their human frailty. Significantly, the "misery" is initially conveyed in terms of the girl-child's identification with the mother and only after that translated to include other oppressed people:

> The child came to a stop beside her mother and stared up at her face as if she had never seen it before. It was the face of the new misery she felt, but on her mother it looked old and it looked as if it might have belonged to anybody, a Negro or a European or to Powell himself. The child turned her head quickly, and past the Negroes' ambling figures she could see the column of smoke rising and widening unchecked inside the granite line of trees. She stood taut, listening, and could just catch in the distance a few wild high shrieks of joy as if the prophets were dancing in the fiery furnace, in the circle the angel had cleared for them. (250–51)

As Sally Virginia recognizes her own and her mother's vulnerability, she is able to see in her mother's face a reflection of age-old suffering, Matthew Arnold's "turbid ebb and flow of human misery," of which she is now a part.

Although this story might be said to be less intensely theological than other O'Connor works, the author obviously means for us to see the boys' burning of the farm as Mrs. Cope's and Sally Virginia's opportunity for grace, for in juxtaposition to Mrs. Cope's proclamation, "This is my place," is the youngest boy's remark, "'Man, Gawd owns them woods and her too" (242–43). Again in this story O'Connor uses an embedded assumption of female weakness to convey the fact of our fallen condition. As Miles and others remind us, in western thought the weakness of the flesh is most frequently signified by the female body, and in this story the connection between female flesh and the land itself deepens the texture of the narrative, leading to the story's powerfully evocative conclusion. The bad boys are not really prophets, but the child imagines that their shouts might be those of "the prophets" Shadrach, Meshach, and Abednego, "dancing in the fiery furnace, in the circle the angel had cleared for them" (O'Connor 251).

As readers, we feel the rightness of her conclusion. Mrs. Cope needed to have her pride and smugness violated; she was, as the saying goes, "asking for it" through her selfishness and her pompous certainty about her work ethic. Even the young boy's revealing remark, "Gawd owns them woods and her too," links the land and the female and would appear to suggest that this "owner," God, whom O'Connor repeatedly presents in images of the sun — the powerful, traditional male god — may penetrate this world (the woods) and "her too." (On several occasions in the story O'Connor makes it clear that the brilliant sunset causes the woods to appear to be on fire. This suggestion prepares the way for the *actual* burning of the woods, caused by God's unlikely agents, the bad boys.) Indirectly, therefore, we have once again the allusion to God/Christ as lover, as suitor, an image as familiar to Christians, especially Catholics, as Bernini's intense fusion of sexual and spiritual in his St. Theresa or Francis Thompson's less intense *Hound of Heaven*. And although we may not take the time to be relieved that neither Mrs. Cope nor the child is physically violated, we may conclude that such a catastrophe was also within the realm of possibility. After all, O'Connor seems to be reminding us that, as humans, we are not self-sufficient and that in a fallen world such horrors are possible.

Just why the author did not conclude with the actual rape of either the mother or the daughter here is purely a matter of speculation. We might conjecture, for example, that rape itself was too far beyond the limits of propriety for even the bold imagination of O'Connor (although *The Violent Bear It Away* contains a homosexual rape) or that the story's actual ending achieves its power through the *suggestion* of what might have happened, or that the tone of the earlier parts of the story was too comic and satirical to allow the story to end in rape. For whatever reason, O'Connor stops short of allowing violence to be done to the women's bodies. Nevertheless, I believe that our perception of their (and our) human frailty or vulnerability, the truth O'Connor is obviously dramatizing in this story, depends on our recognition at some level of the danger inherent to women *in their bodies*. If God allows the burning of the woods (a part of the world's body, traditionally imaged as female) for the chastening of Mrs. Cope's pride, might he not also allow the women's bodies to be wounded? Obviously, the god who countenances such devastation suggests the stern, judgmental, often punitive deity usually associated with the Old Testament and the patriarchal Church.

The frame and scope of the story and especially its violent conclusion cause "A Circle in the Fire" to seem indeed very much a kind of Old Testament narrative. Elaine Scarry in *The Body in Pain* argues that in the Old

Testament the "scenes of hurt . . . tend to occur in the context of disbelief and doubt" and that "through the human body . . . belief is substantiated" by such hurt or wounding (183). She asserts that "God's power of alteration continually re-manifests itself" on the human and on the land (199). The means of God's wounding or hurting are many: "fire, storm, whirlwind, plague, rod, arrow, knife, sword." When the human is wounded in Old Testament narratives, the cause for such hurt is usually a "failure of belief." Those without belief, furthermore, are frequently described as hard of heart or stiff (202). The Israelites, for example, are described as stiff-necked when they offend God as Moses receives the Ten Commandments, and Pharaoh's heart is hardened, causing him to refuse to listen to Moses (203). Thus, Scarry concludes, the human's "withholding of the body—the stiffening of the neck, the turning of the shoulder, the closing of the ears, the hardening of the heart, the making of the face like stone—necessitates God's forceful shattering of the reluctant human surface and the repossession of the interior" (204).

In "A Circle in the Fire," O'Connor appears to be writing out of that Old Testament tradition of divine wounding. Sally Virginia and Mrs. Cope are hurt out of their closed ears and hardened hearts by the fire on the land. That land is what Scarry calls the "source of analogical verification" of God's presence and judgment (201). The female bodies in this story remain intact, but the wound to the land easily suggests the possibility of (or is itself analogous to) the wounding—in this case, sexual violation—of the lone women. The connection O'Connor implies between the women and the land is clear. Her vision here is clearly in keeping with Old Testament narrative with its emphasis on the hurt or the wound that is inflicted on the spiritually deaf and blind, a phenomenon that is present in varying degrees in much of O'Connor's work. The emphasis of the New Testament on healing and recovery, as Scarry describes the shape of New Testament narrative, seems absent here, as it is absent in other O'Connor stories—for example, "The Life You Save May Be Your Own," "Greenleaf," and "A View of the Woods."

By now perhaps it is evident that the questions raised by such a view of the divine (the Old Testament God of the wound or of hurt) are, to some of us, troubling. Surely the use of the female to suggest the flesh's frailty and dependence is traditional in the patriarchy and would have come "naturally" to O'Connor. Yet I cannot help wishing for more of Hopkins's view in O'Connor's works, for more of the sense of God's presence in the world—as

Christ, the God incarnate whose spirit imbues the "meanest" sparkling tree, the speckled cows, and, we are to assume, the most tainted flesh. To put the "lack" in Scarry's terms, the (at best) secondary role played by the New Testament narrative of healing and recovery makes O'Connor's vision troubling. Moreover, in "A Circle in the Fire" O'Connor seems closer to Manichaeanism than in "The River" or "A Temple of the Holy Ghost," for in "A Circle," her attitude toward this world seems at times to be almost sneering or contemptuous. We might indeed question whether Mrs. Cope's sins are sufficient to warrant such a violent comeuppance, although in so doing we might be brought up short by the reminder that even Job, for all of his questioning and in spite of his upright character, finally had to repent in dust and ashes. And Job is, after all, an Old Testament hero, although whether he lacks faith or is hard of heart is unclear. He is forcibly reminded of his creatureliness through a series of wounds inflicted by God.

In contrast to the powerful male-centered stories of the Old Testament, however, O'Connor wrote a number of stories concerned with women alone who are literally visited by males, or some form of "gentleman caller." In addition to the previously discussed "Temple of the Holy Ghost" and "A Circle in the Fire," they are "The Life You Save May Be Your Own," "Good Country People," "The Displaced Person," and "Greenleaf" from the collection *Everything That Rises Must Converge*. In each of these stories women's lives are dramatically disrupted by the intrusion of the male, and although the emphasis in each story is not always on the male as sexual being, O'Connor consistently relies on the assumption of the vulnerability of female flesh to effect the story's resolution. In other words, the stories work on several levels, including the theological, because of the assumption of female weakness with which the reader implicitly identifies. Such an assumption is in the very air we breathe.

"The Life You Save May Be Your Own" begins with the arrival of Tom T. Shiftlet at the farm of Mrs. Lucynell Crater, who peers at his figure ambling up the road and then dismisses him as no threat, because even though she "lived in this desolate spot with only her daughter and she had never seen Mr. Shiftlet before, she could tell, even from a distance, that he was a tramp and no one to be afraid of" (O'Connor 172). Mrs. Crater, another of O'Connor's tough, single-minded farm widows, meets her match, of course, in the form of the handicapped Mr. Shiftlet, who allows her to persuade him to work on the farm, to revive her old car, and, eventually, to marry her "afflicted" daughter, Lucynell. Like Powell in "A Circle in the Fire," Mr. Shiftlet, upon his arrival, gazes at "everything in the yard" (173) and singles out the car as the primary object of his interest. As he pretends to answer Mrs. Crater's questions, he philosophizes about the mystery of human existence, but Mrs. Crater, whom we might call "Lucynell Sr.," is a practical woman and not the least interested in the truths he spouts. However, as readers who acknowledge the wisdom in his words, we also recognize the O'Connor technique of putting in the mouths of the most disreputable characters the most profound truths. In this connection, the Misfit of "A Good Man Is Hard to Find" and Rufus Johnson of "The Lame Shall Enter First" immediately come to mind. Tom T. Shiftlet differs from these characters in that he is the center of this story. Certainly the senior Lucynell is to be deplored for the transparent angling by means of which she hopes to buy both a son-in-law and a man about the farm; her character appears in many ways a doubling of that of Tom T. Shiftlet. Just as she is "ravenous for a son-in-law," he is ravenous for the car, the means of his mobility and thus of his escape from responsibility and any sort of examination of conscience. The calculating mother, who announces that she will not give up her daughter "for a casket of jewels" (177), does just that when Mr. Shiftlet resurrects the car, which will serve as his living quarters and which he likens to a coffin (casket):

> "Why listen, Lady . . . the monks of old slept in their coffins!"
> "They wasn't as advanced as we are," the old woman said. (176)

For $17.50 and the use of the car for their honeymoon, Mr. Shiftlet agrees to marry the retarded, mute "girl" of thirty-two. Thus, on one level the story follows the trickster plot common to American comic literature.

That the con artist ends up abandoning the afflicted girl in a roadside cafe is not surprising, and if the mother were the central character—or even the daughter—the story could end right there, with the horror of the mother's finagling and our speculation about what the daughter's loss might mean to her. However, in this instance the story does not belong to the female characters. Tom T. Shiftlet, who feels "depressed" as soon as he and Lucynell, the newlyweds, leave together in the car, does have a conscience, or so we are led to believe. After he abandons his bride, Mr. Shiftlet encounters the brutally cynical young hitchhiker who serves as the catalyst for his recognition of evil in the world. Echoing the words of the waiter in describing Lucynell as an "angel of Gawd" (181), Mr. Shiftlet piously describes his own mother as an "angel of Gawd" (183), as though preaching a lesson to the hitchhiker, who he perhaps naively assumes is running away from home. Instead of the expected response, however, come the boy's angry words: "You go to the devil! . . . My old woman is a flea bag and yours is a stinking pole cat!" The boy then leaps from the car into a ditch. In this comic reversal, Mr. Shiftlet's own hypocrisy is hurled back at him, and he feels that "the rottenness of the world [is] about to engulf him." So intense is his recognition of the world's evil that he prays, "Oh Lord! . . . Break forth and wash the slime from this earth!" Clearly O'Connor intends for the reader to recognize — in the "guffawing peal of thunder" and the "fantastic raindrops" of the story's last paragraph — that if Mr. Shiftlet's prayer were answered, he would be the first to go, as he "[races] the galloping shower into Mobile" (183).

Thus, the story that at least superficially resembles the plot of "A Circle in the Fire" or "Good Country People" is something else, with its emphasis on the con man and the question of his salvation. Particularly interesting in this variation of O'Connor's most familiar plot is the function of the retarded daughter. Lucynell is described in images of childlike vulnerability, with "her head thrust forward and her fat helpless hands hanging at her wrists." Furthermore, she has "long pink-gold hair and eyes as blue as a peacock's neck" (173); later, O'Connor tells us that Lucynell's eyes are "blue even in the dark" (178). To Mr. Shiftlet's calculated question, "Lady . . . where would you find you an innocent woman today?" Lucynell seems to be the answer. In addition to her obvious virginity, the daughter is, as her mother points out, "the sweetest girl in the world" and "smart too," able to "sweep the floor, cook, wash, feed the chickens, and hoe" (176). Female readers may be especially amused at O'Connor's satirical thrust at this ideal of "innocence," a girl who, in the words of her own mother, won't "sass . . . or use foul language" because she is mute (178). Aside from creating her own wry version of male jokes about the supreme value of the silent woman, O'Connor is underscoring the fact of Lucynell's innocence. It is more than the "innocence" Mr. Shiftlet and Mrs. Crater and most of the rest of us in patriarchal society have been taught to value in women: virginity. Beyond sexual innocence, it is a matter of a kind of innocence of *essence* that might be considered truly angelic. The waiter is correct in identifying Lucynell as "an angel of Gawd," for that is what she is.

Lucynell's innocence, O'Connor implies, is a mysterious gift to those who will recognize it as such. The comparison of the intense blue of her eyes to the blue of a peacock's neck suggests the divine mystery O'Connor associates with the peacock. As both O'Connor's essay "The King of the Birds" and her story "The Displaced Person" demonstrate, the way we view the peacock in some significant way reveals who we are. In "The Life You Save May Be Your Own," O'Connor clearly indicts both Mrs. Crater and Mr. Shiftlet for their attitudes toward Lucynell. Although Mr. Shiftlet abandons Lucynell, her own mother is even more culpable in pretending that Lucynell is normal and forcing her into the traditional womanly role. Both Mr. Shiftlet and Mrs. Crater refuse to look beyond their own selfish, practical designs at the angel of God who has been entrusted to them. O'Connor presents a similar theme in "The Displaced Person" and *The Violent Bear It Away*. Here we conclude that the "test" given to both of the rational, "whole" characters in this story is that of how to "see" Lucynell, who is not responsible for her choices and whose presence on earth is a mystery of the most sacred kind.

In this way the female, though afflicted and perhaps on the surface a part of the comedy, is absolutely essential to the salvation of the male protagonist. The girl's holy innocence shines in the dark; even the waiter in the roadside cafe recognizes, on some level, who she is. Lucynell's importance in this story depends on our understanding the idea of purity, a purity analogous to that of the Virgin, who, we note, is usually associated with the color blue. Through symbolism, character contrast, irony, and plot structure, O'Connor creates anagogical meaning. Moreover, she is not deviating at all from the supreme value placed by the Church on virginity as symbolic of the soul's innocence; the virginal woman is often the metaphor for the soul's purity. Lucynell's role is thus complex. She is both a reflection of the fallenness of the world in her affliction and an emblem of angelic purity. Her value to the "unafflicted" characters in the story, namely, her mother and Tom T. Shiftlet, lies in the way in which each chooses to view her. She is a potentially mediating fleshly presence.

Tom T. Shiftlet, of course, speaks a truth he himself has yet to understand. Like many of O'Connor's male protagonists, including Julian, Asbury, and Rayber, he is the dissociated sensibility who may speak the words that compel his hearer but who is, after all, only mouthing words. When he announces in pontifical terms that he is "a man . . . even if [he] ain't a whole one" and that he has "a moral intelligence!" O'Connor records his own disbelief: "His face pierced out of the darkness into a shaft of doorlight and he stared at

[Mrs. Crater] as if he were astonished himself at this impossible truth" (176). What Mrs. Crater hears in these words is the possibility of a son-in-law, not his preachy announcement of his own morality in the face of human frailty. Even in his description of the making of the automobile, Mr. Shiftlet acknowledges the fragmentation of human endeavor through our modern emphasis on specialization. He aptly notes the lack of unity and purpose characteristic of industrialism:

> "You take now . . . one man puts in one bolt and another man puts in another bolt and another man puts in another bolt so that it's a man for a bolt. That's why you have to pay so much for a car: you're paying all those men. Now if you didn't have to pay but one man, you could get you a cheaper car and one that had had a personal interest taken in it, and it would be a better car." (177)

Later, in the process of bargaining with Mrs. Crater, Mr. Shiftlet reminds us of the separation of man into "two parts, body and spirit" and argues that, although the body is stationery, the spirit "is like a automobile: always on the move, always" (179), an observation that would appear to forecast the story's conclusion and that reiterates the Cartesian dualism decried by Maritain, Tate, and other conservative modernists. The irony of Mr. Shiftlet's statement, however, is evident in the fact that an automobile is not, if we may be pardoned the pun, a valid vehicle for the tenor (spirit) because the man-made car is subject to breakdown and loss. Of course, the car is the objective correlative for Mr. Shiftlet's spiritual wandering and escapism. Moreover, in an obvious parody of Christ's raising of the dead, Mr. Shiftlet resurrects the car. Its body leaves the shed "in a fierce and stately way" with Mr. Shiftlet at the helm, with "an expression of serious modesty on his face as if he had just raised the dead" (178). There is no question that Mr. Shiftlet's miraculous recovery of the car is associated with his conquest of Mrs. Crater and her daughter, Lucynell. He has given new life to all three bodies, although clearly with an eye to having only one of those bodies for his own—that of the automobile.

Just as the Essex failed Hazel Motes in *Wise Blood*, so we assume that Tom T. Shiftlet's means of mobility and escape will eventually fail him, as our carnal bodies will fail us all. A number of critics have observed that the automobile functions in both *Wise Blood* and "The Life You Save May Be Your Own" as emblematic of the modern belief in progress, in O'Connor's view obviously the result of the distorted values of modern technology and secularism. J. O. Tate, in a creatively speculative essay on the source of

Motes's Essex, notes that in *Wise Blood* "a car is a false god" and that O'Connor is punning on the word *Essex* by choosing a name that "fairly hisses SSEX at us" ("The Essential Essex" 54). Contending that Motes is anything but a lover and that his "females are inversions of loveliness, reversals of innocence, negatives of desire" (55), Tate concludes that the only real pleasure for Hazel Motes is, ironically and sadly enough, afforded by the car, which represents for him "the equation of 'freedom' and 'sex' that is the epitome of his 'philosophy'" (51). Clearly, then, through Haze's obsession with the Essex, O'Connor parodies the pervasive modern belief that the car, "a fantasy-projection of self," is also "a status symbol, an assertion of prowess, a declaration of value" (53). In Tate's reading we remark the association of car with body, with flesh — not with spirit, as Shiftlet would have Mrs. Crater believe, but with the fleshly mortality repeatedly associated with the female. Even Tate's language is imbued with this association, as he writes, "Mrs. Watts is, in effect, a 'pre-owned' vehicle, and Sabbath Lily is a bad buy, a lemon, as Hazel discovers" (51) and "If the Essex is no Packard, then Mrs. Watts, with her teeth 'speckled with green,' is no Rita Hayworth, nor is Sabbath anybody's Betty Grable" (53). And just as Tate implies that O'Connor burlesques the idea of Haze's power over the car as his assertion of manliness and control, so we could argue that Tom T. Shiftlet's manhood is greatly enhanced, both in his own mind and in the minds of Mrs. Crater and Lucynell, when he is able to resurrect the car.

In a more recent reading, however, Brian Abel Ragen asserts that, in contrast to the farm that, "with its responsibilities and its deep well, is feminine, the car is masculine" (101). He argues that, because the car stopped running on the very day of Mrs. Crater's husband's death, we must attribute its failure to the fact that the farm is run by women and that "[a]utomobiles, like moving itself, are linked with masculinity" (101).[3] Ragen concludes that Shiftlet uses the mobility provided by the car to head west, as the American (male) protagonist is wont to do, and to escape "from female entanglements," thus "rejecting a chance to redeem his sinful self" (105).

I do not agree with Ragen that Shiftlet's story is one of "grace resisted" (105), for I see the story's ending as ambiguous and deliberately inconclusive. Mr. Shiftlet might indeed be seen as trapped in the body of the car, that is to say, trapped in his own sinful mortality, for his earlier remorse of conscience has only intensified at the story's conclusion. Like the Essex in *Wise Blood*, the car in this story is very much associated with the body. At the story's conclusion, Tom T. Shiftlet's car is shadowed by the turnip-shaped cloud just as his life in the flesh is shadowed by sin and guilt. And if we allow the possibility of such an interpretation, we observe, perhaps without surprise by now, that O'Connor is simply adhering to the commonly held association of the time, one so deeply ingrained as to be unquestioned—that flesh, of which the car is the "embodiment," is somehow inevitably associated with the female. We are certain that, if Tom T. Shiftlet is to be saved, he will eventually have to give up the car, the tangible proof of his manly power and control (after all, he "raised" it from the dead), the symbol of his pride and achievement and, quite significantly, of his conquest and escape. The "resurrection" of the automobile was no real miracle; Christ is the only one who can raise the dead. And somewhere down the road to Mobile, the car that is the extension of Mr. Shiftlet will fail, just as the destruction of the Essex marked the turning point in Hazel Motes's journey.

We might add here that the car and Lucynell are almost ironic reflections of one another; they are curiously linked characters in this story, both suggestive of our "afflicted" human natures. As readers we are able to understand this fact in a way that Shiftlet cannot; such is the way O'Connor's irony works—as a sort of shared secret between writer and reader. In a sense, of course, Shiftlet appears to give new life to both the car and Lucynell. That he wants to abandon the "angel of Gawd" and to place his faith in the "body" of the car is testament to one of the tragic errors of our time.

In "Good Country People," another of the stories centered on the arrival of a "gentleman caller," the focus is on Joy/Hulga, into whose miserable life comes the Bible salesman Manley Pointer. As I have noted elsewhere,[4] this unlikely messenger so aptly named brings the word of her arrogance, dependence, and self-delusion to Joy/Hulga, who learns, at the very least, that she is not as smart as she thinks she is. The avowed atheist who announces that she "see[s] *through* to nothing" (*O'Connor* 280) is obviously in need of both attention and control, and she intends to achieve these ends by seducing the Bible salesman, who to her appears naive and in great need of enlightenment. Of course, O'Connor manages to amuse and horrify us by turning the tables on Joy/Hulga. At the story's conclusion she sits helpless in the hayloft, deprived of the wooden leg and her glasses, the symbols of her sense of her own uniqueness and her intellectual superiority, respectively. These conclusions about the story's meaning are fairly evident and widely accepted.

What is perhaps not so frequently noticed is that this narrative, like "A

Temple of the Holy Ghost," is concerned with the body, especially with the vicissitudes of being female. Images of weight and heaviness throughout the story emphasize the burdens of fleshly life, from the first paragraph in which Mrs. Freeman's expression is likened to "the advance of a heavy truck" and her physical presence to "several grain sacks thrown on top of each other" to the repeated allusions to Joy/Hulga's size—she is described as "a large blonde girl" who "lumbers" into the room on her artificial leg (263). Furthermore, she is "hulking" (264), a "poor stout girl in her thirties" (266), who is "bloated" (268). Manley Pointer's "heavy valise," although presumably weighted down with copies of the Lord's word, is actually rather light and contains the grotesque souvenirs of his conquests. Moreover, Mrs. Freeman serves as a foreshadowing of Manley Pointer in her obsession with the physical, especially details of the freakish and the bizarre. In addition to her preoccupation with the physical conditions of her two daughters, Glynese and Carramae (whom Joy/Hulga dubs Glycerin and Caramel, contemptuously underscoring their disposable sweetness), Mrs. Freeman has "a special fondness for the details of secret infections, hidden deformities, assaults upon children" and "[o]f diseases, prefers the lingering or incurable" (267). She is particularly fascinated by Joy/Hulga's artificial leg and never tires of hearing the story of the violent way in which she lost her real one. In these proclivities, of course, she bears a strong resemblance to Mrs. Pritchard in "A Circle in the Fire" and Mrs. Greenleaf in "Greenleaf," although Mrs. Greenleaf's obsession with the physically horrible, to her credit, underscores her belief in original sin and her need for humble repentance before the majesty of God.

In "Good Country People" the emphasis on the fleshly and the physical, presented largely through images of heaviness and weight, seems curiously related to one of the central concerns of the story, namely, our human inability to see clearly and thus to name clearly. Although Joy/Hulga boasts that she "see[s] *through* to nothing," the story proves that her estimation of her own powers of perception is greatly overrated: she has been completely deceived. Clearly another dissociated sensibility,[5] Joy/Hulga, in her habit of judging others on a very superficial basis, resembles her own mother, Mrs. Hopewell, whose language or means of describing reality, as has frequently been noted, consists of one cliché after another. Even the wily Bible salesman, who is not above using a cliché or two himself, responds to Mrs. Hopewell's series of clichés with a clear awareness of language:

"Why!" she cried, "good country people are the salt of the earth! Besides, we all have different ways of doing, it takes all kinds to make the world go 'round. That's life!"

"You said a mouthful," he said. (271)

The banality of Mrs. Hopewell's thinking is evident in this series of platitudes, a fact that Joy/Hulga recognizes and that we recognize as well. Concerned that her daughter has missed the "normal" good times enjoyed by young women and even envious of Mrs. Freeman's two "normal" girls, Mrs. Hopewell is completely baffled by Joy/Hulga. She thinks that, if only her daughter "would . . . keep herself up a little, she wouldn't be so bad looking," noting that "[t]here was nothing wrong with her face that a pleasant expression wouldn't help" (267). That truism, so frequently directed by our mothers to those of us who grew up female in the South (perhaps rivaled in popularity by only "Pretty is as pretty does"), reflects Mrs. Hopewell's sense of Joy/Hulga's misery, her chronically dyspeptic attitude, which her mother apparently attributes to the fact that her daughter has a doctorate in philosophy. After all, "[y]ou could say, 'My daughter is a nurse,' or 'My daughter is a school teacher,' or even, 'My daughter is a chemical engineer.' You could not say, 'My daughter is a philosopher.' That was something that had ended with the Greeks and Romans." Clearly Mrs. Hopewell does not know how to describe her daughter, not even to herself, for Joy/Hulga has completely defied acceptable female behavior.[6] In her defiance, moreover, she associates her mother with the superficiality and banality of polite society and accuses her of lacking self-knowledge: "Woman! do you ever look inside? Do you ever look inside and see what you are *not*? God!" (268).

Ironically, the daughter accuses the mother of the very failure of perception or of *seeing* that she herself exhibits, and certainly, to follow through on O'Connor's irony, neither woman is God. Although the intellectual daughter is not guilty of the top-of-the-head thinking that enables Mrs. Hopewell to fill silence with statements that she has never really examined but has appropriated as part of her store of prefabricated language, Joy/Hulga is guilty of jumping to conclusions about the Bible salesman on the basis of his appearance and the way he uses language. Like her mother, she will attempt to impose her will on another. After all, when Mrs. Hopewell hired Mrs. Freeman, she decided how to "handle" her: "Since she was the type who had to be into everything . . . she would not only let her be into everything, she would *see to it* that she was into everything—she would give her the responsibility of everything, she would put her in charge," for although she has "no bad qualities of her own," she is "able to use other people's in such a constructive way that she never [feels] the lack" (264). Similarly, Joy/Hulga imagines that she seduces the Bible salesman and that, as a result, "she [has] to reckon with his remorse":

> True genius can get an idea across even to an inferior mind. She imagined that she took his remorse in hand and changed it into a deeper understanding of life. She took all his shame away and turned it into something useful. (276)

This dream of control is soon destroyed, however, as the mind she has dubbed inferior is able to seduce her into revealing the most intimate and fragile part of herself. Thus Joy/Hulga's categories, like those of her mother, prove insufficient. As Manley Pointer departs the hayloft, she cries, "Aren't you just good country people?" and in more accusatory tones exclaims, "You're a Christian! . . . You're a fine Christian! You're just like them all—say one thing and do another," only to learn from her departing suitor that he does not "believe in that crap." He counters, from his own store of clichés, "I may sell Bibles but I know which end is up and I wasn't born yesterday and I know where I'm going!" (282–83).

Westling and others have pointed out the obvious autobiographical impulse in this story, and I see no need to reiterate that point here. Indeed, since Westling's book was published, Sally Fitzgerald has provided, in the chronology of O'Connor's life, the statement that in 1953 O'Connor met and fell in love with a Danish textbook representative, Erik Langkjaer (*O'Connor* 1246). Fitzgerald records that in 1954 O'Connor was "[d]istressed by . . . Langkjaer's decision to return to Denmark" and that in 1955 she wrote "Good Country People" (1247–48). We can only surmise that O'Connor's disappointment figures in her treatment of Joy/Hulga's response to the Bible salesman. In any event, I indicated earlier my agreement with Westling that O'Connor's rebellion against acceptable female behavior—even in the matter of the protagonist's willful change of name—is an important factor in this story. That rebellion is checked, certainly, by the crafty Manley Pointer, so that our last image of Joy/Hulga is a pathetic one. Significantly, her intellectual arrogance is punished through her body, for though O'Connor might be again accused of avoiding the matter of rape, she does make it clear that Joy/Hulga is "violated."

As Pointer looks at the limb that he has just removed, O'Connor describes his eyes as "like two steel spikes" (282), an obvious image of penetration. Again O'Connor uses the frame of the arrival of the suitor (who is clearly in this case the messenger) at the home of the female protagonist to suggest our common human frailty and our need to recognize our dependence on God. Moreover, in a story centrally concerned with the physical difficulties of women's lives, O'Connor seems once again to associate the weakness of the flesh with being female. Joy/Hulga may have "sinned" in her arrogant thinking, in pigeonholing individuals on the superficial basis of the way they talk, but she is overtly punished in her flesh. Her categories of language are shattered because the world is not as she has seen it to be; Manley Pointer is not "good country people," nor is he "a fine Christian." The shattering of the categories of her frail human language is equated with the loss of her limb, with physical helplessness — a necessary condition, we are led to infer, for the salvation of her soul. Now the stout Joy/Hulga, deprived of her leg, is literally pounds lighter, a fact suggesting that she has lost that part of herself that stood in the way of her acknowledging God's majesty and mystery.

Once again in this story, as in "A Circle in the Fire" and "The Life You Save May Be Your Own," the author depends on our common assumption of female weakness and vulnerability to effect the comically successful and theologically appropriate ending. Oddly enough, although Joy/Hulga's linguistic categories and even her thinking are shattered, the story achieves its effect by both relying on and reinforcing conventional assumptions of female subordination. Like Mrs. Cope in "A Circle in the Fire," Joy/Hulga has received her comeuppance. Mrs. Cope, who has viewed her land as an extension of herself, sees that land aflame, and Joy/Hulga, who has considered her leg as the essence of her self, loses that leg — and we as readers experience catharsis. Because of our own conditioning in seeing the flesh as weak, we are satisfied that these women have been suitably punished. We are left with the image of Joy/Hulga *waiting*.

The reader may be inclined to interject here that Joy/Hulga's punishment seems no different from that of some of the dissociated characters who are male, such as Asbury and Julian, for example. To that point I would only say that each of those male "intellectuals" — Rayber, Julian, Asbury, Sheppard, Thomas — seems imbued with a kind of Prufrockian effeminacy. These male characters are markedly different from Dudley and Tanner ("The Geranium" and "Judgment Day," respectively), O. E. Parker, and even Francis Marion Tarwater and Hazel Motes, who seem instinctively repelled by the suggestion of effeminacy; the Dudleys and the Tanners seem instead to be horrified by the weakness they associate with the life of the mind and with belief.

For Mrs. McIntyre in "The Displaced Person," the "gentleman caller" is the priest, who brings to the farm both the actual displaced person, Mr. Guizac, and word of the Displaced Person who is Christ. At the outset of the story, Mrs. McIntyre, like Mrs. Cope, is immensely satisfied with her own ability to manage affairs on *her* place, and, like both Mrs. Cope and Mrs. Hopewell, she knows how to use people to her own advantage. Only when the actions of the displaced person threaten to disrupt the efficiency of her farm does Mrs. McIntyre begin to experience helplessness. Her hesitation in firing Mr. Guizac is the result of her tormented conscience, and her eventual complicity in his death suggests that her selfishness has overcome that conscience and the words of the priest, who has served as her *pointer* to salvation.

Mrs. McIntyre also sees the land, the world's body, as an extension of herself; she asserts time and again, "This is my place" (*O'Connor* 314), as though her utterance of the words will establish the undisputed truth of the statement. In "A Circle in the Fire," Mrs. Cope's visitors bring her the message that the land belongs to God; in "The Displaced Person," the priest implies the need for humility before the mystery of God's creation, particularly in his response to the beauty of the peacock.

But Mrs. McIntyre knows no humility. She believes, in the clichéd language of the judge, her late husband, "One fellow's misery is the other fellow's gain" (299). She is proud of her accomplishment in managing the farm single-handedly and is unable to see that her use of others is a form of dehumanization with the same roots as Hitler's denial of the humanity of the Jews, as O'Connor's frequent use of allusions to the boxcars and the concentration camps makes clear. Because Mrs. McIntyre is yet another dissociated sensibility, an individual whose mind is separate from her heart, she is capable of seeing others only in terms of their value to her own goals and purposes. Early in the story O'Connor suggests that in the microcosmic world of the farm exists the same capacity for denial of the humanity of others as is found in the world at large, the macrocosm, whose collective machinations are the subject matter of newsreels and the catalyst for a public outcry of horror and protest.

The entire first section of the narrative (which was originally the complete story, published in the *Sewanee Review* in 1954) is devoted to Mrs. Shortley and concludes with her stroke. Functioning in large measure as a foil to Mrs. McIntyre, Mrs. Shortley acts on the basis of fear and ignorance, so that when the displaced person and his family arrive, she associates them with Europe, with its lack of progress and advancement:

> Mrs. Shortley recalled a newsreel she had seen once of a small room piled high with bodies of dead naked people all in a heap, their arms and legs tangled together, a head thrust in here, a head there, a foot, a knee, a part that should have been covered up sticking out, a hand raised clutching nothing. Before you could realize that it was real and take it into your head, the picture changed and a hollow-sounding voice was saying, "Time marches on!" This was the kind of thing that was happening every day in Europe where they had not advanced as in this country, and watching from her vantage point, Mrs. Shortley had the sudden intuition that the Gobblehooks, like rats with typhoid fleas, could have carried all those murderous ways over the water with them directly to this place. If they had come from where that kind of thing was done to them, who was to say they were not the kind that would also do it to others? (287)

Mrs. Shortley is unable to make any sense of history. The newsreel images of destruction and human carnage mean little to her except to convince her that the Guizacs come from a place that progress has not touched and that they likely pose a threat to *her place*. Moreover, she associates the priest and his church with Europe, where "[t]here was no telling what all they believed since none of the foolishness had been reformed out of it" (288). Indeed, as she informs Mr. Shortley, the Europeans are "full of crooked ways" because "[t]hey never have advanced or reformed" and have "the same religion as a thousand years ago" (297).

When the priest comes to the farm, Mrs. Shortley hides and watches, waiting for him to leave. We infer that her "vision" comes as the result of the high blood pressure that will kill her and that the vision is partly informed by images from her intense Bible reading. The "giant figure facing her" is "the color of the sun in the early afternoon, white-gold," vague in shape but with "fiery wheels with fierce dark eyes in them, spinning rapidly all around it." When she shuts her eyes to look at it, the figure becomes "blood-red and the wheels [turn] white," and she hears the word "Prophesy!" Significantly, her first "prophetic" words reiterate the newsreel images of brokenness and fragmented bodies: "The children of wicked nations will be butchered. . . . Legs where arms should be, foot to face, ear in the palm of hand. Who will remain whole? Who will remain whole? Who?" (301). The "fiery wheels with fierce dark eyes" might very well be an image of the peacock's tail with all of its eyes; after all, the story opens with Mrs. Shortley being pursued by the peacock, of whom she takes no notice and whom she regards as "[n]othing but a peachicken" (289).

Certainly the story's opening paragraph signals us that another soul is being "wooed" by a very persistent suitor, a "gentleman caller" whose pursuit and mysterious beauty Mrs. Shortley is perfectly capable of ignoring:

> The peacock was following Mrs. Shortley up the road to the hill where she meant to stand. Moving one behind the other, they looked like a complete procession. Her arms were folded and as she mounted the prominence, she might have been the giant wife of the countryside, come out at some sign of danger to see what the trouble was. She stood on two tremendous legs, with the grand self-confidence of a mountain, and rose, up narrowing bulges of granite, to two icy blue points of light that pierced forward, surveying everything. She ignored the white afternoon sun which was creeping behind a ragged wall of cloud as if it pretended to be an intruder and cast her gaze down the red clay road that turned off from the highway.
>
> The peacock stopped just behind her, his tail — glittering green-gold and blue in the sunlight — lifted just enough so that it would not touch the ground. It flowed out on either side like a floating train and his head on the long blue reed-like neck was drawn back as if his attention were fixed in the distance on something no one else could see. (285)

Here again we have an image of woman waiting. In this case, however, Mrs. Shortley, staring into the distance, completely ignores God's mysterious presence in the form of the peacock who stands right behind her. These opening paragraphs afford more than a glimpse into what will transpire in the rest of the story. Both Mrs. Shortley and Mrs. McIntyre — one of whom, because of her size, is momentarily viewed by the narrator as "the giant wife of the countryside" and the other of whom, we quickly learn, genuinely believes that because of her pride in her achievements, she *is* that giant wife — are protective of their places and capable of viewing everything and everybody else primarily in relationship to the fulfillment of their own goals. Although Mrs. McIntyre is better educated than Mrs. Shortley and obviously of a higher social class, neither woman is capable of understanding the atrocities Hitler is committing in Europe beyond the impact of these events on her own life.

Mrs. Shortley's real vision of her true country comes only as she is dying. Then, as the family travels to an unknown future in the packed car, the light fades from her eyes, and she appears to be looking inside herself. Finally, as though in an attempt to make herself whole (and in a repeat of the imagery of separated body parts associated with her earlier in this section), she "suddenly grab[s] Mr. Shortley's elbow and Sarah Mae's foot at the same time and [begins] to tug and pull on them as if she were trying to fit the two extra limbs onto herself" (304). The question she asked at the conclusion of her first "vision" — "Who shall remain whole?" — reverberates, and we recognize that Mrs. Shortley is acting out, in her dying, her awareness of her *own* fragmentation or lack of wholeness. Her large size is emphasized in the last lines of this first part of the story, in which O'Connor suggests that despite that physical presence, Mrs. Shortley is "short" a thing or two as she "contemplate[s] for the first time the tremendous frontiers of her true country" (305). These words take us back to the earlier description of the peacock sitting in the tree, with his tail hanging "in front of [Mrs. Shortley], full of fierce planets with eyes that were each ringed in green and set against a sun that was gold in one second's light and salmon-colored in the next." Moreover, O'Connor tells us that Mrs. Shortley "might have been looking at a map of the universe but she didn't notice it any more than she did the spots of sky that cracked the dull green of the tree" (290–91). Ironically, Mrs. Shortley is having another kind of vision, one in which she sees "the ten million billion" Poles "pushing their way into new places over here and herself, a giant angel with wings as wide as a house, telling the Negroes that they would have to find another place" (291). Mrs. Shortley is unable to see the "map of the universe" displayed by the peacock, her "suitor," for she is completely focused on her own narrow, selfish interests. O'Connor implies that, had she read the "map," she might have known the frontiers of that "true country" earlier.

The structural parallels between the story of Mrs. Shortley and that of Mrs. McIntyre are perhaps rather evident. Just as the peacock pursues Mrs. Shortley, so the priest pursues Mrs. McIntyre with the Good News of salvation. The figures of the peacock and the priest unite all three parts of the story, which is, on the anagogical level, concerned with the importance of the soul's readiness to receive God's grace, in whatever unlikely form that grace may come. The priest, alone among the characters, acknowledges the mysterious beauty and sanctity of the peacock. In the first part of the story, he calls the attention of the assembled group to the peacock; as he tiptoes toward the bird, he looks "down on the bird's back where the polished gold and green design [begins]," whereupon the peacock "[stands] still as if he had just come down from some sundrenched height to be a vision for them all" (289). And in the story's third part, just as Mrs. McIntyre concludes her attempt to justify firing Mr. Guizac, the priest sees the cock again, this time with his tail spread: "Tiers of small pregnant suns floated in a green-gold haze over his head." The priest is described at this moment as "transfixed, his jaw slack," and he announces, much to Mrs. McIntyre's consternation, "Christ will come like that!" seeing the moment as like "The Transfiguration" (317). Even the announcement of Christ's coming, of course, reiterates the importance of the soul's correct posture.

Once again, O'Connor uses female protagonists to suggest mortal disobedience and male "suitors," the peacock and the priest, as the bearers of good tidings. And just as we saw that the ways of thinking, and the language used to express that thinking, of Mrs. Cope, Sally Virginia, Mrs. Hopewell and Joy/Hulga had to be shattered, so both Mrs. Shortley and Mrs. McIntyre struggle to hold on to the world as they have described it against the onslaught of change and the possibility of new meaning. As we observed earlier, the matter of language is crucial to many of O'Connor's stories, the author suggesting that the simple comfort afforded us by our ways of talking about and thinking about things often has to be relinquished in order for the Word to enter.

Underscoring all of O'Connor's comments about language seems to be the notion of the difference between the words that we as humans utter and shape and organize, usually to attain our own ends, and the Word. That Mrs. Shortley is capable of this series of lies that attempt to elevate the status of her husband — "It is no man . . . that works as hard as Chancey, or is as easy with a cow, or is more of a Christian" (296) — should not surprise us. Although again and again Mrs. Shortley demonstrates her fear of the foreigners' language, thereby assigning great power to that language, we infer that she places little value on the relationship between her own words and the reality they signify.

As Mrs. Shortley ponders the oddness of the names of the Guizac children and the name Guizac itself, she wonders if people who cannot speak English will "know what colors even is." Our human habit of creating slogans by which we are able to classify reality and more comfortably cope with events is evident in Mrs. Shortley's memory of the piles of broken bodies in the newsreel, information that she does not know how to cope with except perhaps through the words of the "hollow-sounding voice" that says, "Time marches on!" (287) Surely these disastrous events warrant more than such a cliché; O'Connor implies, however, that neither Mrs. Shortley nor Mrs. McIntyre is able to recognize the full humanity of the Poles and other Europeans who are being persecuted and killed. The fact of fleshly human reality is clearly connected to the failure of language, a fact we noted as early as our discussion of "A Late Encounter with the Enemy." Indeed, both Mrs. Shortley and Mrs. McIntyre are guilty of thinking of Mr. Guizac as "the displaced person" rather than as a person with a name, a family, and a life; they cannot separate him from the threat he represents (in Mrs. Shortley's thinking) or (in Mrs. McIntyre's thinking) from the idea of his usefulness and, later, his challenge to the status quo.

Integrally tied to the difficulty both Mrs. Shortley and Mrs. McIntyre experience in seeing the Pole as a real person are his strange religion and his association in their minds with, as Mrs. Shortley puts it, "all them bodies" in Europe. Furthermore, the stereotypical attitudes that both women demonstrate toward the blacks on the place underscore and intensify their dilemma. Mrs. Shortley, for example, announces that Mrs. McIntyre "ain't any better off [with Mr. Guizac] than if she had more niggers," to which her husband responds, "I rather have a nigger if it was me" (292). When Mr. Guizac discovers that Sulk has stolen a turkey, Mrs. McIntyre must educate him "that all Negroes would steal." Believing that she now has a hired hand on whom she can depend, Mrs. McIntyre declares, "For years I've been fooling with sorry people. Sorry people. Poor white trash and niggers," as though the very naming of the category — "sorry people" are "poor white trash and niggers" — is sufficient to establish her superiority to these human beings and to announce their failure in meeting *her* needs. For her part, Mrs. Shortley, privy to these remarks, is consoled that she herself must not therefore be "trash" in Mrs. McIntyre's eyes or Mrs. McIntyre would not discuss such people with her. After all, "[n]either of them approved of trash" (293). O'Connor obviously satirizes our human tendency to treat others condescendingly and to indicate that condescension in our use of language: "sorry people," "white trash," and "niggers." Of course, to see others solely in terms of their usefulness to the achievement of our goals and to allow our language to indicate our judgment in that regard is to close off the possibility of encounter with the incarnational Christ, whose definition of charity underlies this story: "For I was hungry, and ye gave me meat; I was thirsty, and ye gave me drink; I was a stranger, and ye took me in; naked, and ye clothed me; I was sick, and ye visited me; I was in prison, and ye came unto me" (Matthew 25:35–36). "Inasmuch as ye have done it unto one of the least of these my brethren, ye have done it unto me" (Matthew 25: 40).

One troubling observation that we might make at this point is that O'Connor's refusal as an artist to engage in any sort of social or political commentary leads her to use the Holocaust as a metaphor to further her Christian vision. One could argue, I think, that as O'Connor finds in Hitler's destruction of the Jews and other groups a useful metaphor for the sinful human soul, she avoids seeing any connection between the individual's experience of God's grace and the necessity for that individual to assume political responsibility as a means of taking Christ's words seriously—into the world. O'Connor's fiction, her essays, and her letters attest to her own disavowal of commitment to act on behalf of social or political justice. The analogue here is the much discussed silence of the Roman Catholic Church during and after the Holocaust. In a recent article in the *New Yorker*, James Carroll asserts that Pope John Paul's insistence today on papal infallibility at the same time that he deplores the violations of the humanity of the Jews during the Holocaust is "the great paradox of his papacy" (67). The Church's claim that it alone represents the absolute authority of God on earth and that those who are outside the Church receive no salvation leads to the "diminishment," indeed the "demonization," of the other (67). For Carroll, as well as for theologians Karl Rahner and Hans Küng, such rigidly authoritarian religious ideas are largely responsible for the dissension and wars between nations. For these thinkers, humanity's very survival is the issue (68).

O'Connor, however, as a dutiful daughter of the traditional Church, is prevented from seeing the logical outcome of her own argument—that even the Church is capable of refusing to see the *whole* of humanity; instead, it sees from its own "infallible" and condescending position. Thus, in "The Displaced Person" O'Connor can take Mrs. McIntyre to task, but O'Connor seems never to have questioned the authority of her own Church and the diminishment of others that results from the Church's unbending assertion of infallibility. We remember that Mr. Guizac is not himself a Jew; even in that fact or writerly choice O'Connor seems to evade the central issue of the Holocaust. This displaced person—as we shall see—becomes in effect the means of Mrs. McIntyre's salvation. What matters most to O'Connor appears to be the bringing of the soul to the one true Church, not the broader implications of the diminishment of the "other" or the other's difference that is promulgated by the Church's claim to absolute authority. I shall deal with this issue more fully in chapter 5.

In keeping with the story's original section depicting the fall of Mrs. Shortley, the remainder of the story clearly demonstrates O'Connor's anagogical vision, especially as it uses the concrete from which to launch its transcendent vision. Like her hired help, Mrs. Shortley, Mrs. McIntyre is impervious to the peacock's beauty and sees the bird as just "[a]nother mouth to feed," announcing that she has let the peacocks "die off" (289). Her assignment of value to anything is determined by the usefulness of that thing or that person to her scheme of things. Thus, she is soon ready to dismiss Mr. Shortley when she realizes what the energetic Mr. Guizac can do for the farm. On several significant occasions O'Connor describes Mrs. McIntyre's gaze itself as dehumanizing, as, for instance, when she responds to Mrs. Shortley's claim that her husband is "over-exhausted" with the rejoinder that if that is the case, Mr. Shortley "must have a second job on the side" and then looks "at Mrs. Shortley with almost closed eyes as if she were examining the bottom of a milk can" (295). In a conversation with the old black, Astor, Mrs. McIntyre sees "[b]ars of sunlight [fall] from the cracked ceiling across his back and cut him in three distinct parts" (305), a clear indication that she is incapable of seeing the whole man.

Furthermore, her statement that Mr. Guizac is her "salvation" (*O'Connor* 294) is an obvious bit of irony in the extremely limited meaning she gives to salvation. When she discovers Mr. Guizac's plan to marry his cousin to Sulk in order to get her to America, Mrs. McIntyre confronts the displaced person and looks "at him as if she were seeing him for the first time," as indeed she is:

> His forehead and skull were white where they had been protected by his cap but the rest of his face was red and bristled with short yellow hairs. His eyes were like two bright nails behind his gold-rimmed spectacles that had been mended over the nose with haywire. His whole face looked as if it might have been patched together out of several others. (313)

The simile comparing Mr. Guizac's eyes to "bright nails" underscores the suggestion that Mr. Guizac is a Christ-like messenger who has come to penetrate the soul of Mrs. McIntyre, just as Joy/Hulga's soul must be "ravished" by the word that the fake Bible salesman brings to her.

The fact that Mr. Guizac's face seems a composite of "several others" implies his connection with all of humanity. Mrs. McIntyre will not understand this connection, however, although here she does at least seem to see the man as a real, flesh-and-blood human being. Her acknowledgment of Mr. Guizac's humanity does not last long, however, for she is aghast at the displaced person's plan. Like Joy/Hulga at the moment of the loss of her leg to the Bible salesman, Mrs. McIntyre experiences the shattering of her language categories. In a passage heavy with irony, she wonders "how a man who calls himself a Christian . . . could bring a poor innocent girl over here and marry her to something like that [a black]," and she looks "into the distance with a pained blue gaze" (314). Moreover, at the conclusion of the second section of the story, she watches a chastened and bewildered Mr. Guizac mount his tractor and continue his mowing:

> When he had passed her and rounded the turn, she climbed to the top of the slope and stood with her arms folded and looked out grimly over the field. "They're all the same," she muttered, "whether they come from Poland or Tennessee. I've handled Herrins and Ringfields and Shortleys and I can handle a Guizac," and she narrowed her gaze until it closed entirely around the diminishing figure on the tractor *as if she were watching him through a gunsight.* (315, my emphasis)

The suggestion of the last simile is that Mrs. McIntyre senses that she possesses the power of life and death over Mr. Guizac. Further, the violence of Mr. Guizac's death and her collusion in that death are forecast in this passage. Finally, this paragraph concludes with another description of Mrs. McIntyre's leveling gaze: "She opened her eyes to include the whole field so that the figure on the tractor was no larger than a grasshopper in her widened view." As she asserts her control and maintains, as Mrs. Cope does in "A Circle in the Fire, "This is my place," Mrs. McIntyre sees Mr. Guizac as little more than a speck on the horizon (315).

When she thinks of her struggle on the farm, Mrs. McIntyre is proud of her accomplishments in managing others, from "tenant farmers and dairymen" to "moody unpredictable Negroes" to the "incidental bloodsuckers, the cattle dealers and lumber men and the buyers and sellers of anything who drove up in pieced-together trucks and honked in the yard" (309–10).

She concludes that the judge, the one of her three husbands for whom she had felt considerable fondness, would have commended her skill. The judge's legacy, in addition to "the mortgaged house and fifty acres" (309), is a collection of sayings with which she likes to sprinkle her conversation, most notable among them being "One fellow's misery is the other fellow's gain" and "The devil you know is better than the devil you don't" (299). Both of these adages reveal the judge's and Mrs. McIntyre's outlook. The first suggests, of course, that the suffering of others can be put to use; while as an individual I may certainly acknowledge "misery," such recognition is actually impure when it is tainted by the consideration of how another's pain may be to my advantage. Mrs. McIntyre uses this cliché to justify her good fortune in acquiring the displaced person, with whose suffering she obviously does not identify very fully. "The devil you know is better than the devil you don't" clearly implies a real need for vigilance in a world filled with "devils," known and unknown, but when the statement is used by Mrs. McIntyre and others in this story, its theological implications are denied. As readers, however, we perceive O'Connor's irony: Mrs. McIntyre's "devil" is indeed somebody she knows—herself. One way of interpreting the statement in light of what happens is to conclude that knowing one's own propensity for selfishness and inhumanity is the first step toward understanding that evil exists in the world and toward coping with the devil one doesn't know. Certainly Mrs. McIntyre would not be able to see how her own use of other people for her own purposes, her denial of their humanity, bears any resemblance to Hitler's persecution of the Jews and others in his effort to establish the master race.

Thus, once again O'Connor establishes the connections between the heart's disposition, language, and action. The help on the farm are so accustomed to hearing these statements that they echo Mrs. McIntyre, and the judge and his language attain a kind of ironic immortality. If the judge and his words can be said to represent the beliefs of the patriarchy, O'Connor may seem to subvert those lessons through her chastisement of the selfish, uncharitable Mrs. McIntyre. Because she is guilty of complicity in the death of Mr. Guizac, we see that the selfishness and manipulation of such secular philosophies as those of the judge—which Mrs. McIntyre obviously espouses—are clearly deplored by O'Connor. However, because the force that is actually in contention with the judge and his values is the Church, represented by the priest, we can hardly say that O'Connor is, in the last analysis, rebelling against the essential power of the patriarchy.

The third section of the story concerns Mrs. McIntyre's battle with herself over what the priest suggests is her moral obligation to the displaced person. O'Connor tells us that she "looked as if something was wearing her down from the inside." She is physically changed by her struggle and, perhaps surprisingly, seems indifferent to matters of the farm's upkeep. Yet she still intends to fire Mr. Guizac, telling the priest how she has constantly fought to hold on to the farm, "always just barely making it against people who came from nowhere and were going nowhere, who didn't want anything but an automobile." In her view these people are all alike, "whether they [come] from Poland or Tennessee" (321). In other words, to the end she is capable of reducing others to their usefulness to her, of seeing her help as "other" and "them." Even in her tormented dreams, the language of "us" and "them" prevails. One night, for example, she dreams that the priest comes to visit and says, "Dear lady, I know your tender heart won't suffer you to turn the porrrrr man out. Think of the thousands of *them*, think of the ovens and the boxcars and the camps and the sick children and Christ Our Lord" (322, my emphasis), to which she responds that she is "a logical practical woman," that the displaced person will leave and make even more money, and that "all *they* want is a car" (323, my emphasis).[7]

On the morning that she finally decides to give Mr. Guizac his notice, Mrs. McIntyre finds him working on the tractor and thinks that perhaps there will be time in the thirty days left in his tenure for him to "get the fields turned over," thus demonstrating that she intends to use him until his time is up. We should not be surprised, therefore, that as she stands there watching the displaced person, she feels "the cold . . . climbing like a paralysis up her feet and legs." Moreover, because Mr. Guizac is working under the tractor, she sees not his face but "only his feet and legs and trunk sticking impudently out from the side of the tractor" (325). We surmise that the deed she has come to do (give the man his notice) and the deed she actually does (allow him to be run over by the tractor) are each possible only because she has refused to see the *whole* man in all of his humanity. Significantly, immediately preceding the sentence describing the slipping of the brake on the large tractor is a statement underscoring Mrs. McIntyre's severely limited vision: "Mrs. McIntyre was looking fixedly at Mr. Guizac's legs lying flat on the ground now." In the ensuing sentences we are given to understand that Mrs. McIntyre, Mr. Shortley, and Sulk are silent conspirators in the death of the displaced person, and we cannot help being reminded of the complicity of many Germans—through their refusal to verbalize what they knew or at least suspected was happening—in the deaths of hundreds of thousands of Jews. (Parenthetically, we likely realize something that O'Connor herself would not have acknowledged: the near silence of the Roman Catholic Church during the Holocaust.) As is appropriate, Mrs. McIntyre's fate includes her loss of voice. Now she who would not speak out cannot speak. O'Connor once again emphasizes the potential of language: Mrs. McIntyre's silence enables her to be "rid" of the problem of the displaced person once and for all; we recall that "[o]f all the things [Mrs. McIntyre] resented about him, she resented most that he hadn't left of his own accord" (325).

The judge's adage that "one fellow's misery is the other fellow's gain" is proved fallacious on the literal level, although we might argue that the suffering of the Christ-like displaced person may ultimately be the impetus for the salvation of Mrs. McIntyre's soul. At the time of the "accident," Mrs. McIntyre is described as seeing the figure in black, the priest, administering the Eucharist, the Word, to the dying man, although she does not grasp what is happening and she feels "she [is] in some foreign country where the people bent over the body [are] natives, and she watche[s] like a stranger while the dead man [is] carried away in the ambulance" (326). Perhaps Mrs. McIntyre's profound distress resembles that of O'Connor's readers, who—offered O'Connor's incarnational vision—simply do not understand "what is happening." Repeatedly O'Connor employs a trope of the incarnation to suggest her own aims—the physical impression made by the crucifix on the child's face in "A Temple of the Holy Ghost," Parker's tattooed body in "Parker's Back," the "word" hitting Mrs. Turpin in "Revelation."

In "The Displaced Person" Mrs. McIntyre loses everything, including her own health, after Mr. Guizac's death, and her only visitor in her illness is the priest. The story concludes by uniting once again the image of peacock and priest; this "gentleman caller" feeds breadcrumbs to the peacock (who has been, in a manner of speaking, another such caller) prior to his visits to Mrs. McIntyre during which he "explain[s] the doctrines of the Church" (327). The priest brings the Word—not the clichéd, self-serving fallen language of a fallen humanity—to the humbled soul, and we have every reason for optimism that, even in her weakness and affliction, Mrs. McIntyre is receptive to God's grace. Certainly the implication that Christ, the lover of souls, is the Suitor represented by the priest deepens the story's meaning. I believe, furthermore, that the work is successful in large measure because O'Connor trades on the conventional idea of woman's role. As Westling and others have noted, Mrs. McIntyre oversteps her bounds as a woman, and while we may agree that O'Connor in the last analysis checks her own impulse toward rebellion by punishing Mrs. McIntyre, we may also conclude that the assertive, manipulative woman proved an apt vehicle for O'Connor the Catholic in describing our human arrogance in ignoring the suitor, the lover who is Christ.

In keeping with her orthodoxy, O'Connor uses one of the Church's most pervasive metaphors—the soul as female, pursued by Christ, the "gentleman caller." If we as readers are uncomfortable with O'Connor's treatment of women in these stories, our discomfiture may result from our conviction that for centuries in the west women have been subjugated and denied their power. O'Connor, however, did not challenge the subordinate role of woman; indeed, she found in the idea of woman's dependent status a compelling metaphor for the soul's necessary dependence on God, a yielding that is epitomized in Mary's words at the Annunciation: "Behold the handmaid of the Lord: be it unto me according to thy word" (Luke 1:38). Noting Evelyn Underhill's discussion of the soul of the sinner as the bride of Christ in *Mysticism*, Frederick Asals cites O'Connor's indebtedness to the mystics and to the Song of Solomon throughout her work (223 and n. 33). Both the mystics and the Song of Solomon (at least as the Church reads this work) convey the soul as female, seeking, or being sought by, the suitor or the bridegroom who is Christ. Perhaps nowhere is O'Connor's use of this metaphoric structure more evident than in the late story "Greenleaf," which depends for its theological meaning on our recognition of Christ as suitor come to woo the sinner.

As only one of two stories in *Everything That Rises Must Converge* with a female protagonist and as one of O'Connor's last works imaging the pursued sinner as female, "Greenleaf" has been somewhat controversial. Some critics claim that Mrs. May experiences no real revelation because of the hardness of her heart or, on the other hand, that, because of the hardness of her heart, Mrs. May's revelation arrives too late to signal conversion. Asals, for example, suggests that Mrs. May "seems to harbor no longing, however suppressed for the divine" (223) and that, although she is clearly identified with the bride of Christ, "it is a role she fatally resists" (223). Westling, too, is concerned about "the lack of interior development in Mrs. May's character to prepare her for the spiritual revelation she is supposed to experience in the final scene" (166). Although both Asals and Westling rely heavily on analysis of the mythic underpinnings of the story, both pagan and Christian, neither commentator finds the story satisfactory. Westling, for example, writes,

> Never are we shown that [Mrs. May] has the slightest understanding of Greenleaf reverence or the bull's significance. She simply fears the social and economic mobility of the Greenleafs, is horrified by Mrs. Greenleaf's obscene form of worship, and is afraid the bull will ruin her herd of cows because he is not purebred. In a literal sense all that transpires is that she is killed by the bull because none of the men around her will help her control it. We are told that she has a vision of unbearable light as she dies, but all its significance comes from outside her, in the author's manipulation of symbols which have no reflection in her mind. In her final vision, her protective tree line is a "dark wound in a world that was nothing but sky"; her green pasture, her farm, her very self, have been obliterated. (166)

For his part, Asals is not troubled by O'Connor's use of symbols, although he finds in the story's ending an Augustinian fusion of "love and vengeance" — "Mrs. May's revelation measures the fullness of her denial: she is the only O'Connor character who pays for her vision with her life" (223).[8] Unlike Westling, Asals does not question the authenticity of the vision in terms of the development of the character of Mrs. May; he is, rather, convinced that the story "mark[s] an extreme limit in O'Connor's work" in that the "violent overpowering of the self by a God unknown and apparently undesired appears nowhere else in [O'Connor's] fiction" (223–24). Although Asals briefly considers the possibility that O'Connor is dramatizing the "irresistibility of grace," he reminds us that in O'Connor's next published story, "A View of the Woods," Mr. Fortune is shown to be quite capable of resisting grace and that such stories as "The Enduring Chill," which demonstrate conflict within the protagonist's divided will, suggest a struggle that we do not find within Mrs. May (224).

Asals concludes, therefore, that for O'Connor the operation of God's grace is indeed "frightening" and suggests "the realm of terrifying mystery" (224) wherein O'Connor's own asceticism decrees "that *only* suffering has value in God's eyes" (225). Citing passages from the author's letters and other nonfiction writings, Asals asserts that O'Connor saw herself as a prophet and that, although she was drawn to the sacramental view of the world, she yielded to an "ascetic imperative" (226) in determining her prophetic function. That prophetic impulse often caused O'Connor's fiction to center on "the relationship of man with God rather than with his fellow man" and required "the infliction of a searing grace, the onset of a saving pain" (226–27). By this way of thinking, the prerequisite for God's grace is suffering. Asals's argument is compelling in light of what he calls O'Connor's "native asceticism" (226) and his assertion that in O'Connor's mature fiction, she presents "mortification not of the body, but of the mind." Asals believes that O'Connor rebelled against the emphasis on rationalism, even as that emphasis underlay the Thomistic synthesis, favoring the freeing of the imagination as the means of opening the spirit to the possibility of God's grace (220–21). O'Connor had, Asals argues, a "deep mistrust of the mind" (222), and in the fiction after *Wise Blood* she used her characters' contact with physical reality as a means of precipitating vision to signal a turning away from the discursive intellect, which faculty, indeed, she often identified with the demonic (222, 229). For Asals, then, O'Connor's God is one from whose gaze all of us would rather be released: "Demanding everything, valuing only our diminishments, bringing not peace but a sword, O'Connor's Deity corresponds to no recognizable humanistic value." This deity is indeed a "Christian version of the fierce and awesome God of the prophets," demanding nothing less than total surrender (228). Asals seems to conclude that Mrs. May, because of her refusal to surrender, is fatally punished.

We might add to Asals's conclusions a reminder that Mrs. May is another pursued (female) sinner and that, like other O'Connor women, she too is obsessed with power and control. She is awakened, by the bull's chewing, from a dream of being consumed. In fact, she has dreamed that everything she has is eaten "until nothing was left but the Greenleafs on a little island all their own in the middle of what had been her place" (*O'Connor* 502–3). The bull, which belongs to the Greenleafs, is associated with them and especially with the power and virility of O.T. and E.T. as they contrast with Mrs. May's ineffectual "boys." The animal is a "scrub" bull, and at one point, Mrs. May thinks of the Greenleafs as "scrub-human" (507). The force that Mrs. Greenleaf seems to summon from the earth as she pleads, "Jesus, stab me in the heart!" is identified with the power of the bull in Mrs. May's consciousness. As she comes upon Mrs. Greenleaf in her paroxysm of ecstasy, Mrs. May feels "as if some violent unleashed force had broken out of the ground and was charging toward her" (506). This image of violence, of course, foreshadows the penetration of the bull's horns at the story's climax and is intensified by later allusions to the sun as a bullet "ready to drop into [Mrs. May's] brain" (515). The night before she decides to have Mr. Greenleaf shoot the bull, Mrs. May dreams again of the threat of the bull:

> Half the night in her sleep she heard a sound as if some large stone were grinding a hole on the outside wall of her brain. She was walking on the inside, over a succession of beautiful rolling hills, planting her stick in front of each step. She became aware after a time that the noise was the sun trying to burn through the tree line and she stopped to watch, safe in the knowledge that it couldn't, that it had to sink the way it always did outside of her property. When she first stopped it was a swollen red ball, but as she stood watching it began to narrow and pale until it looked like a bullet. Then suddenly it burst through the tree line and raced down the hill toward her. She woke up with her hand over her mouth and the same noise, diminished but distinct, in her ear. It was the bull munching under her window. Mr. Greenleaf had let him out. (519)

The wall of her brain is likened to the wall of her property, inside which Mrs. May evidently feels safe and where beauty and tranquillity reign. The sun, however, noisily and frighteningly intrudes, and although she assures herself of her safety for a time — the sun will sink "outside of her property" as it always does — she experiences the transformation of the sun from red ball to bullet (with obvious sexual implications) with the power to "burst through the tree line." The obvious associations of Christ-sun-bullet-bull represent a curious merging of pagan and Christian myth and again suggest, more emphatically than in any other O'Connor work, the author's reliance on the familiar idea of Christ as suitor or bridegroom. Asals's observation that the "patient god" who came to court Mrs. May early in the story becomes, by the story's conclusion, a "wild tormented lover" (O'Connor qtd. in Asals 223) enables us to see the intensity of the divine pursuit. O'Connor implies that Mrs. May's resistance is the reason for her lover's torment.

When we review all of O'Connor's published fiction, we find that — except for Ruby Turpin in "Revelation" — not a single female protagonist seems to experience the agony of a soul yearning for belief and certainty. Although many of the central characters who are female can easily be accused of pride and selfishness, none really embodies what Asals and others see as the typical conflict in O'Connor's fiction "between reason and faith, between the demands of the intellect and the hunger of the soul" (213). That urge for belief that we find in Hazel Motes, Francis Marion Tarwater, O. E. Parker, for example, is really not a part of the consciousness of the female protagonists. Joy/Hulga Hopewell could not really be described as a soul hungering for belief as much as a soul convinced of its own superiority to belief. Although in "Revelation" Ruby Turpin knows that Mary Grace has brought her a message, we do not have the feeling from the outset of the story that Mrs. Turpin is an anguished soul; she, like the grandmother in "A Good Man Is Hard to Find," is simply smug, convinced that God has rewarded her for her cleanliness, her industry, and her good works. She is, in some respects, an extension of the comedy of Mrs. Cope, Mrs. Hopewell, and Mrs. McIntyre, although the latter is not, it might be argued, essentially comic. Mrs. Greenleaf is obviously a religious fanatic whose presence in the story serves as a comic foil to Mrs. May's own lack of belief and, further, her horror at Mrs. Greenleaf's excesses, which are even linked in her own thinking to sexual indulgence: "She thought the word, Jesus, should be kept inside the church building like other words inside the bedroom. She was a good Christian woman with a large respect for religion, though she did not, of course, believe any of it was true" (506). It is noteworthy that the word *Jesus* is embarrassing to Mrs. May, especially as she hears it emanating from Mrs. Greenleaf in her spiritual passion. Moreover, Mrs. May consoles herself in the face of the superiority of the Greenleaf boys' achievements to her own boys' achievements by remembering Mrs. Greenleaf "sprawled obscenely on the ground" and by saying to herself, "Well, no matter how far they *go*, they *came* from that" (507).

Mrs. May's association of religious excess, sexuality, and childbearing with Mrs. Greenleaf represents a vulnerability that she considers female and weak, a condition that she would obviously like to avoid. Not for her the helplessness and timidity often considered part of the southern female role. Mrs. May is proud of her ability to "handle" Mr. Greenleaf, proud of her "iron hand." No matter that Scofield mocks her and seizes her arm to reveal "her delicate blue-veined little hand [dangling] from her wrist like the head of a broken lily" (510–11), she is a practical woman with fierce determination. Like her female antecedents in the earlier stories, Mrs. May sees "Greenleafs" as *other* and as the force with which she must contend to maintain power and control ("She reminded herself that you could always tell the class of people by the class of dog" [513]), although, significantly, she thinks of her struggle as one with the Greenleaf men, not with the women.

Thus in O'Connor's anagogical vision we see a female protagonist whose demeanor rebels against the prescribed and approved behavior for women and whose smugness and control are shattered by the arrival of the "gentleman caller." What we do *not* find in this protagonist may be just as revealing as the recurrent pattern already described; we find no evidence of a soul in agony, of a soul searching for belief in a secular, atheistic world. O'Connor thus uses the female to suggest apparently contradictory elements of human experience — the Church's teaching about the sacredness of the human body and, as a corollary, its emphasis on the fallenness of the flesh, and the Church's recurrent metaphoric use of the soul as female pursued by the divine Lover. In male-centered narratives, the female is flesh, fallen, the obstacle who must be overcome as the male moves toward salvation. In those narratives with female protagonists, the emphasis is on the pattern of the pursuit of the female soul by the "gentleman caller," the divine suitor. In none of these narratives do we see a female protagonist in great spiritual struggle, as we do with Hazel Motes and Francis Marion Tarwater. Instead, in all cases the female characters appear useful to the lesson of the narrative in their very flat, almost allegorical embodiments. Although sometimes these women rebel against social convention and restraint, I believe that the recurrent emphasis in O'Connor is on the necessity for the soul of the female — which rarely agonizes over God's existence or struggles with meaning — to be in readiness, in waiting. More importantly, that soul must be resigned to its weak and subordinate role. O'Connor clearly adopted the attitude of the Church toward women, in all probability without question.

I see from the standpoint of Christian orthodoxy. This means that for me the meaning of life is centered in our Redemption by Christ and what I see in the world I see in its relation to that. I don't think that this is a position that can be taken halfway or one that is particularly easy in these times to make transparent in fiction. — Flannery O'Connor, "The Fiction Writer and His Country," *Mystery and Manners*

It's well to remember that the serious fiction writer always writes about the whole world, no matter how limited his particular scene. For him, the bomb that was dropped on Hiroshima affects life on the Oconee River, and there's not anything he can do about it. — Flannery O'Connor, "The Nature and Aim of Fiction," *Mystery and Manners*

It is suffering, and suffering alone, that makes available to man the burning grace of a purifying mercy, and the return of this merciful agony to its Source is the only gift of value man can offer God. As for Hopkins, the world is in a double sense "charged with the grandeur of God," yet for O'Connor it is not beauty that we must give back, but pain, the *imitatio Christi* of the crucified self. — Frederick Asals, *Flannery O'Connor: The Imagination of Extremity*

Jesus was radical not in his lust for sacrifice but in his power of mutuality. Jesus' death on a cross, his sacrifice, was no abstract exercise in moral virtue. His death was the price he paid for refusing to abandon the radical activity of love — of expressing solidarity and reciprocity with the excluded ones in his community. Sacrifice, I submit, is not a central moral goal or virtue in the Christian life. Radical acts of love — expressing human solidarity and bringing mutual relationship to life — are the central virtues of the Christian moral life. That we have turned sacrifice into a moral virtue has deeply confused the Christian moral tradition. — Beverly Wildung Harrison, "The Power of Anger in the Work of Love: Christian Ethics for Women and Other Strangers"

5

Communities
The Historic, the Orthodox, the Intimate

In the critical penchant for and comfort in labeling, many commentators describe the difference between O'Connor and other southern and American writers by establishing Hawthorne as O'Connor's predecessor and the tradition of the romance as her genre. In the context of the twentieth century, the argument goes, O'Connor's fiction is anomalous, surely closer to allegory than to realism, and perhaps closer to parable than allegory. By this way of thinking, allusions to historical events — the Civil War, the Holocaust, the civil rights movement, for example — may seem to ground the stories in time and place, but the narratives defy the limitations of history, embodying "universal" themes. J. O. Tate, for example, in fascinatingly detailed and sometimes firsthand accounts of O'Connor's Milledgeville source material, concludes that O'Connor eschewed the readily accessible matter of southern history to pursue a larger vision. Tate asserts that O'Connor did not read the Agrarian writers; in fact, she finally read *I'll Take My Stand* only in the last year of her life. Although she was acquainted personally with John Crowe Ransom, Robert Penn Warren, Andrew Lytle, Allen Tate, and Caroline Gordon, she did not read very much of their work. Tate notes that she never mentions Ransom's work and that she refers only to Warren's *All the King's Men* and Tate's *Ode to the Confederate Dead*. With respect to Tate's *Ode*, surely one of the landmarks of modern southern literature, O'Connor notes only "the color imagery, not the substance or the references" ("On Flannery O'Connor" 27).

Tate notes that O'Connor in her letters actually misrepresents the seriousness of Lance Phillips's Milledgeville secession "pageant" produced in 1961, asserting that O'Connor's "accomplished ability to sniff the stink of banality in the air, her sensitivity to vulgarity, led her in this case to isolate the Centennial from its historical and local context, and to see what she wanted to see" (31). Tate's point, of course, is that O'Connor's "piety" was not that of "Southern historical memory"; instead, hers was "the piety of world-historical consciousness as embodied in the Hebrew Bible and the Gospels, the writing of the Church Fathers, the institutional memory of the Roman Catholic Church as an embodied communal image of the history of the Western world extending all the way back to the sacred history that begins with the first chapter of Genesis" (36). Such a view of O'Connor—in this instance so grandly expressed—would appear to leave little room for quibbling. If O'Connor made much fun of the local centennial celebration, if indeed she even distorted its success to provide grist for her mill, isn't that to be allowed or even condoned in a writer who sees through or beyond it all to the eternal verities?

Tate's observations are amplified theologically by John Desmond's *Risen Sons: Flannery O'Connor's Vision of History*, in which Desmond places O'Connor squarely in the tradition of Catholic eschatology. Although the material Tate provides in the way of enlightening particulars of middle Georgia history and custom is missing from Desmond's expressly theological study, both commentators reflect the ongoing tendency to place O'Connor's work in the patriarchal tradition. The male "tradition" — as even Desmond's title *Risen Sons* implies — is grounded in the Bible and in the authority of historic Roman Catholic teaching. Certainly, in comments on her own craft and its relationship to her faith and to her region, O'Connor facilitated the placement of her work in the spiritual tradition of the patriarchy. To a large extent, she ensured that her work would be read as she wanted it to be read, for traditional critics inevitably build their case on O'Connor's own statements of faith and intention in the essays and letters.

Without dwelling on the contradiction between the New Critics' idea that the work is autonomous and the idea or practice of using extrafictional material as the primary means of explaining that work, we would nonetheless observe that these traditional readings encourage the tendency to schematize and dogmatize the fiction and simultaneously appear to close the door to other ways of reading that may be insightful and helpful. Even my own methodology in this study may be suspiciously traditional in its structure — reviewing the criticism, supporting my rebuttal of others' interpretations through reliance on established "authority," attempting to maintain objectivity and detachment, arguing on the basis of the textual analysis of images, symbols, and the use of language — for such was the approach of my literary education. However, because of the challenge of recent developments in criticism, feminist theological criticism in particular, I want to continue to consider O'Connor's presentation of human experience from some distinctly nontraditional angles. I want to consider especially various ways by which the idea of "community" may be construed. On the way to these considerations, I will be alluding to more conventional readings in an attempt to demonstrate both divergence from and convergence with my own ideas.

That O'Connor saw human history "from the standpoint of Christian orthodoxy" is an established fact; her fiction repeatedly emphasizes human weakness and dependence on divine mercy. Yet to concentrate on O'Connor's reflection of conventional patriarchal notions of history is, I believe, to narrow our sights unduly and to overlook what is arguably the most significant history of all, the story of our human connectedness, a history that Allen Tate might have conveniently dismissed as "the long view"[1] but one that nonetheless remains of utmost concern to many. Flannery O'Connor's depiction of human relatedness, or the failure of humans to relate, must be a part of our considerations. I am certain that the alienation from O'Connor that some readers experience results from their sense that the darkly comic world of this writer's imagining has little to do with what Tennyson called "the little, nameless, unremembered acts of kindness and of love" that show forth the divine. Some readers experience discomfort with a world that is described in no uncertain terms as ugly and hostile and are convinced that something of supreme importance is missing in the world that O'Connor presents. Because the matter of fiction evolves from our common human stories, our own history, we had best begin with O'Connor's relationship to the history of her region.

For a writer of O'Connor's generation in the South, the matter of southern history as subject for fiction was problematic. Surely Faulkner's vision of the South, in which the Mississippi writer allowed himself great liberty in re-creating and dramatizing the troubled history of the region, was a hard act for any young writer to follow. Faulkner's broad canvas, in which the colors of past and present are blurred in both sweeping brushstroke and meticulous detail, depended on the author's confident knowledge of southern history and his bold and ambitious genius. Any student of O'Connor's early drafts, moreover, can detect from time to time the stylistic influence of Faulkner, especially in O'Connor's sporadic attempts at stream of consciousness. She was astute enough, however, to realize that she must move on, that her style must be her own. As she later quipped, "The presence alone of Faulkner in our midst makes a great difference in what the writer can and cannot permit himself to do. Nobody wants his mule and wagon stalled on the same track the Dixie Limited is roaring down" (*Mystery and Manners* 45). Moreover, the overwhelming popular success of Margaret Mitchell's *Gone with the Wind* and the disdain of literary scholars for that novel set a precedent for subsequent southern writers, particularly for female southern writers who sought to be taken seriously by academic critics.

As we have previously noted, O'Connor from time to time had good fun with Mitchell's work, relying on the common disparagement of the book in academic circles (for example, what J. O. Tate calls "the cotton-pickin', eye-battin', sashayin', whoop-de-doo of Margaret Mitchell" in "On Flannery O'Connor" 34) to carry her comic attacks on its popular success. In "The Enduring Chill" Asbury's mother echoes Regina O'Connor's wish that her writer-child would produce another *Gone with the Wind*, both fictional and real mothers thereby revealing their obvious lack of educated literary judgment. For decades Mitchell's novel has been an easy target for academicians, literary critics, and historians because of its faulty historicism, banality, and sentimentality. In spite of the fact that the novel received a Pulitzer Prize and the annual award of the American Booksellers Association, in O'Connor's time *Gone with the Wind* was dismissed from the canon of serious literature almost as easily as a Barbara Cartland romance would be today. The novel's popularity — enhanced, of course, by the 1939 release of the blockbuster film — has only increased over the years; Scarlett, Rhett, and Melanie are American household names. Many who grew up in the South in the 1930s, 1940s, and 1950s boast of having read the compendious work ten, fifteen, and twenty times; some can still recite whole passages from the book, while others know the movie line for line.

Faulkner's literary achievement to the contrary notwithstanding, *Gone with the Wind*, for better or worse, became the preferred treatment of fictional southern "history" in these years. O'Connor was acutely aware of the achievement of her fellow Georgian, although certainly, like most of us who received graduate degrees in literature and the fine arts in the decades following the novel's publication, she learned the habit of literary snobbery by which immense public popularity often becomes a book's primary offense. Although the reviews at the time of the novel's publication were generally good, most scholars and critics today fail to note that fact, preferring to dismiss the work as a perennial best-seller that appeals primarily to an unsophisticated popular taste. After all, in the first six months of its publication *Gone with the Wind* sold a million copies, and the novel remains one of the best-selling books of all time. Obviously, O'Connor would not emulate the visionary profundity of Faulkner's historical perspective, nor would she go to the other extreme and aim for nostalgic immersion in the complicated history of her region. Her work would stake out its own territory, as we have previously noted.

The story most often discussed as exemplary of O'Connor's retreat from the matter of southern history is "A Late Encounter with the Enemy," in which the author ridicules the obsessive and sentimental southern attachment to "the War Between the States," the veneration accorded soldiers of the Confederacy, and the human penchant for family status and obsession with geneaology that, although perhaps not peculiarly southern, W. J. Cash described as crucial in the South's maintaining a closed, cohesive, if not repressive society. O'Connor mercilessly satirizes Sally Poker Sash's determination that her 104-year-old grandfather, attired in a Confederate general's uniform, sit on the stage at her graduation from the state teachers' college.

However, O'Connor clearly suggests that for Sally Poker the presence of the old "general" signifies security in a changing world, a world in which "nothing had been normal since she was sixteen" (*O'Connor* 252). She is a spinster schoolteacher with very little identity save that provided by her grandfather's renown. After all, he participated in the premiere of what most readers assume to be the film version of *Gone with the Wind*, a landmark occasion in Atlanta history, and Sally Poker likes to say that he "was the hit of the show" (254). The granddaughter, however, has an unpleasant memory of the gala evening, for she discovered only when she was onstage in her finery with General Sash that she had neglected to change her Girl Scout oxfords. Surely, through the character of Sally Poker, O'Connor manages sharp criticism of foolish family pride and even indirectly of public education in Georgia: "For the past twenty summers, when she should have been resting, she had had to take a trunk in the burning heat to the state teachers' college; and although when she returned in the fall, she always taught in the exact way she had been taught not to teach, this was a mild revenge that didn't satisfy her sense of justice" (252). Her vindication would come, she believed, when the General—who, of course, was not a general at all but "probably a foot soldier," though "he didn't remember what he had been"—sat behind her on that stage. She intended "to hold her head very high as if she were saying, 'See him! See him! My kin, all you upstarts! Glorious upright old man standing for the old traditions! Dignity! Honor! Courage! See him!'" (253).

This foolish pride in ancestry is lampooned by O'Connor, as is the premiere of *Gone with the Wind* itself. She uses that occasion to demonstrate the human folly inherent in attempts to glorify the past; she mocks the scantily clad "usherettes" in their Confederate caps and short skirts, the silly pride of the United Daughters of the Confederacy who lead the applause for the General and rise in respect when he walks to the stage, and the delight of the audience with the General's wit—"How I keep so young. . . . I kiss all the pretty guls!" (256). John Desmond and other critics rightly conclude that General Sash, in his efforts to escape the "black procession" (259), is actually attempting to evade the reality of history, which includes, of course, the reality of death. Desmond notes that O'Connor once again uses comic action to underscore the futility of that attempt (89). One such comedic touch lies in the fragment of the graduation address that the old General hears—"If we forget our past . . . we won't remember our future and it will be as well for we won't have one" (*O'Connor* 260)—a hilarious, nonsensical distortion of Santayana's statement that those who do not learn from history are condemned to repeat it. This idea is ironically epitomized by the General himself, for he has learned absolutely nothing from history and his own part in it.

False pride, the foolishness of attempting to live solely in the present, and the closing off of the mind to spiritual reality certainly receive the brunt of O'Connor's savage wit in "A Late Encounter with the Enemy." Because language itself is the measure and record of human experience and history, the General sees words as enemy soldiers, coming in for the attack. Words are our connection with events and with individuals, and they possess the capacity to open us up to both responsibility and possibility. The fact that General Sash cannot remember his family or even "what he had been" is consonant with his refusal to confront the "dreary black procession of questions about the past." Like many of us, he prefers parades to processions (253), a fact clearly suggesting that his avoidance of history is catastrophic in terms of his relationships with others — his participation in community, the possibility of his experience of what Allen Tate calls "communion"[2] — and in terms of his own salvation. Critics have neglected to comment on the wretched relationship between the General and his granddaughter in this story, not recognizing perhaps that his connection to her (and hers to him) is also part of the matter of "history" presented by O'Connor. The old General experiences no human connection, and therefore it is natural that words, the means of describing that connection, are his enemy.

Unlike the Grandmother in "A Good Man Is Hard to Find," General Sash does not finally reach out to acknowledge human community. Instead, as the hole in his head widens, he sees the words flying at him "like musket fire" and "the entire past [opens] up on him out of nowhere and he [feels] his body riddled in a hundred places with sharp stabs of pain and he [falls] down, returning a curse for every hit" (261). A curse is, of course, the distortion or perversion of language. Thus the Civil War "hero" who is presumably venerated by his community only appears to have escaped time; in fact, time has gone on for the General for so long that he has lost any sense of its meaning (if he ever possessed that sense) and certainly any sense of who he actually is. O'Connor also suggests that all of us southerners who indulge in prideful distortion of the past are just as foolish as the General or Sally Poker. "A Late Encounter with the Enemy" may certainly be read as O'Connor's antidote to that foolishness.

We might even see the echo of Tate's *Ode to the Confederate Dead* in the story; after all, the old "general" appears to be a comically exaggerated form of that very dissociation of sensibility Tate presents in the *Ode*. The modern speaker of the poem, standing at the gate of a Confederate cemetery, cannot begin to imagine the conviction of the Confederate soldiers, "the furious murmur of their chivalry," their ardent devotion to the Cause (*Ode* 69). He is, instead, the antihero, who, like Prufrock, can only conceptualize and agonize — and that, even, in elliptical, allusive language so private as to be almost inaccessible. General Sash may well be O'Connor's comic gloss on Tate's poem. If that is so, we are not surprised to see O'Connor echoing Tate's and Eliot's description of the modern malaise. Like Walker Percy, O'Connor writes out of that conservative theological tradition by which the modern (male) psyche is seen as divided against itself, cut off from the "short view" of history, that is, the eschatological one. O'Connor's General is thus a comic version of the antihero of Tate's poem as well as the ridiculous embodiment of the southern veneration of history, especially as recorded in the popularity of *Gone with the Wind*.

More recently, however, the work of feminist critics such as Anne Goodwyn Jones causes us to reassess the achievement and reputation of Margaret Mitchell and other southern women writers and to reconsider the contributions of these writers, particularly to a female literary tradition. Jones is particularly concerned with *Gone with the Wind* as expressive of Mitchell's experience of womanhood in the South, for, although Mitchell felt that her novel concerned southern history and presented "a realistic depiction of the South, the antithesis of what she called (scornfully) a 'Thomas Nelson Pagish' novel" (319–20), Jones argues that the book is thematically focused on "southern ladyhood" (341) and on "the definition and role of women, men, and community" (338). For example, as I suggested earlier, Mitchell's personal ambivalence toward acceptable female behavior in the South is at the root of the conflict between Scarlett and Melanie. The jazz-age milieu and the example of female strength Mitchell found in her own suffragist mother, Maybelle, account for much of the character of Scarlett, while "Melanie Wilkes comes right out of the South's expectations for its young ladies as late as the 1930s" (333). Maintaining that Mitchell "found it imaginatively impossible to unify her conception of woman" (333), Jones cites Mitchell's comment that she had intended for Melanie to be the "heroine" of the book, "the ideal Southern woman," but that "somehow Scarlett had simply taken over" (Mitchell qtd. by Jones 333). Acknowledging that the book's readership over the years has been predominantly female, Jones suggests that women, perhaps especially southern women, are drawn to the novel in large part because of the conflict between Scarlett and Melanie or because of the tension created by two sharply different views of womanhood. Furthermore, the easy dismissal of the book by the largely male literary establishment might in part be accounted for on the basis of its "female" subject matter.

From its opening sentences, Jones asserts, the novel is concerned with gender distinctions; Scarlett's face is "'too sharp' a blend of her mother's feminine features and her father's masculine ones" (338) to be considered beautiful, although Scarlett clearly has the wherewithal to survive—precisely because she is *not* Melanie. Jones writes,

> Mitchell herself intended the novel's subject to be the conditions for survival: who makes it through a traumatic, world-destroying event, who doesn't, and why. As a novel whose subject is southern history, *Gone with the Wind* describes the downfall of the Old South and the beginnings of the New; looked at from this angle, the characters embody historical forces. Scarlett, for example, represents Atlanta, the New South, and finally post–Civil War America. (339)

The conflict in Scarlett, then, is that between dependence and self-reliance; she desires power and control and thus is unable to be the dependent woman necessary to a man like Rhett Butler (344–46). Perhaps surprisingly, Jones points out that Melanie also "rebels against the conventional mores that define the lady," although in her case, the rebellion is in the name of "a higher, more 'Christian' ideal," unlike the rebellion of Scarlett, who "rebels for materialistic, 'selfish' reasons" (346). Scarlett naturally associates power with the realm of the male, and throughout the novel it is evident that "cold objective knowledge and concern with larger issues are exclusively the province of males" (347), another indication of Mitchell's own ambivalence toward the female. After all, the only women Scarlett consistently admires are her mother and Mammy. With the exception of Melanie, for whom she does gain respect over the years, Scarlett finds other women "spineless and weak, dependent" (344).

Darden Asbury Pyron also suggests the complexity of Mitchell's attitude toward the female experience, arguing that "[s]ex and gender was the heavy load" for women (283) and that Mitchell's "own struggle for autonomy and integrity" was projected onto the fiction. In particular, Pyron asserts, Mitchell's mother, the suffragette Maybelle, is at the novel's center, *not* as the model for the character of Scarlett (as Anne Jones had claimed) but rather as the model for Rhett Butler. In response to her idealization of Ashley Wilkes, Rhett advises Scarlett that the "real heroes" are "people with spunk and determination—like Scarlett herself" (Pyron 264). His advice is strongly reminiscent of Maybelle Mitchell's lecture to her rebellious daughter in 1907, when young Margaret expressed her dislike of school:

> In one version of the story, Mitchell related that her mother had populated these crumbling mansions [on the Jonesboro road] with equally sad and dependent aged virgins: "charming, embroidering, china-painting, one-time belles, who, after the war had deprived them of their means, degenerated pitifully." All these people had lived securely once, but their world had exploded. "And she told me that my own world was going to explode under me someday, and God help me if I didn't have some weapon to meet the world." That weapon was education. (Pyron 264)

On another occasion, Mitchell's mother urged, "[G]o to school and learn something that will stay with you. The strength of women's hands isn't worth anything but what they've got in their heads will carry them as far as they need go" (46).

Whether we agree with Pyron that Rhett's admonitions and indeed his nurturance echo the character of Mitchell's mother, we may acknowledge that his abandonment of Scarlett on that fateful trip home to Tara is the catalyst for Scarlett's independence and strength in the face of catastrophe (267). Much in the way that a child is terrified by the absence of the protective mother, Scarlett is terrified to be without Rhett. Yet, comparing Scarlett's experience to the fact of birth, Pyron maintains that issues of "autonomy, independence, and self" for women are all related to questions of motherhood and womanhood (268). Indeed, Pyron asserts that the "overarching themes" of *Gone with the Wind* are "the fundamental conflicts between parents and children—specifically mothers and daughters—and the conflicted nature of womanhood itself" (265).

Jones's and Pyron's discussions of *Gone with the Wind* are especially significant because of their reminder that Mitchell uses a conflicted female protagonist to present the major event in southern history. Furthermore, we can hardly afford to ignore Scarlett's spirited rebellion. Both Jones and Pyron observe that matters of gender identity and responsibility are at the heart of this work, a fact that many readers of the novel have failed to see. To recognize and to name those female conflicts is perhaps to account for—for the first time—the overwhelming appeal of the novel. Certainly its bold presentation of the major event in southern history through the conflict within a female protagonist is also tremendously appealing.

Without overestimating the importance of this novel, we should be reminded that its publication in 1936, when Flannery O'Connor was eleven years old, was a signal event in the history of Georgia and the South. Moreover, the novel's focus on gender roles (a fact of which all of us as young readers were certainly aware, although, to be sure, we lacked then the terminology by which to verbalize or analyze that awareness) underscored some important differences between the sexes, most notably the "fact" that women are incapable of abstract thought. Anne Goodwyn Jones writes,

> Although Scarlett has the "male" mind for business, although Rhett has the "female" mind for character, no women in the novel can see—as can Rhett and Ashley—the larger implications of history and of their actions. No woman can think abstractly. In a novel written by a woman (who of course imagines their abstract thinking), this reinforces once again the suspicion that Mitchell sees her voice as essentially "masculine" just as she has Scarlett wanting not just to have or to love but to *be* Ashley and Rhett. (348)

Thus, the "way out" of the conflicts of womanhood was the desire to leave one's sex altogether, to find identity through the objectivity and power that are male. Therefore, although a woman cannot become a man, she can dream about and strive for masculine freedom and control. Such is the conflict within Scarlett, a dilemma that surely reflects that of Margaret Mitchell herself and that is typical of the conflict in many thinking southern women in the first half of the twentieth century.

I have suggested, as early as the first chapter of this work, that O'Connor herself experienced just such ambivalence. *Gone with the Wind* surely added to that confusion: a popular novel written by a Georgia woman in the aftermath of the first wave of women's suffrage about a brassy Georgia woman caught in the cataclysm of the Civil War. As the novel closes, the rebellious Scarlett O'Hara receives her comeuppance and yet remains fiercely determined, looking hopefully to the future and to the sustenance of the land. The reading public was immediately captivated (and continues to be captivated) by Scarlett's spirit and resourcefulness, in short, by her defiance of the traditional role of the southern lady. For any thinking female reader, therefore, *Gone with the Wind* presents a mixed message. On the other hand, for a young, female southern writer entering adolescence at the time of the novel's publication, *Gone with the Wind* must have been exemplary, if only in its sweep, its daring, and its success. As time passed, however, the novel was censured for its popularity and its misrepresentation of southern history, and the young, female southern writer, now in graduate school studying writing technique, came to despise it and perhaps even to despise Scarlett O'Hara. In fact, we might conjecture, the young writer was rewarded for her decision to eschew southern history, the ragged narrative cloth of her region. Her territory would be elsewhere. As J. O. Tate concludes, O'Connor's "intense religious concentration . . . released her to cultivate a world-historical imagination that we might compare to that of Hegel, Spengler, Yeats, and Voegelin" ("On Flannery O'Connor" 39).

Thus, although O'Connor is usually linked with other southern writers of the academic literary renaissance at Vanderbilt in the 1920s, the fact remains that her fiction is distinctive in its rejection of what Lewis Simpson in *The Brazen Face of History* calls "the aesthetic of memory" characterizing the work of William Faulkner, Robert Penn Warren, and Eudora Welty (240). Simpson maintains that O'Connor, whose devout Christianity removes her from the central tradition of the literary imagination of the South, denies the complexity of the modern consciousness (247–48). On the other hand, John Desmond responds to Simpson's criticism of O'Connor by reminding us that her eschatological view of history holds that the human consciousness alone is an insufficient barometer of reality. Desmond asserts that in her fiction O'Connor relies on what Etienne Gilson, echoing Augustine, calls "metaphysical memory," and that history for O'Connor is thereby defined far more broadly than the record of observable reality (87). Basing his comments on the thought of Claude Trèsmontant, Desmond describes the positive "creative act that began history" as the center of O'Connor's fiction. Countering the assertions that O'Connor's vision is essentially Manichaean, Desmond argues that for O'Connor matter is inherently good and salvation is not a matter of the transcendence of the physical (9–11). History *is* metaphysical reality: "An event is therefore both a fact and a sign; it is a sign with meaning because it indicates the direction of the ongoing genesis of history, its movement toward maturation" (9). Moreover, because "history began in a divine creative act," there can be "no dualism, no division between the temporal and the eternal, the mundane and the supernatural" and "mystery is intelligible . . . a proper subject of knowledge; it can be known as mystery" (9). Because Desmond's work is exemplary of the traditional Catholic approach to O'Connor and especially of her view of history, a closer look at his argument is in order.

Desmond argues that O'Connor is not a Manichaean, essentially because, as a devout Catholic, she *could* not be. In contrast to Greek philosophy, Desmond reminds us, Christianity teaches "the biblical view [that] contemplation is intimately bound to the sensible, especially through the Incarnation" and that "the affirmation of divine love is the heart of a dynamic conception of history—history moving progressively toward its ultimate completion" (12). Desmond's conclusions are consonant with William Lynch's idea of art as incarnational—the word made flesh—and compatible with statements O'Connor herself made in letters, lectures, and essays concerning the Christian basis of her art.

To his credit, Desmond acknowledges early in his book that O'Connor struggled with this vision of history throughout her career, constantly seeking the means by which history could be made to "live" in a work of fiction (12–16). He concludes that O'Connor's answer to the perplexing question of the relationship of reality (and Reality) to fiction lay in her use of "the doctrine of the analogy of being" (16), whereby "the historical analogue" derives from the reality of the story itself, a lesson O'Connor learned from the Hebrew storytelling tradition and found reaffirmed in the theory of Lynch and others (24). Desmond's observation that the structure of some of O'Connor's stories involves a "descent for the character, almost always brought about by a kind of violence" (30) is extraordinarily helpful in explaining the effect of such stories as "A Good Man Is Hard to Find." The "displacement"—or, to use the more traditional term Desmond also offers, the "fall"—brought about by the "action of descent" elicits "a new and radical realization of the full possibility of human beingness, the kind of possibility for free *action* created by Christ's descent into and transfiguration of history" (30). Thus, the "central question" suggested by this displacement in all of O'Connor's stories, according to Desmond, is "what does it mean to be a person in history, *in this moment?*" (31)

Desmond argues that O'Connor's answer to that question begins to be clear in "The Peeler" (1949), which marks a turning point in O'Connor's development because it gives "explicit . . . treatment to the theme of Christian redemption" and develops what would become "the central image in all her major fiction: seeing and vision, sight and blindness" (39). From this point on, Desmond posits, O'Connor claimed her territory; unlike her contemporaries, the so-called postmodernists, she would not write "spatialized" narratives or attempt to subvert "the inherent consecutiveness of narration" (42). Instead, she would concentrate on the "problem of the metaphysical dimension of image-making" (43), devoting the rest of her life — in both fiction and in nonfictional commentary — to this "larger theological perspective" that is based on the idea of the Incarnation and that suggests "a whole way of seeing reality as concrete, yet freely open to transfiguration" (45). According to this view, the image itself is of crucial importance; O'Connor's task was to find "ways to create the incarnational image" that would serve as "the medium of revelation" (46). The statue of the artificial nigger and the peacock in "The Displaced Person" are examples of images that embody the best "anagogical possibilities" (47–50), both suggesting the importance of vision — the way in which different characters perceive and respond to the image — to salvation. (Although Desmond does not say so, his emphasis on the characters' ability to see suggests the medieval doctrine of use and its underscoring of the importance of individual free will, a view completely compatible with his Catholic reading of O'Connor.)

Responding to critical attacks on the bleakness and ugliness depicted in the world of *Wise Blood*, Desmond argues that the novel presents distortion that is "in fact literally realistic and verifiable" as it dramatizes Hazel Motes's "attempt to escape history" (54–55). Unwilling to acknowledge his connection with fallen humanity and therefore with human history, Haze attempts to deny sin and guilt and the need for redemption; in other words, he seeks to establish a kind of self-sufficiency apart from any spiritual order. Thus Haze's conflict is between two opposing views of history: the modern or "gnostic" view by which the world is seen as "desacralized" and which is symbolized by Haze's car, his hats, the peeler, and the mummy, for example (59); and the sacramental view, which asserts that time and event are crucial inasmuch as they reveal numinous reality and the "full mystery of the redemptive process at work" (60). When Haze recognizes that he is not clean, O'Connor implies that his vision of history is "altered" (57). However, Desmond concludes that the novel fails because O'Connor is unable to find images that effectively evoke "the numinous" (59). On the other hand, according to Desmond, *The Violent Bear It Away* more effectively demonstrates the conflicting views of history, demonstrating in the conflict of Francis

Marion Tarwater the second "axial breakthrough" in human consciousness, the change occurring between 1200 and 1700 which posited that man is "the supreme agent in history, creating and governing events solely through the power of secular reason" (101).

Relying on the thought of Voegelin, Jaspers, and others whose work, he avers, profoundly influenced Flannery O'Connor, Desmond describes the first "axial breakthrough" as occurring between 800 and 300 BCE, at which time—through divine revelation—man came to see himself "as a participant in a transcendent and divine reality beyond the order of nature and society" and "called to a personal relationship with the divine being, who initiates the call out of love for His creation" (96). Humanity now is able to see itself as "in partnership with God" and as able to "co-create history and be responsible for it" (97). Furthermore, "the Christ event" (97) to which this enlightened consciousness led changed the very meaning of consciousness, causing it to be open "to the mysterious, to the reality more real than things" (98). The "Christ event" is, in Desmond's view, at the center of O'Connor's fiction and is repeatedly in conflict with that historical consciousness by which the human is placed at the controls, "man" the measure of all things, and the capacity of human reason exalted (the result of the second axial breakthrough). Indeed, Desmond asserts, O'Connor's use of violence is necessitated by the probability of human "closure" to metaphysical reality:

> The task [O'Connor] set herself as a writer was to represent faithfully the fact of historical consciousness, which she saw as dominating the modern temper, and yet represent it in such a way *both* to show clearly how it is a deformation of being and at the same time to reveal the possibility of breakthrough to a higher, more complex level of consciousness. Such a revelation would at least open her characters—if only in defeat—to the possibility of self-transcendence and a more authentic personality rooted in the divine. In the stories . . . violence becomes the means of disrupting closure in order to create these possibilities, for a world of possibility is a world governed by the mystery of being that she so forcefully reveals to the reader. (103)

Thus the homosexual rape of young Tarwater in *The Violent Bear It Away* marks the turning point for Tarwater's conversion, for by means of this violent act the boy comes to acknowledge the same "radically evil denial of being and personhood which he committed in drowning Bishop" (115). The self-sufficient consciousness is thereby overcome and "replaced by a consciousness open to mystery" (115) in a work described by Desmond as "the fullest development of [O'Connor's] anagogical vision and the most complete identification of thought and technique" (111). To a discussion of that novel I shall return presently.

What I believe we find in Desmond's careful reading of O'Connor's historicism and his analysis of the aesthetic task entailed by that dynamic eschatological vision is a very commendable and certainly valid attempt to place O'Connor's imagination of the outrageous in a framework consonant with her private and public statements of authorial intention and belief. There is nothing surprising in Desmond's approach or in his conclusions, there is little that traditional Catholic or Christian readers would find heretical or even objectionable, and there is a commendable freshness in approach to some of the fiction.

What is remarkable, however, is that nowhere in his entire study does Desmond allude to events in O'Connor's own life as any key to developments or changes in fictional technique. Furthermore, he obviously does not heed the New Critics' warning about the intentional fallacy; early in the book he establishes his belief that what O'Connor said she was going to do in her fiction and what she said she had done in that fiction are what is actually there. For example, noting changes in O'Connor's fiction after 1955 — less use of "the harsh cartoonlike style of characterization and . . . of the staged quip or the bizarrely comic action" (64) — Desmond contends that the tone of the stories becomes less caustic. He argues that O'Connor places "greater emphasis on depicting the process of redemption in relation to the universal social order, the corporate body of the human community moving through history" (64). However, Desmond offers no real explanation for this change in tone and focus, not so much as a moment's speculation. Moreover, in this same context, we are led to wonder just why — if O'Connor is really concerned with the *human* community — the stories are so singularly lacking in any positive picture of that community.

Can we be faulted if we ask just why it is that many commentators on O'Connor's work seem to sit outside or above the stories themselves as they weave their theories, especially the theological ones, by which light we are enjoined to read everything? Because of her own public comments emphasizing the theological import of her fiction, is O'Connor herself inadvertently responsible for our spinning out theories that neatly cover, even disguise, the angularity and complexity of her vision? Are our failings as readers attributable to our own inability to *see*? Is seeing believing? Surely as we pore over such finely argued theories as Desmond's, we experience from time to time the sense that such critics are wrapping O'Connor's stories in such heavy cloaks that the actual body beneath seems nearly to disappear! Or, to suggest another analogy, that we are Mrs. Hopewell reading the passage in Joy/Hulga's book and finding herself confronted by words that seemed to her "like some evil incantation in gibberish" (*O'Connor* 269). Doubtless O'Connor would have taken her satirical pen to all of our theories about her stories, although, as I have just suggested, her own comments in essays and lectures may have inadvertently been the catalyst for just such theorizing.

Of course, O'Connor's stated theological motives, often used to illuminate the fiction, are orthodox, based on the belief that absolute truth, by definition, does not bend to changes in societal mores, to the satisfaction of individual whim, or to the convenience of believers:

> When we talk about the writer's country we are liable to forget that no matter what particular country it is, it is inside as well as outside him. Art requires a delicate adjustment of the outer and inner worlds in such a way that, without changing their nature, they can be seen through each other. To know oneself is to know one's region. It is also to know the world, and it is also, paradoxically, a form of exile from that world. The writer's value is lost, both to himself and to his country, as soon as he ceases to see that country as a part of himself, and to know oneself is, above all, to know what one lacks. It is to measure oneself against Truth, and not the other way around. (*Mystery and Manners* 35)

This statement is rather typical of what many O'Connor readers exulted in finding in *Mystery and Manners* when it was published in 1969. Here, after all, was a way to "explain" the fiction, as though we could now see the skull beneath the skin.

In these essays and lectures O'Connor maintains that, although the writer is immersed in her region, she must experience a necessary detachment from that region and, simultaneously, from herself—in order to experience humility in the face of human limitation. Or, to put it another way, the successful regional writer is able to use the raw material her "country" provides her in order to transcend that "country" and approach universality. Universality, of course, has traditionally been defined as the promotion of the values of the dominant institutions within the patriarchal culture. The

Church is the institution whose values O'Connor espouses, and therefore — the author's statements to the contrary about the primacy of storytelling as *art* notwithstanding — the raw materials of history and region and personality are subordinated to that institution, rather in the way that the medieval scholastics viewed art as the handmaiden to philosophy. The imagination must learn obedience.

If I seem to be belaboring the obvious here, I am simply attempting to account for and even to justify "orthodox" readings of O'Connor and, at the same time, to suggest that other readings, even other Christian readings that might be labeled "heretical" in light of the standard O'Connor herself set, are nonetheless possible.

As we noted earlier, John Desmond argues that *The Violent Bear It Away* represents the "full development of a complex consciousness from an internal perspective." In Francis Marion Tarwater, O'Connor "created her fullest and most mature dramatization of the development of Christian consciousness and personality in relation to history" (111). Desmond's view — that the novel "is about the vocation of the word, the prophetic artist's call" (111) — certainly seems well supported by the bare facts of the narrative.

Young Tarwater, like Hazel Motes who moves "backwards to Bethlehem," resists for a time the spiritual education of his great-uncle and fights his call to prophecy, only to move inexorably to the consciousness of his own sinfulness and to a vision of his mission, to "GO WARN THE CHILDREN OF GOD OF THE TERRIBLE SPEED OF MERCY" (*The Violent Bear It Away* 478). Not surprisingly, of course, O'Connor again uses a male protagonist in whom to embody this spiritual struggle, and the familiar framework of the journey is circular. Young Tarwater, as though acting out Eliot's dictum in the *Four Quartets*, arrives where he started from (Powderhead) and "knows the place for the first time"; that is to say, he now knows the meaning of his great-uncle's words and consequently of his own life. His soul has been burnt clean, and he is ready: "His singed eyes, black in their deep sockets, seem already to envision the fate that awaited him but he moved steadily on, his face set toward the dark city, where the children of God lay sleeping" (479).

Although we may well acknowledge the validity of Desmond's assertions that Tarwater's "vocation to be a prophet will define his place within and relationship to history" and that, "like the prophetic artist, his mission is to create and interpret history in the light of its transcendent purpose" (112), we may find such assertions disturbing. We may, in fact, agree with Frederick

Asals's argument that the boy's conformity to God's will "requires a psychic ravaging so radical that the boy's recognition that he has been chosen leaves him . . . 'in despair,' and his final acquiescence to that will renders him both 'forever lost' to all 'his own inclinations' but one and an outcast on the face of the earth" (192). Asals adds that acknowledging that "alienation from the world is traditionally Christian" does not suffice to explain "the mixed tone of the novel's ending and the dark coloration of O'Connor's fierce Christianity." He concludes that this novel "reveals the divine to be at least as terrifying as the demonic" (193), a statement that, I believe, does a great deal to explain the discomfiture of many readers of *The Violent*, even the Christian ones. Further, if we speculate, with John Desmond, that this novel is concerned with the prophetic *artist* who is Flannery O'Connor herself, we may be even more disturbed by the suggestion of what O'Connor's "fierce Christianity" implied about her own vocation.

As Tarwater makes his way to the city to pursue his calling, we might well ponder his attitude toward the world to whom he believes he has a mission. After all, although his great-uncle, Mason Tarwater, did not hate the sinful world, we question whether he ever loved it. Although O'Connor's narrator asserts that, in the evolution of his prophecy, the old man "had learned enough to hate the destruction that had to come and not all that was going to be destroyed" (333), we are not at all convinced that simply not hating the sinful world is tantamount to loving it. The old man's relationship with the boy was surely not conventionally affectionate. When the old man dies, we do not feel that young Tarwater is overcome with grief. He is simply eager to escape the burden of burying his great-uncle and of the stringent command to follow the will of God (involving specifically the baptism of the child Bishop), a stern directive issued to him by the old man. In fact, throughout the novel the possibility of the experience of human relatedness is repeatedly subverted, the most obvious case being Rayber, Tarwater's uncle, whose emotional and spiritual paralysis is symbolized by his hearing aid and his glasses.

Rayber's compelling love for the dimwitted Bishop threatens, in his view, to annihilate him. We are given to understand, moreover, that this "horrifying love," this "curse that lay in his blood," is actually his love for God as the divine is manifested in creation—for example, in the afflicted child or in "the absurd old man's walk of a starling crossing the sidewalk." Because this emotion defies control and thus any "use" Rayber might put it to, he is "terrified" by its onslaught, for he knows that, although the feeling is "completely irrational and abnormal," it is "powerful enough to throw him to the ground in an act of idiot praise" (401):

> He was not afraid of love in general. He knew the value of it and how it could be used. He had seen it transform in cases where nothing else had worked, such as with his poor sister. None of this had the least bearing on his situation. The love that would overcome him was of a different order entirely. It was not the kind that could be used for the child's improvement or his own. It was love without reason, love for something futureless, love that appeared to exist only to be itself, imperious and all demanding, the kind that would cause him to make a fool of himself in an instant. And it only began with Bishop. It began with Bishop and then like an avalanche covered everything his reason hated. He always felt with it a rush of longing to have the old man's eyes — insane, fish-coloured, violent with their impossible vision of a world transfigured — turned on him once again. The longing was like an undertow in his blood dragging him backwards to what he knew to be madness.
>
> The affliction was in the family. It lay hidden in the line of blood that touched them, flowing from some ancient source, some desert prophet or pole-sitter, until, its power unabated, it appeared in the old man and him and, he surmised, in the boy. Those it touched were condemned to fight it constantly or be ruled by it. The old man had been ruled by it. He, at the cost of a full life, staved it off. What the boy would do hung in the balance. (401–2)

This passage demands our attention because of its ambivalence. At first we believe that Rayber fears the loss of control that would follow his yielding to divine love, a loss of control that he could only define as "madness." We find that fear understandable in him, for Rayber is a supremely rational man seeking to escape the family "affliction." However, that Rayber considers the old man to have been "ruled" by love implies a definition of love that would seem to subordinate human relationship and human connection to the dictates of a fierce and demanding God who must constantly be satisfied with our allegiance. This deity is, of course, far closer to the commonly held view of the wrathful and punitive Jehovah of the Old Testament than to the New Testament Christ, who, in what could surely be called the greatest example of mutuality the world has ever known, gave his life for the fallen creation.

Like Jacob, old Tarwater has wrestled with his God, and the greatest responsibility enjoined in him by divine love — and the greatest gift he can bequeath his nephew and his great-nephews — is an intense spiritual education that begins with baptism. Thus, for the old man and for young Tarwater, earthly food can never satisfy. The image of the heavenly bread recurs throughout the novel and culminates in young Tarwater's vision of the old man seated in the multitude, "impatiently" awaiting the bread of life. At this moment young Tarwater knows that his hunger is like the old man's and "that nothing on earth [will] fill him." Moreover, he experiences the hunger "as a tide . . . rising in himself through time and darkness, rising through the centuries," and he knows that "it rose in a line of men whose lives were chosen to sustain it, who would wander in the world, strangers from that violent country where the silence is never broken except to shout the truth" (478). Although at the end of the novel young Tarwater is headed to the city and turned toward God's plan for him, he is not turned toward God's creation. He will continue to find it difficult to look into the eyes and faces of all of us who are, in our own way, as afflicted as Bishop. For this reason, we will likely experience no sense of community, certainly no communion, with his sort. He will likely be found preaching on street corners, a "freak" in the eyes of the world but in O'Connor's eyes "a figure for our essential displacement" (*Mystery and Manners* 45). If, as John Desmond suggests, we read Tarwater's journey toward prophecy as symbolic of the journey of O'Connor as "prophetic artist," we may have further explanation for the alienation from her vision experienced by many readers. Like Tarwater's "congregation" on some anonymous city street, we as O'Connor's readers may very well not feel a sense of connection — much less communion — with her stringently prophetic fiction.

At this point traditional theologians will undoubtedly rush in to admonish me, to assert that O'Connor was dramatizing in extreme terms the desperate crisis of faith in our time and that she is only underscoring the central fact of Christian teaching: that all human love and relatedness have their true origin in God's love for creation, for the salvation of which God gave his only son. They would remind me that any human connectedness or human affection that is not based on that divine standard — for example, any humanistic or secular attempts at love or charity or even social betterment, however well intentioned — are thin simulations or imitations, and as such are justifiably the object of O'Connor's satire. O'Connor saw all around her, they would surely add, evidence of the extremely misguided notions of the social scientists and psychologists who believe, as Rayber wants to believe, that all human problems have rational human solutions. These theological critics would cite O'Connor's and Walker Percy's mutual distaste for secular humanism. As I myself have done on occasion, they will refer to O'Connor's statement in her introduction to *A Memoir of Mary Ann* that compassion or "tenderness" that is "detached from the source of tenderness" has, as its logical outcome, "terror" and ends "in forced-labor camps and in the fumes of the gas chamber" (*O'Connor* 227). As Richard Giannone puts it, "humankind wants love on its own soft terms," while O'Connor writes from an understanding of "the violence of love." Giannone, another Catholic commentator and one of the most biblically literal in his reading of O'Connor, observes, "Love is not a cultural nicety; it does not ratify one's desire; nor does it make one fit in or feel good," and he reminds us that, for a Christian writer like O'Connor, love is "the Word made flesh," revealing "the individual's duty that furthers the divine plan for all creation" (131).

Giannone describes that divine love as one that "cuts and burns to prepare for the glory to come" (131). Indeed, he continues to focus on the image of cutting in *The Violent Bear It Away* by asserting that the turning point in young Tarwater's spiritual journey occurs at the revival led by the child evangelist, the sharpness of whose name — Lucette — evokes the image of cutting and causes Tarwater to experience "the rite of emotional circumcision as the girl's preaching cuts the covenant in him to accept the burden of experience." In a radical extension of his metaphor, Giannone writes, "In the moment when the prepuce of Tarwater's heart is cut [in his experience of Lucette Carmody's ministry], he is ready to see Rayber through affection." However, because Rayber has had quite a different experience of Lucette's ministry, he misses the chance to respond to Tarwater's openness to affection and the chapter concludes with the "failure of love" (132). Giannone's use of a male sexual ritual (circumcision) to explain O'Connor's idea of the severity of divine love is harsh, although perfectly in keeping with the overwhelmingly patriarchal and orthodox emphasis in O'Connor's fiction and in most of the traditional criticism of that work. Paradoxically, we also note that the girl preacher's words, her use of language, "cut" and "burn" ("circumcise") the male protagonist's heart to begin to prepare him for his prophetic ministry, much in the way, we might argue, that the words of O'Connor's fiction cut and burn us. Lucette Carmody may therefore be seen as another suggestion of the prophetic artist.

Like Giannone, other Christian commentators on O'Connor are also at pains to demonstrate the relationship between the author's Christianity and her "imagination of extremity." Ralph C. Wood, certainly one of the most sensible of the traditional readers of O'Connor, presents in his study *The Comedy of Redemption* two chapters on O'Connor significantly titled "O'Connor as a Satirist of the Negative Way" and "O'Connor as a Comedian of Comic Grace." Wood suggests an intense conflict within the author herself between the satiric impulse and the experience of divine love. Wood emphasizes that, for O'Connor, "the summons to belief is a perilous thing" and that the "forgiveness of sins engenders a water-walking faith that is able to traverse both the river of despondency and the lake of woe." To pay no heed to God's gracious forgiveness "is to fall into the abyss of divine abandonment called hell" (88). Thus, for O'Connor's characters, "the stakes are not merely high; they are absolute" (89).

> God is at once the Archer and the Target of all creation. The cosmos is the arrow which God flings primordially out of himself and eschatologically back unto himself. The arc of God's grace describes a gigantic circle wherein the divine goodness encompasses everything. Sin is the free deflection of life's true trajectory, causing the will to turn in upon itself (*incurvatus in se*) in hideous parody of the divine circularity. Salvation, by contrast, is to will what God wills. By the grace made available through Christ, we are enjoined to align our lives with the pattern of the universe itself. (91)

While we note that Wood, in describing God, echoes William Lynch's images of penetration, we see that God is also imaged in traditional female terms, as the recipient of the arrow, the object of the chase, and the circle — ideas at least as old as the Renaissance. Although Wood is himself a Protestant reader, his commentary for the most part conforms to the traditionalists' readings as, for example, he points up the necessity for "obedience and sacrifice" in the "lifelong penance" that is the individual's life in Christ. Indeed, for Wood, O'Connor's idea that "God's mercy shatters before it rebuilds" creates "a deep affinity" between O'Connor and southern fundamentalist Protestants (91–92). Moreover, Wood spends some time in explaining the rather complicated relationship between O'Connor's fiction and the work of Teilhard de Chardin. He argues that, although O'Connor was in agreement with Teilhard's idea that the natural order is "a sacramental reality that reveals the godward urgency and movement of every living thing" (92), her stories were not in accord with Teilhard's "scientific mysticism." They instead proposed "an enduring struggle of good against evil that can be temporarily won with the intervention of transcendent grace, but that shall finally end only with an apocalyptic closure" (93).

Wood believes that O'Connor's "dark estimate of human sinfulness is closer to Augustine than to Teilhard" and that O'Connor is like C. S. Lewis and T. S. Eliot in her belief that the modern age "represents a surrender of the grand medieval synthesis of biblical faith and classical culture" (92). However, Wood notes that, because of O'Connor's repeated attacks on human sin and unbelief, on how "overrighteous unbelievers and smug half-believers must be blasted by the withering winds of God's grace," she ran the risk—up to the end of her career—of "conceiving the Gospel as ill tidings rather than glad news" (126). He finds in O'Connor's last works, most notably in "Revelation," the happy counter to this negativism.

I find great integrity and comfort in Wood's observations, particularly because I know the care with which he has read and taught O'Connor over the years, and I believe that his reading is consonant with O'Connor's stated intent. Nevertheless, for me, Wood's commentary, although far better grounded in the literature and the life than either Desmond's or Giannone's work, is also troubling in its acceptance of O'Connor's treatment of human relatedness and human love.

O'Connor's fiction, and the traditional criticism of that fiction, espouses a kind of "tough love" whereby the soul's primary objective, the love of God, appears to have little to do with the joys and vicissitudes of earthly encounter in and of themselves; or, put another way, human engagement is valuable primarily insofar as it directs the soul to salvation. The ragged figure of Jesus that Hazel Motes and Francis Marion Tarwater flee does not appear to be present in the human beings encountered by either solitary figure. Certainly in *Wise Blood* there is not a shred of the love Rayber feels for Bishop in *The Violent,* and even that love, O'Connor implies, is Rayber's way of controlling his love for God's creation so that it will not, in his view, overwhelm him with its intensity. Tarwater rebukes Buford Munson's sympathetic touch. Although he has wanted to believe that Rayber loved him "like a daddy" (*The Violent Bear It Away* 375), that is, enough to come to Powderhead and attempt to rescue him, Tarwater rejects Rayber's offer, however misguided, to be a friend and a father to him. Furthermore, he repeatedly repels Bishop's gestures of affection.

O'Connor's underscoring of the similarity of the novel's three male characters, all of whom are "marked" by God's hand and spend their lives responding, either positively or negatively, to that singling out, suggests an "affliction in the blood" that will not be denied. Old Tarwater wrestles with God; Rayber vigorously attempts to deny God in creating an atheistic humanism compatible with his own very evident personal needs; and young Tarwater, resolutely determined to "act," follows the urging of both uncles: He baptizes Bishop even as he drowns him. Both of these actions constitute Tarwater's response to what appear to be autocratic commands. Old Tarwater's obsession that Tarwater baptize Bishop and Rayber's belief that doing away with Bishop would simply be an improvement on nature are similar in their profound disregard for the humanity of both Tarwater and Bishop. In each case, the child becomes the vehicle for the accomplishment of adult belief.

While it is very possible, from the Christian perspective, to regard what the old man does to save the soul of Francis Marion Tarwater (and indeed Bishop) as the greatest act of human love, we may decry the old man's *use* of the boy. The old man, after all, turns Francis Marion away from the possibility of any human connection and insists that the boy's duty is to baptize Bishop. We may also decry Rayber's use of Tarwater in getting back at the old man for the way he feels old Tarwater exploited him. Indeed, in a passage very much reminiscent of Salinger's depiction of Holden Caulfield in *Catcher in the Rye* (and which, in fact, may be O'Connor's parody of Caulfield), Rayber imagines fleeing with Lucette Carmody and all the world's exploited children to "some enclosed garden." There he will teach them the truth "and let the sunshine flood their minds" (414). Yet Rayber is no less guilty of exploiting the children than the old man whom he bitterly resents.

Is Tarwater's "call," the call to prophecy, to be assessed differently from the call of any Christian to belief? That is to say, are the stringency and the violence of his summons simply metaphoric expressions of the hard way of the prophet, or is O'Connor suggesting that conversion itself is just such a fierce and absolute matter? Much commentary on the novel underscores the "universality" of Tarwater's condition; that is, just as Tarwater clings to the hope of avoiding his destiny, so each of us holds fast to the possibility of avoiding acknowledgment of God's grace. By this reading, Tarwater becomes a kind of Everyman, with added emphasis on the *man*. After all, old Tarwater did not see fit to kidnap Rayber's sister when she was a child, in order to baptize her and raise her in God's truth, and in old Tarwater's mind, she, like the old man's own sister who was Rayber's mother, becomes no more than a "whore," just as Rayber's wife, Berenice Bishop, is repeatedly referred to as "the welfare woman." I am afraid that, as we observed earlier, the spiritual journey of import for O'Connor was the male journey; she had learned the lessons of the patriarchy quite well. Tarwater's journey is the "universal" one, and in accomplishing his goal, he will not be deterred. O'Connor sets the stage for this determination in the first chapter in which she presents the terror of the child Tarwater who fears that, as in the case of his great-uncle, the "bottom [has been] split out of his stomach" and that only the bread of life will "heal or fill it" (343).

A number of commentators have pointed out that Tarwater's early idea of his prophecy is a cerebral one, by which he means to avoid the "threatened intimacy of creation" (343). The child Tarwater practices the same kind of disciplined shutting out of reality that Rayber uses to control his experience of divine love. This connection underscores both the similarity of the two characters and the idea that, contrary to what Tarwater and Rayber intend, divine love entails the love of all creation. As the boy conceives it,

> It was as if he were afraid that if he let his eye rest for an instant longer than was needed to place something—a spade, a hoe, the mule's hind quarters before his plow, the red furrow under him—that the thing would suddenly stand before him, strange and terrifying, demanding that he name it and name it justly and be judged for the name he gave it. He did all he could to avoid this threatened intimacy of creation. When the Lord's call came, he wished it to be a voice from out of a clear and empty sky, the trumpet of the Lord God Almighty, untouched by any fleshly hand or breath. He expected to see wheels of fire in the eyes of unearthly beasts. (343)

This passage would seem to anticipate that Tarwater will inevitably have to confront the sacred in all creation and, like Adam in the power he possesses to name and be judged by his "naming," Tarwater will be judged by his capacity to be immersed in this "intimacy" of creation. As a child, however, he seeks to avoid that possibility, preferring to think of his call to prophecy in the Old Testament context: dramatic, otherworldly, unmistakable.

Of course, the conclusion of the novel presents Tarwater's call as predicated on the certainty of his own sinfulness and his acknowledgment of the power of evil. He can only be grateful before God's mercy and heed his uncle's command to enter the city and prophesy to the sleeping children of God. Undoubtedly, Tarwater will never experience the intimacy of creation that is community and communion with others, for O'Connor does not seem to attach importance to such human connection. She suggests instead that the way of the Christian is necessarily solitary, that the journey to salvation is a lonely, arduous one, and that witnessing to divine truth may well lead to ostracism and even persecution. If Tarwater's journey is also that of the artist with prophetic vision, then we may infer that O'Connor saw the task of such an artist as also difficult and solitary, capable of being misunderstood, and without the warmth and amenities of community acceptance. The prophetic artist is thus a kind of "freak" by society's standards, set apart, in some sense a pariah.

However, O'Connor's letters do not seem to testify to such a personality. She clearly valued and depended on her friendships and her family relationships, and she delighted in Milledgeville's generous offerings of the comic and the bizarre. Her advice about writing—though, as we have noted, often proffered with an authority that may be bewildering to the reader—is usually deliberate and practical, emphasizing discipline and hard work and demonstrating her own willingness to read others' work. In the letters her remarks on religious belief are thoughtful, often tough-minded, emphasizing the importance of the community of believers and the essential role of the Church as teacher and guide. The letters to Maryat Lee are especially warm; as Jean Cash has suggested, Lee represented the antithesis of O'Connor's conservatism and may have been attractive to O'Connor for the very flamboyance of her difference from Milledgeville society and the expectations of southern female propriety ("Maryat and Flanneryat" 60–64). Surely O'Connor's warm, often playful letters to Lee, all of which are not included in either *The Habit of Being* or the Library of America edition of O'Connor's works, are evidence of O'Connor's capacity for deep, caring friendship. Yet we must remember that O'Connor's most profound relationships—with the exception of the complex one with her mother—are conducted by mail. Although there certainly were members of the Milledgeville community with whom O'Connor shared interests, her primary relationships (with Maryat Lee, "A," Cecil Dawkins, and the Fitzgeralds, for example) were long-distance ones.

In spite of the presence of GSCW in Milledgeville, the community did not offer O'Connor many opportunities for the kinds of literary and theological exchanges she enjoyed with her correspondents. The literary group that met regularly at Andalusia, consisting of some of the most serious readers and would-be artists in the community, undoubtedly provided O'Connor the opportunity for some exchange,[3] and her visits from out-of-town friends such as Louise Abbot were salutary. Nonetheless, given the limitations of a small southern town, we conclude that, either by choice or circumstance or a combination of both, O'Connor relied primarily on an epistolary community for the experience of closeness. That she needed such closeness and felt deprived of it is evident in her letter to "A" in which she contrasted her own need for people with that of her father: "Needing people badly and not getting them may turn you in a creative direction, provided you have the other requirements. He [her father] needed the people I guess and got them. Or rather wanted them and got them. I wanted them and didn't. We are all rather blessed in our deprivations if we let ourselves be, I suppose" (*Habit of Being* 169). The unusual candor of this statement is revealing and touching, and the tentativeness of the added qualifier ("I suppose") suggests that O'Connor may have struggled a bit to see her need for people as a blessing.

In this regard the letters stand in sharp contrast to the fiction. In fact, because the letters reveal the human and caring O'Connor and allow her to state her intentions in a straightforward fashion, many critics, including Sally Fitzgerald, urge readers to read the letters before they read the fiction. Ralph Wood advocates that *The Habit of Being* "be read in tandem with [O'Connor's] fiction in order to comprehend the unity of her art, her faith, and her life" (*Comedy of Redemption* 83), while Clara Claiborne Park makes the outrageous suggestion that the letters be read *in lieu of* the fiction. Without dwelling on the fact that O'Connor herself would doubtless have been horrified to witness even the publication of the letters, to say nothing of her certain rejection of their use as gloss on or substitute for the fiction, we can nonetheless observe what many of the proponents of the letters discern: the very darkness of the fiction seems to demand a palliative.

I submit, furthermore, that the need for such explanation and softening exists primarily because O'Connor is a Christian artist. After all, who suggests that readers of Edgar Allan Poe, Shirley Jackson, or Joyce Carol Oates resort to extrafictional material to explain or soften these writers' dark imaginings? The discrepancy between O'Connor as a writer of Christian concerns and the bleakness of the fiction, the absence from it of simple goodness and love, is problematic for many readers, who, at the risk of being accused of trivializing the fiction, miss in O'Connor any genuine sense of the possibilities for human growth and understanding, any celebration of the delight of human exchange and community. To be sure, the denigration of human relationships is more the rule than the exception in O'Connor's fiction. While I want to believe, as I have asserted in an earlier chapter, that

O'Connor's adherence to the idea of art as incarnation would suggest an emphasis on the divine presence in the here and now, I must conclude that in the fiction O'Connor does not seem to find that presence in relationship. Most often she presents immanence in the figure of the solitary individual (usually a child or an "afflicted" character who may function in an almost angelic capacity) or sometimes suggests the divine presence in the natural world (the trees, the sun). In the fiction, rarely, if ever, does a parent-child relationship, a relationship of romantic love, or a friendship show forth divine goodness and love.

Who are the naturally lovable characters in O'Connor's fiction? Surely one could argue that such strong and memorable characters as the grandmother, Mrs. McIntyre, and even General Sash, Hazel Motes, and the great-uncle and nephew Tarwater in a sense become lovable to us as readers through the extent to which we invest in their struggles and identify with them. We might surmise that these characters were lovable to O'Connor in that sense as well. All of us who have read O'Connor over the years have laughed to recognize ourselves among certain of her fictional folk, although we may have initially resisted the impulse to see ourselves there. Further, O'Connor in the letters has testified that she herself *is* in many of those characters, from Enoch Emery to Joy/Hulga. Yet reader identification with a character — for whatever complicated reasons — is not synonymous with finding that character lovably presented by the author. The comedy carries our laughter, for which, as a matter of fact, sometimes we almost have to apologize, especially to those readers who find O'Connor's work perverse and offensive.

We might surely argue that the children in O'Connor's work, although they are frequently depicted as possessing the wisdom and indeed the cynicism of adults, are often very winningly presented. Their attractiveness and lovable qualities, however, are not essentially manifested in relationship to other characters but rather are conveyed to the reader through O'Connor's skillful use of such devices as compelling plotline, interior monologue, and comic perspective. In other words, for the most part the *reader* perceives the lovable nature of the character; *other characters* for the most part do not interact lovingly with the attractive child. While that is much of O'Connor's point — in the modern waste land we cannot see God's goodness in others — we as readers may yearn for the "conversion" that will result in changed relationships, in addition to what O'Connor suggests are changes in the individual's awareness of sin and dependence on God. The child in "A Temple of the Holy Ghost," for example, is attractive in her honesty, her innocence, and perhaps above all in her desire to be good. Without creating a romantic, sentimental picture of childhood, O'Connor manages here to give us a child who is one of her most sympathetic creations. Sally Virginia in "A Circle in the Fire" and Nelson in "The Artificial Nigger" are darker versions of the child in "A Temple." Their motivation is closer to that of O'Connor's adult children—Joy/Hulga ("Good Country People"), Asbury ("The Enduring Chill"), Julian ("Everything That Rises Must Converge"), Scofield and Wesley ("Greenleaf"), and Thomas ("The Comforts of Home")—who seek retaliation against the parent figure and some measure of power over their own lives. In "The River" young Harry/Bevel, who bumbles about rather like an old man, is compelling in the simplicity of his urge "to count." He bears marked similarity to Norton of "The Lame Shall Enter First," whose grief over the loss of his mother is as movingly described as anything in O'Connor's fiction. Norton is another version of the child Bishop of *The Violent Bear It Away*, the story fashioned from an early draft of the novel in which Sheppard figures as the Rayber character, determined to save Rufus Johnson from a life of crime and from his "primitive" fundamentalist belief. Indeed, Bishop and Norton are two of O'Connor's most lovable characters, and they are both, O'Connor makes clear, essential to the salvation of their earthly caretakers.

Anticipated by the earlier character of the afflicted daughter, Lucynell Crater, in "The Life You Save May Be Your Own," Bishop possesses a kind of radiance that, O'Connor suggests, partakes of the divine. Early in the novel Tarwater remembers the resemblance of Bishop and old Tarwater: "The little boy somewhat resembled old Tarwater except for his eyes which were grey like the old man's but clear, as if the other side of them went down and down into two pools of light" (*The Violent Bear It Away* 344), and when he sees the child after his great-uncle's death, the child's breathing is described as "closer to [Tarwater] than the beating of his own heart." The child is a mysterious figure of timeless innocence. O'Connor writes that Bishop "stood there, dim and ancient, like a child who had been a child for centuries" (388), suggesting both the child's deficiency (he will never mature, never be more than a child) and, most significantly, the presence of eternal innocence among us, whether or not we are capable of perceiving that innocence and its importance. Although both Rayber and Tarwater want to dismiss Bishop—Rayber calls Bishop "a freak of nature"—Tarwater clearly acknowledges that if Bishop's humanity (and indeed Bishop's life) is dismissed, then his and Rayber's lives are insignificant as well. Perhaps nowhere is Tarwater's struggle with Bishop's innocent presence and his need to believe that Bishop is no more than an animal (hence, soul-less) more succinctly presented than in this passage:

> Tarwater was glaring at the dark walls of the room. "He's like a hog," he said. "He eats like a hog and he don't think no more than a hog and when he dies, he'll rot like a hog. Me and you too," he said, looking back at the schoolteacher's mottled face, "will rot like hogs. The only difference between me and you and a hog is me and you can calculate, but there ain't any difference between [Bishop] and one." (403)

Tarwater, unable to follow Rayber's admonition that he simply "forget Bishop exists" (403), cannot finally deny Bishop's humanity; near the end of the novel, even as he attempts to do the deed that his uncle could not manage—drown the child—he baptizes him. Sadly and ironically, we are not sure that Tarwater actually allows himself to *see* the child until the last hours that Bishop is alive. As Rayber and the two boys check into the Cherokee Lodge, Tarwater attempts once again to rebuff the child, who has reached out to touch him. O'Connor writes, "The instant the child touched him, the country boy's shoulders leapt. He snatched his touched hand up and jammed it in his pocket. 'Leave off!' he said in a high voice. 'Git away and quit bothering me!'" (426). The desk clerk remonstrates with Tarwater, warning him to "mind" how he talks to "one of them there," and when Tarwater asks, "Them there what?" she responds, "That there kind," and gazes "at him fiercely as if he had profaned the holy" (426–27). Clearly O'Connor means for us to see that Tarwater, like his uncle Rayber, has profaned the holy. As Bishop makes his slow way up the stairs, he is followed by Tarwater "so directly that he might have been attached to him by a tow-line." Suddenly the child turns and sits down on the stairs, planting himself directly in Tarwater's way and sticking his feet out for his shoes to be tied. Now Tarwater is forced to look at him and to tie his shoes. When he finishes his task, we sense that Tarwater is not able to dismiss Bishop quite as easily as he might have done earlier, for O'Connor tells us that he says to the child, "Now git on and quit bothering me with them laces" but now "in a querulous voice" (427).

Bishop is now much more than the assignment given to Tarwater by the old man. He is a flesh-and-blood human being needing love and attention. In drowning the child, Tarwater will ultimately reject the possibility of providing that love. Further, as Desmond and others have observed, Tarwater's own violation by the homosexual stranger will later demonstrate to him the enormity of his own sin. Just as he is *used* by the stranger who, O'Connor suggests, may literally feed off him ("[The stranger's] delicate skin had acquired a faint pink tint as if he had refreshed himself on blood" [472]), so he has taken Bishop's life in a perverse determination to show Rayber and himself that he can *act*. As if responding to the paralysis of will described by Eliot, Tate, and others in their diagnosis of the modern malaise, O'Connor allows Tarwater to do what the cerebral, atheist Rayber cannot. Tarwater may thus be viewed as O'Connor's ironic antidote to the Prufrockian antihero, although Tarwater's action tragically reflects his profound confusion. His baptism of the child even as he murders him dramatizes Tarwater's inability to yield completely to the real "temptation" embodied in the stranger's wily words. This double action of murder and baptism also allows us to view Bishop's death as a sacrificial catalyst by means of which Tarwater's soul will be saved, his prophetic mission confirmed.

The strong physical resemblance of all four male characters in the novel is strongly underscored in the spiritual similarity and kinship between Tarwater and Rayber. "The schoolteacher," as Rayber is repeatedly called by the old man and then by Tarwater himself, "suffer[s]" the child to crawl onto his lap (418), this verb an ironic play on Christ's admonition, "Suffer the little children to come unto me, for of such is the kingdom of heaven." In this same scene, O'Connor presents a memorable vignette of the father and son, the child "sprawled and grinning" in the father's lap, with his "white head fitted under his [father's] chin." The picture is most moving, however, because of the father's fear of that "hated love" which "gripped him and held him in a vise" (418), a fear that prompts him to recall the day when he had tried and failed to drown the child. As I have mentioned earlier, Rayber believes that he must keep under control his love for the idiot child, for fear that if that love were allowed to spread from the child to the rest of creation, it would annihilate him. After Tarwater leaves with Bishop in the boat, Rayber realizes that he no longer wants to rehabilitate Tarwater and that he will simply be relieved to be rid of him. At the same time, he considers momentarily the possibility of placing Bishop "in an institution for a few weeks," but "he [is] shaken and [turns] his mind to other things." He falls asleep and dreams that he and Bishop are in the car pursued by a "lowering tornado-like cloud" (454), an underscoring of Rayber's subconscious recognition of the perilous condition of both his and Bishop's souls, the sense that danger is imminent.

Thus Tarwater's drowning-baptism could surely be seen as the acting out of Rayber's weak, antiheroic will. By denying Bishop's significance to Tarwater, Rayber is indeed in large measure responsible, O'Connor suggests, for the murder of his own child. Furthermore, Rayber has largely contributed to Tarwater's commission of the crime, and therefore he has failed his nephew in the most profound way. Finally, because he has lost the only thing on earth that he allowed himself to love, Rayber is relegated to a complete and horrifying numbness for the rest of his life:

> He stood waiting for the raging pain, the intolerable hurt that was his due, to begin, so that he could ignore it, but he continued to feel nothing. He stood light-headed at the window and it was not until he realized there would be no pain that he collapsed. (456)

For both Rayber and Tarwater, therefore, Bishop has signified that "threatened intimacy of creation" by means of which each believed that he would lose control. For Rayber the death of this innocent child means the end, the abyss, the fall into the very nothingness that he himself espoused. For Tarwater, on the other hand, the child's death marks the beginning of his conversion, for he has been unable to shake "the bleeding stinking mad shadow of Jesus" and thus is stalked by guilt. The encounter with the homosexual rapist confirms Tarwater's knowledge of the existence of evil. We note that Tarwater has not learned the love and forgiveness of God through any experience of human love; as Lucette Carmody prophesied, the love of God that Tarwater experiences "cuts" and "burns."

Just as we see that, for such characters as Hazel Motes, Tom T. Shiftlet, and Francis Marion Tarwater, God's love cuts and burns, so we conclude that for Flannery O'Connor the lessons of God's love are hard ones, not found, to be sure, in a sentimental piety, nor even in the usual sorts of communal affirmation and human connectedness by which most of us would feel that we as humans understand something of the love of God. Lucette Carmody's exhortation to her congregation might well be O'Connor's own to her readers: "Listen you people!" she cried, "the world knew in its heart, the same as you know in your hearts and I know in my heart. The world said,

'Love cuts like the cold wind and the will of God is plain as the winter. Where is the summer will of God? Where are the green seasons of God's will? Where is the spring and summer of God's will?" (413). The "summer will of God" is surely missing from O'Connor's fiction, which presents divine love "plain as the winter." Encouraged by the New Critics to create an unsentimental and impersonal art, O'Connor rebelled against the facile, sticky piety often associated with religious fiction in the minds of many Catholics. Instead, she used her skill at satire to cut away any suspicion of sentimentality, often even eviscerating sentiment itself. In similar fashion, she declared her separation from traditional expectations of southern womanhood; she became a writer who refused to write the romantic (or even "pleasing") narratives that typically appeal to a female audience.

While I do not mean to suggest a completely calculated, conscious effort on O'Connor's part to settle on the toughest possible approach to the world through her fiction, I do believe that, like Rayber and Tarwater, she came to see that, for her, the experience of the "intimacy of creation" was inappropriate, perhaps even a weakness. Bishop's squatting on the stairs and boldly offering his shoes to be tied is an image, I think, of a vulnerable and needy creation reaching out to the writer O'Connor. Tarwater's response to Bishop may in a sense be read as O'Connor's rebuke to the soft, yielding side of her sensibility, indeed to that radical love that would look the afflicted child in the eye, tie his shoes (as Tarwater does), and lift him in the arms of compassion and love. Moreover, just as Tarwater's urge for control over his own life leads him to defy his great-uncle's command and to drown the child, so O'Connor in the fiction often has to present the violent deed, to draw the large and startling figure, in order to assert her control and to get our attention. The analogy is not a perfect one, of course. Tarwater is a murderer, after all. Unlike Rayber, however, Tarwater fulfills his prophetic mission, as O'Connor herself does, largely through the boldness of his defiance, a defiance that seems to mean a turning away from homespun notions of community and everydayness and toward an otherworldly or metaphysical reality. Because it is singularly focused on the final state of the soul, the journey of the prophetic artist, like that of the prophet, is based on self-denial and self-sacrifice and usually demands the sorts of gestures that alienate the prophet from community—and perhaps alienate a certain kind of reader from the fiction.

In "The Lame Shall Enter First," Sheppard, Rayber's counterpart, attempts to reform Rufus Johnson, to no avail. As malevolent as many of his practices may seem, Rufus Johnson functions as both a prophet and a devil, eating the word of God, knowing full well that only God's love and mercy can save him. Yet, like Tarwater in his efforts to counter Rayber and his great-uncle, Rufus causes the death of an innocent child, Norton, through his efforts to defy Sheppard. We have no sense, of course, at the conclusion of "The Lame Shall Enter First" that Rufus's soul will ever be saved; O'Connor's focus here is on Sheppard who, though similar to Rayber in his secular humanism, does not lose his capacity to feel as Rayber does. When Sheppard recognizes with complete disgust his own arrogance in ignoring his own child's needs to "[stuff] his own emptiness with good works like a glutton" in order "to feed a vision of himself," the moment arrives too late to save Norton, who has hanged himself in an attempt to reach his mother. Sheppard's view of the empty bed, the fallen tripod and telescope, and the child's body hanging "in the jungle of shadows" constitutes a tragic recognition that Rayber never experiences. Sheppard's anagnorisis is usually interpreted to signify his acknowledgment of evil: he sees "the clear-eyed Devil, the sounder of hearts, leering at him from the eyes of Johnson" [*O'Connor* 632]. Obviously Sheppard's atheistic humanism, what we might call his system of *unbelief*, prevents him from seeing the sacredness of his own child. Only through the violent destruction of his habit of abstracting his son—a destruction achieved through Norton's death—can Sheppard ever be saved.

Perhaps "The Lame" is in part a cautionary tale in which O'Connor might at least inadvertently be presenting a warning to herself. O'Connor's own beliefs—by which the eyes of her fiction seem always on the horizon, on last things, on human choice under the aspect of eternity—might be challenged by Sheppard's tragic vision of an innocent life lost by reason of his inability to see the actual human face of his child before him. As a matter of fact, O'Connor may have inherited this profound distrust of abstraction from the Fugitives and the Agrarians. Although she may not have responded to this theme in such poems as Ransom's "The Equilibrists" or Tate's "Last Days of Alice," she would almost certainly have found it in Tate's prose. In his 1936 essay "Religion and the Old South," Tate asserts that the northern industrialist has succeeded in "making a society out of abstractions" and proposes that the southerner may "take hold of his tradition" only "by violence" (184). O'Connor was undoubtedly familiar with this essay and with its argument as well as with Tate's idea that, at its base, southern religion was "a convinced supernaturalism . . . nearer to Aquinas than to Calvin, Wesley, or Knox" ("The Profession of Letters in the South" 150). With all of these ideas O'Connor would have been in agreement; they certainly seem to underlie the structure of "The Lame Shall Enter First." As was the case in *The Violent Bear It Away*, in "The Lame Shall Enter First" Sheppard, who never actually *sees* Norton, instead generalizes about him, sewing up his life in a series of condescending generalizations: "The boy's future was written in his face. He would be a banker. No, worse. He would operate a small loan company. All he wanted for the child was that he be good and unselfish and neither seemed likely" (*O'Connor* 595). Sheppard's attention is instead focused on rehabilitating Rufus Johnson, the clubfooted juvenile delinquent whose poverty and miserable family life serve Sheppard as object lessons in instructing his son Norton.

Clearly implying that Sheppard's inability to cope with the problems of his own grieving son is the result of his refusal to confront his own devastation over the death of his wife, O'Connor presents a character whose expression of feelings is blocked and whose solace is "intellectual" activity, as is frequently the case with characters in O'Connor's work. The dead wife's room has not been disturbed; moreover, Sheppard's purchase of the telescope and his belief that the scientific study of the stars will open the delinquent's eyes to his human potential are symptoms of his malaise. A man with a dissociated sensibility, like Rayber, Sheppard thinks that with the telescope "he had made it possible for [Rufus's] vision to pass through a slender channel to the stars" (609), and he expects that the new shoe he has ordered for the boy's clubfoot will "make the greatest difference in the boy's attitude" (610). Rufus's attitude toward the new shoe, however, is completely disdainful, and to Sheppard's encouragement to consider a career as an astronaut he replies, "I ain't going to the moon and get there alive . . . and when I die I'm going to hell" (611). Rufus's certainty about the truth of the Bible is as unshakable as Sheppard's belief in progress. Despite the boy's wickedness, we are certain that, like the Misfit, he has the knowledge that O'Connor considers essential to salvation.

The story is Sheppard's, however, not Rufus Johnson's and not Norton's. It is Sheppard who experiences God's cutting and burning love. In this case also, a child's death serves as the catalyst for the salvation of the central character. O'Connor's implication that Sheppard could learn his lesson in no other way may seem to some a harsh judgment; we may in fact wonder whether Sheppard deserves such a harsh punishment for his "crimes." However, we know that O'Connor was contemptuous of what she considered to be superficial social solutions to human problems and often took to task social workers, psychologists (like Rayber, whose testing of old Tarwater elicits scathing satire), educators, and others who would reduce life's difficulties to a matter of secular compassion or "tenderness" that is theoretical and "detached from the source of tenderness" who is Christ (*Mystery and Manners* 227). Sheppard's wrongheaded philosophy becomes symptomatic of the age; his soft altruism is, for O'Connor, dangerously misguided, even tragic. The death of the child confirms this fact.

In Flannery O'Connor's lifetime there were, of course, a number of committed Christians, Protestant and Catholic alike, who defined Christ's love not primarily in terms of otherworldly concerns — the human experience seen always *sub specie aeternitatis*, life as the road to somewhere else, human vision constantly tuned to the contemplation of last things and the soul's disposition — but in terms of the lessons in mutuality Christ exemplified. We remember O'Connor's interest in Simone Weil and Edith Stein, both radical thinkers whose identification with human suffering and persecution led them to extravagant gestures of solidarity and heroism. Weil especially interested O'Connor, who admired her courage and intelligence even as she acknowledged that Weil was "a trifle monstrous" (*Habit of Being* 522). Most significantly perhaps, as I have demonstrated elsewhere, Weil's aversion to abstraction and her distrust of science as a kind of "religious idolatry" were stances with which O'Connor could readily agree ("Flannery O'Connor, the Left-Wing Mystic, and the German Jew" 47). O'Connor was clearly impressed by Weil's intense search for God ("Simone Weil is a mystery that should keep us all humble, and I need it more than most" [*Habit of Being* 189]), yet Weil's refusal to convert to Catholicism and her conviction that the Roman Catholic Church exacted control and punished disobedience were disturbing positions in O'Connor's eyes. But it was Weil's identification with the poor and the suffering that became the major reason for her refusal to join the Catholic Church. For Weil, the Church seriously neglected to identify with human suffering because of its tendency to set its sights abstractly on the otherworldly and not on the here and now. Thus, the distrust of the process of abstraction shared by Weil and O'Connor (and, earlier, T. S. Eliot and Allen Tate) appeared not to be sufficient grounds for O'Connor to question the authority and rigidity of the Church and its teachings; nor was this distrust sufficiently strong in O'Connor to move her to condone (or even evince respect for) the kind of political action that characterized Weil's life.

Similarly, in the United States, Dorothy Day and the Catholic Worker Movement, surely anticipating today's liberation theology, reflected the same commitment to political and social justice. The Catholic Worker Movement began in 1940 and has continued, long past the death of Day herself, to the present time. From as early as 1953 O'Connor was aware of Dorothy Day's activities. A letter to Sally and Robert Fitzgerald alludes to a conversation O'Connor had in early 1953 with a friend of William Lynch, a Danish book salesman (presumably Erik Langkjaer, with whom, Sally Fitzgerald claims, O'Connor was in love [*O'Connor* 1247]). Langkjaer, although not a Catholic, was much interested in Dorothy Day. However, Langkjaer "couldn't see he said why [Day] fed endless lines of endless bums for whom there was no hope, she'd never see any results from that, said he." O'Connor's light mockery ends in the wry but certainly truthful conclusions that "Charity was not understandable" and that "Strange people turn up." O'Connor had not heard of Day's *Conversations at Newburgh*, and in another letter to the Fitzgeralds she alludes to Langkjaer's objection to Day's activities with a strange ambiguity: "[The Cheneys] wanted to know what *Conversations at Newburgh* were but I couldn't enlighten them. Is it some more philosophers and bums and priests conversing at a retreat at one of those farms or what?" (*Habit of Being* 58)

Day's socially committed Catholicism clearly became an easy target for O'Connor's searing satire, and matters were not helped when Dorothy Day refused to allow Caroline Gordon's novel *The Malefactors*, one of whose characters is obviously based on Day, to be dedicated to her. Moreover, she threatened to "burn every copy she could get her hands on if she had her way." Once the dedication was withdrawn, O'Connor reports to the Fitzgeralds, "Miss D. begins to like the book better" (*Habit of Being* 135). Later O'Connor underscores Caroline Gordon's intention to treat Day fairly in the novel, insisting on Gordon's great respect for Day (*Habit of Being* 167). In fact, although she also professed to admire her, O'Connor's own reaction to Day was complex.

In a letter to "A" in 1957, she recounts Dorothy Day's visit to Koinonia, an Americus, Georgia, experiment in Christian communal living in which blacks and whites resolved to work and live together (and which, in spite of efforts of the Ku Klux Klan and other racists, still continues today):

D.D. had been to Koinonia and had been shot at. All my thoughts on this subject are ugly and uncharitable — such as: that's a mighty long way to come to get shot at, etc. I admire her very much. I still think of the story about the Tennessee hillbilly who picked up his gun and said, "I'm going to Texas to fight fuhmuh rights." I hope that to be of two minds about some things is not to be neutral. (*Habit of Being* 218)

Being of two minds is not to be committed to one side or the other, that much is certain. The ambivalence evident in this letter is, I believe, typical of O'Connor and of many of her white southern contemporaries, who wanted to be dissociated from the headlined racism surrounding school segregation but, at the same time, feared those outsiders whose commitment to social justice in the South was threatening and more than a little irritating to them. Later in 1957 O'Connor clipped Dorothy Day's own account of her visit to Koinonia in the *Catholic Worker* and sent it to "A" with this revealing comment: "It would have been all right if she hadn't had to stick in her plug for Their Way of Life for Everybody" (*Habit of Being* 220). O'Connor apparently sees Day as something of the proverbial "outside agitator" and suggests in the preceding remark that the standards of charity may be relative.

Only once in O'Connor's letters does she allude to Lillian Smith, the controversial Georgia writer whose outspokenness regarding civil rights and women's issues caused her to experience the same kinds of harassment visited upon Koinonia. Until recently, Smith has been largely ignored by southern readers, although her novel *Strange Fruit*, published in 1944, was forbidden to many of us who grew up in the South in the 1950s because of its treatment of miscegenation. Furthermore, her intensely personal *Killers of the Dream*, an analysis of the racial and sexual conditioning of young white girls in the South, argues from a Protestant perspective the immorality of white male supremacy and clearly anticipates the emphasis on the social gospel of the last decades. O'Connor's reference to Smith merely acknowledges Denver Lindley's report of a compliment paid by Smith to O'Connor for a speech she had given to a gathering of Georgia writers in 1955 (*Habit of Being* 123). At no time in the letters is there any indication that O'Connor had any reaction to Smith's bold political and social stands, although we assume that O'Connor as an avid newspaper reader was well aware of the efforts on behalf of blacks made by her fellow Georgians Lillian Smith and Ralph McGill.

Of even greater concern are the contents of the unpublished letters from O'Connor to Maryat Lee, made available in 1990 for the use of scholars in the O'Connor Collection at Georgia College & State University. Although O'Connor often couched her barbs to Lee in comically affectionate language, the underlying current of racism in these letters is difficult to ignore or to rationalize. Indeed, the matter of O'Connor's attitude toward blacks was of significant concern to her Catholic friend Sally Fitzgerald, who, in the introduction to *The Habit of Being* in 1979, takes pains to acknowledge that O'Connor, whose "tongue could take on a quite unsaintly edge," possessed "an area of sensibility . . . that seems to have remained imperfectly developed, as her letters suggest" (xviii), namely, her attitude toward blacks. What Fitzgerald does not indicate, however, is that *The Habit of Being* does not include the O'Connor letters that are most likely to be labeled racist, i.e., many of those to Maryat Lee. Be that as it may, in the *Habit of Being* introduction, Fitzgerald proceeds to defend O'Connor from the charge of racism. She cites O'Connor's indignation at the crude remark of a white bus driver to a group of blacks as the catalyst for her becoming "an integrationist." Fitzgerald continues by asserting that, had O'Connor lived, she would have known "greater personal empathy with the blacks who were so important a part of the tissue of the South, and of the humanity with whose redemption she was so truly and deeply concerned." Fitzgerald notes that O'Connor's concerns were not those of writers committed to "large social issues" (xviii) and that, while O'Connor was respectful of southern blacks, she "disliked the stridency of the militant movement and some of its spokesmen, although she recognized the need for, and approved of, Martin Luther King's crusade." Fitzgerald adds that, because the blacks at Andalusia "were as primitive as some of the whites she wrote about," they may have "served as trees obscuring her view of the social forest" (xix).

However, Catherine R. Moirai, a Milledgeville acquaintance of O'Connor and a fellow Catholic, in a review of *The Habit of Being* in 1982, decries Fitzgerald's defense of O'Connor in the introduction to the letters. Moirai argues that O'Connor's "comprehension of racial issues rarely went beyond a question of good manners" (133). Commenting on O'Connor's October 1963 letter stating that the Milledgeville public library had been integrated for a year — unbeknownst to those seeking racial change — Moirai reminds us that nine Negroes with library cards is hardly integration. She observes that O'Connor "did not say (and perhaps she did not know) that the library tables were removed to prevent black and white patrons from sitting together," thus creating "an 'integration' designed in every way to accommodate racism." Obviously a disaffected Catholic, Moirai challenges O'Connor's own words in the letters concerning her intention in "The Artificial Nigger" (to "suggest" the "redemptive quality of the Negro's suffering for us all") by declaring that the statement is imbued with "arrogance": "Like the Pope discussing the glories of motherhood, Flannery O'Connor was finding benefit and meaning in someone else's situation, in a pain she would not share" (134). In a pointed summation of her objection, Moirai writes, "The church might provide Flannery with the idea of 'the redemptive quality of the Negro's suffering for us all,' but not of *her* suffering for the Negro" (137). Perhaps most important, Moirai condemns Fitzgerald's attempts "to deny or gloss over that racism even while she admits it" (134). Indeed, Alice Walker's essay "Beyond the Peacock: The Reconstruction of Flannery O'Connor," first published in *MS.* magazine in the 1970s, underscores the context of racism with its sharp differences in socioeconomics for O'Connor and Walker in central Georgia in the 1940s and 1950s. Walker, who grew up some twenty miles from where O'Connor lived, compliments O'Connor on her presentation of black characters, proclaiming O'Connor's wisdom in not presuming to think for African American characters and thus, one infers, to engage in dangerous stereotyping. Walker and Fitzgerald therefore appear (at least in the 1970s) to excuse O'Connor from racism for similar reasons, although we may still find troubling Fitzgerald's contention that O'Connor perceived black consciousness as different ("other") from white consciousness.

Fitzgerald's apologia for O'Connor's treatment of blacks in the fiction and her references to them in the letters published in *The Habit of Being* ends on this curious note:

> [O'Connor] evidently felt unable to "get inside their heads," in her own phrase. This may have been humility. In her letters, she uses the prevailing locution of the South as easily, and as unmaliciously, as it often occurs there, among blacks and whites alike. It was simply natural to her in her time and place. And if she did not live to envision fully and dramatize their role in the divine comedy, it was perhaps because it was her well-met responsibility to her gift to give dignity and meaning to the lives of individuals who have far fewer champions, and enjoy considerably less sympathy, and are far lonelier than they. (*Habit of Being* xix)

I assume that those other individuals referred to by Fitzgerald in the last sentence above are the poor whites with whom O'Connor is concerned in much of her fiction. If that is the case, Fitzgerald would have real difficulty proving that any people in the South have, historically, had fewer champions than the blacks. Furthermore, the argument that O'Connor was simply not concerned with "large social issues"—that she was not a political writer— would certainly be countered by arguments that *all* writing is political, per- haps most especially that which upholds the status quo. In fact, Catherine Moirai argues that social issues *are* present in O'Connor's work: "Displaced persons, poor white Southerners, poor black Southerners, white ladies with cold blue eyes—whoever we write about, we are also writing about the soci- ety that forms them. The way we write, what we say about the characters and their surroundings, will reflect our attitudes" (137). Indeed, one of the epi- graphs to this chapter suggests that O'Connor realized the interrelatedness of all experience and the far-reaching impact of major historical events, as is clearly evident in a story like "The Displaced Person." One does not have to subscribe to the social gospel of contemporary Christianity to understand the lessons of history concerning the subjugation of blacks in the South: that the Christian churches for the most part abdicated their responsibility to decry the inhumanity of slavery and, later, of discrimination and segregation.

Fitzgerald has continued to defend O'Connor against charges of racism, even when those charges are presented by one of O'Connor's most devoted and sensitive Christian readers, Ralph Wood. In a carefully argued delinea- tion of the difference between O'Connor's personal "opinions" and her public "convictions," published in the *Flannery O'Connor Bulletin* in 1994, Wood asserts that O'Connor privately seems to have absorbed many of the white prejudices of the time, as is evident in some of the unpublished let- ters to Maryat Lee referred to earlier. In her fiction, Wood argues, O'Con- nor demonstrates that true Christian charity is not consonant with racism. "Everything That Rises Must Converge" and "The Artificial Nigger" prove Wood's point. He states, however, that O'Connor adamantly refused John Crowe Ransom's suggestion to change the title of "The Artificial Nigger" because of his concern about its potentially controversial impact ("Where Is the Voice Coming From?" 111).

In a letter to the *Flannery O'Connor Bulletin* the following year (1995), Fitzgerald corrects Wood's assertion about the title of "The Artificial Nigger" by presenting as evidence the actual correspondence between O'Connor and Ransom. Fitzgerald's letter does acknowledge that Wood had no access to the O'Connor-Ransom exchange (it is not included in *The Habit of Being*) and that she herself was at fault for not providing Wood with the letters, especially when she had actually heard an earlier version of Wood's paper at the April 1994 O'Connor symposium at Georgia College & State University in Milledgeville and had at the time recognized that she possessed information to counter Wood's claim of O'Connor's resistance to the title change.

For Fitzgerald to focus at length on this misstatement on Wood's part is, however, for her to miss the forest for the trees. Any reader of the O'Connor-Lee correspondence, available in totality only in the O'Connor Collection in Milledgeville, is acutely aware of O'Connor's use of the "n" word, her occasional telling of a racist joke, and her preoccupation with Maryat Lee's liberalism. In fact, as I have argued elsewhere,[4] a good part of the impetus for O'Connor's creation of Julian in "Everything That Rises Must Converge" derives from Lee's account of a bus ride from North Carolina to New York at the height of the civil rights movement. Just why certain of O'Connor's letters to Lee—namely, those with the most damaging racial references—were omitted from *The Habit of Being* is a mystery.

Analysis of the content and tone of the O'Connor-Lee letters might allow a reader to conclude that O'Connor is merely putting on the "mask" or the guise of the southern white racist in order to tweak Lee's liberalism, for in no other correspondence does O'Connor use such language. However, Lee is arguably O'Connor's most intimate correspondent, and the reader might thus conjecture that O'Connor was more relaxed with Lee, more likely to let her hair down, than with others. In fact, several of Lee's letters to O'Connor suggest that Lee, a lesbian, had declared her love for O'Connor early in their friendship, only to be rebuffed by O'Connor, who was not a lesbian. However, as more than one critic has observed, Lee evoked a complex response in O'Connor; she admired Lee's rebellion against southern convention (especially against the expectations of white southern womanhood), although she was aware that, locally, Maryat Lee was seen as bizarre, a misfit, even foolish. In spite of Maryat's local image—or perhaps in part because of it—O'Connor was her friend and became the devil's advocate with her on the race issue, playing and joking in a way that surely reflects the prevalent attitudes toward race among white citizens of Milledgeville. Nevertheless, when one reads the unpublished correspondence between the two, one often finds it difficult to laugh.

As students of language well understand, the joke itself is one of the most obvious indicators of social value, hierarchy, and attitude. For example, many jokes in patriarchal society are centered around put-downs of women. Similarly, the dominant white society, especially in the southern United States, commonly makes jokes about black intelligence, motivation (or the presumed lack thereof), and physiognomy. O'Connor inherited that tradition as surely as she inherited and claimed for her own the literary tradition of the white male. The strength of that white male tradition is attested to in remarks that Alfred Kazin recently made about Allen Tate, one of O'Connor's friends and literary forebears: "[Tate] was the best of the southern critics and the most intransigently reactionary. He was a gentleman—racist even when professing Catholicism; once he actually refused to shake hands with Langston Hughes" (32). Students of O'Connor cannot help being reminded of O'Connor's refusal to meet James Baldwin in Georgia. Furthermore, if we accept Ralph Wood's distinction between O'Connor's opinions and her convictions, we must conclude that O'Connor—at the height of her career and just as the civil rights movement was raising awareness of deeply rooted racism in the South—struggled in the light of her Christian faith to embody in her fiction her own dilemma, as well as that of the so-called New South. O'Connor was not of the generation of the Fugitives (Davidson and Tate being the most adamantly conservative of the group), and although she inherited that tradition, in most cases embracing it, her own ambivalence on the race issue is evident. Perhaps the flamboyant and sometimes foolish Maryat Lee had something to do with O'Connor's apparent reluctance to adopt unquestioningly the conservative position. Surely the positions of other white southern writers outside the Fugitive tradition, including Faulkner with his moderate stance, had their impact, too.

Some readers of O'Connor's work might argue that the writer's private opinions are not relevant to the achievement of her fiction, that what matters ultimately is what the fiction conveys of the charitable Christian outlook on race and, for that matter, on other human struggles. There is certainly a measure of wisdom in that admonition, and, as a reader schooled in the New Criticism, I admit that I have found it troubling to hold expectations of the life of the author in addition to expectations of the fiction. When, however, O'Connor's letters and essays are used, as they frequently are, to demonstrate her devotion to her faith and even to suggest an almost saintlike demeanor, I must rebel. Those who make such claims for O'Connor as a person of faith should be aware that the published letters are incomplete and that some of those unpublished letters point to the genuine humanity, the human foibles, of this writer, particularly with respect to race and the civil rights movement. Furthermore, as I have tried to suggest, reading a writer's letters with discernment is often beset with difficulty; innuendo, tone, and the presence of irony are paramount considerations in evaluating any writer's private utterances.

Some might interject that such literary discernment is needed in reading any writing. However, when we consider that letters are not written with the goal of public scrutiny, that they are essentially casual and unrevised, and that they are composed with a particular idiosyncratic reader in mind, we must conclude, I believe, that the use of traditional *literary* approaches to letters is, at best, fraught with problems. This is not to say, of course, that a writer's private correspondence is without value to students of that writer's work. I am suggesting, nevertheless, some of the variables that should be weighed as we peruse personal correspondence. Not the least of those variables is a determination of the completeness of the correspondence prior to using letters to support a particular thesis. Further, when that thesis concerns the wholeness—indeed, even the slippery matter of the *sanctity* — of a writer's life, extra caution seems called for. I am inclined to conclude that statements based on letters and anecdotal evidence about a writer's private life should always be qualified or stated tentatively, as I have tried to do in this study. Although one might not necessarily agree with those "stern Shakespearean scholars [who] may say that *Hamlet* would be the same whether Shakespeare were sitting or standing" (Gittings 19), surely a certain wariness in evaluating a writer's letters and other private utterances is called for.

What does it mean, therefore, to say that in many of her beliefs and attitudes Flannery O'Connor was not a saint, that is, that she may have failed sometimes in her personal life to live up to ideals of Christian solidarity with racial, social, and political outcasts? I do not believe that the power of her fiction will be damaged by such an observation. In fact, I strongly believe that students of O'Connor's work will likely experience the deepening impact of that fiction in light of knowing something of O'Connor's own personal, social, and literary background; her commitment to Roman Catholicism; and her interaction with her "intimate" community, the membership of which ranges from the savvy and practical businesswoman Regina Cline

O'Connor to the devout Catholic apologist Sally Fitzgerald to the renegade, rebellious Maryat Lee and the brilliant and eccentric Betty Hester ("A"). To shut the door to the possibility of such knowledge and investigation is to deny O'Connor her full humanity and to reduce her life and her work to pious platitude or to dogmatic exemplum.

Epilogue
The Obedient Imagination

By the phrase "the obedient imagination" I have intended to suggest something of an oxymoron—the paradox by which the devout Catholic writer creates and explores fictive worlds and yet works within the limits of faithful obedience to the hierarchical Church. I have meant, furthermore, to suggest a kind of tension that necessarily comes from that paradox; the imagination, by definition free-ranging and risk-taking, is reined in by the teaching and guidance of the Church. In her own view, Flannery O'Connor's devout Catholicism enabled her to possess the freedom to write, to put on "the habit of art" (*Habit of Being* 136), and to express such convictions as the following:

> I believe that the writer's moral sense must coincide with his dramatic sense and this means that moral judgment has to be implicit in the act of vision. Let me make no bones about it: I write from the standpoint of Christian orthodoxy. . . . I write with the solid belief in *all* the Christian dogmas. I find that this in no way limits my freedom as a writer and that it increases rather than decreases my vision. (*Habit of Being* 147)

The writer's "dramatic sense" I take to refer to the capacity of the imagination to explore, to invent, and to bring that "invention" to life. The "moral sense," of course, refers to the conscience; more specifically, to those inclinations to goodness and to the holy that are shaped, guided, and taught by the authority of the Church. O'Connor's statement is therefore an excellent, concise summary of her authorial intention as a Catholic writer. One might well argue that O'Connor's very success as a fiction writer depends on the tension in her work between her powerful imagination and her ultimate obedience to the Church.

Thus, O'Connor's sense of obedience was formed chiefly by the Roman Catholic Church. Certainly the teaching of the Church was complemented by her upbringing as a white southern woman in a mannered society with high expectations for its females to "do pretty." Although O'Connor rebelled to a certain extent against those expectations in both her life and her work, she remained, in significant ways, a true daughter of the white, conservative, patriarchal South. Furthermore, her literary education, greatly influenced by the modernist male writers, by the male New Critics and their emphasis on the impersonality of the artist, and by her reading in Catholic aesthetic thinkers like William Lynch, helped to create in her a habit of art that was strong, disciplined, and obedient.

As is illustrated in Man Martin's humorous flowchart (page 247), the plots of O'Connor's stories may appear to follow a similar pattern. Indeed, when many of these stories are reduced to brief plot summaries, the reader understands a certain predictable unpredictability, or unpredictable predictability. By story's end, the reader is prepared for the worst. This characteristic is now inextricably associated with O'Connor's short stories, and my observation of that fact is certainly not meant as a criticism. At least a few of the stories, however, do not fit this pattern; in fact, the last story that O'Connor

Flannery O'Connor Computer

Simply follow the lines to compose your own Flannery O'Connor masterpiece

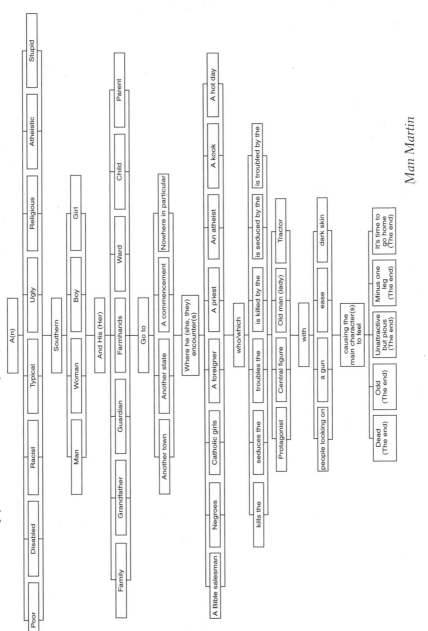

Man Martin

completed before her death, "Parker's Back," defies the plot delineated by Martin's flowchart and, in my view, is a fitting conclusion to O'Connor's lamentably brief career.

"Parker's Back" brings together most of the concerns of O'Connor's canon, and it presents what might be seen as a parable of obedience. It stands alone among O'Connor's work, however, because of its tone and narrative stance. Here is less, far less, of the fierce narrator of the earlier work, as I shall try to demonstrate.

O. E. Parker possesses the same urge for the holy that characterizes Hazel Motes and Francis Marion Tarwater. His "urge" exists on a far more primitive level than that of Motes or Tarwater; it begins in an epiphanic sense of wonder when, in his youth, Parker views the tattooed man:

> Parker had never before felt the least motion of wonder in himself. Until he saw the man at the fair, it did not enter his mind that there was anything out of the ordinary about the fact that he existed. Even then it did not enter his head, but a peculiar unease settled in him. It was as if a blind boy had been turned so gently in a different direction that he did not know his destination had been changed. (*O'Connor* 658)

This incident marks the start of Parker's journey to salvation. His obsession thereafter with tattoos is O'Connor's way of dramatizing his wonder at creation, his need to celebrate it in the only way he knows how. As other commentators have observed, Parker's tattoos begin with representations of the inanimate, move to the animate and human, and end with the divine — in the figure of Christ imprinted (one wants to say "impressed") upon his back. Parker's youthful experience with the tattooed man at the fair is only the beginning of his conversion, his being "turned." His later experience of the call in the field resembles that of Moses at the burning bush. Having earlier considered placing a tattoo of God on the only undecorated part of his body in order to get the attention of his strict wife, Sarah Ruth, Parker is now convinced that this is his mission.

Parker's grave error, however, is in placing his faith and hope in Sarah Ruth and what she represents — a stringent, joyless church that narrowly defines obedience as denial of pleasure, as recognition of the ubiquity of sin and the necessity for punishment. She disapproves of all of his tattoos as "[v]anity of vanities" (660) and is especially horrified, at the story's conclusion, by the tattoo of Christ ("Idolatry! . . . Idolatry!" [674]). She does not find pleasure in the physical, she dislikes colors, and she forbids herself to experience any joy in life. Therefore, when Parker returns from town, having suffered the pain of two days' worth of tattooing and the subsequent humiliation of public mockery of the tattoo, he expects his wife to understand and to justify his action.

Parker's initial sight of the Byzantine Christ in the picture book at the tattoo parlor somehow directed him: "GO BACK" (667). The "all-demanding eyes" of the Christ are so compelling to Parker that before they are finally etched on his back (as the last element of his tattoo), he undergoes a horrible night at the Haven of Light Mission:

> He longed miserably for Sarah Ruth. Her sharp tongue and icepick eyes were the only comfort he could bring to mind. He decided he was losing it. Her eyes appeared soft and dilatory compared with the eyes in the book, for even though he could not summon up the exact look of those eyes, he could still feel their *penetration*. He felt as though, under their gaze, he was as transparent as the wings of a fly. (669, my emphasis)

The next day, when the eyes of Christ have been added, Parker is forced by the artist to look at the tattoo. At first reluctant to do so, Parker finally submits: "The eyes in the face continued to look at him—still straight, all-demanding, enclosed in silence" (670). After quickly consuming a pint of whiskey and getting embroiled in a fight (one might add, for Christ's sake), Parker finds himself sitting on the ground and contemplating his soul: "He saw it as a spider web of facts and lies that was not at all important to him but which appeared to be necessary in spite of his opinion. The eyes that were now forever on his back were eyes to be *obeyed*. He was as certain of it as he had ever been of anything" (672, my emphasis).

Parker's next thought is a misguided but understandable one: He will find Sarah Ruth. He reasons, "She would know what he had to do. She would clear up the rest of it, and she would at least be pleased" (761). Although Sarah Ruth does force Parker to speak his full name, Obadiah Elihue, before she allows him to enter the house—a requirement that, the reader infers, will allow Parker to discover his true Christian and prophetic identity—she is ultimately not the appropriate spiritual guide for Parker. Denouncing the tattoo as idolatry because God "don't *look*. . . . He's a spirit. No man shall see his face" (674), Sarah Ruth seizes the broom, beats Parker across the shoulders, and causes him to flee the house. When she looks out, her eyes harden when she sees "him—who called himself Obadiah Elihue—leaning against the tree, crying like a baby" (675).

Sarah Ruth is mistaken in her condescending view of Parker, although she sees more than she knows when she perceives him as "crying like a baby." I believe this descriptive phrase contains perhaps the most important words in the story, for in it is contained the essence of the experience of spiritual rebirth, of being "born again," as Protestants might describe it. Moreover, the phrase points to Parker's profound need for spiritual guidance and teaching, needs that O'Connor believed could be filled only by the Roman Catholic Church.

In his essay "The Vision of the Way," an excerpt from his 1945 book *The Heart of Man* (in O'Connor's private library), Gerald Vann reminds us that the Ten Commandments forbid certain actions because they are "sins against love" (282), arguing that Christ came to offer us abundant life as we live in love (283). Sarah Ruth's life-denying, primitive position is clearly opposed to the teaching of the Church in this regard. She does not see that virtue is based in "humility," by means of which the new Christian embodies "the dependence and smallness of the child." Vann further asserts that the Christian duty is "to rediscover the world" and "to show . . . the unity of the family of creation" (286). Parker's tattooed body surely demonstrates the fullness and unity of creation; Sarah Ruth's disapproval of the tattoos suggests her disapproval of the world and the flesh—a disapproval that, of course, reflects the Manichaean heresy.

O'Connor, however, rather obviously expresses her own disapproval of Sarah Ruth and her form of spirituality. In perhaps the clearest repudiation of Manichaeanism in all of her works, O'Connor presents Sarah Ruth's foolishness in rejecting creation, denying joy. Vann states that desire for joy is a part of the experience of God's love (288). Furthermore, he states that "still today the Church's office and privilege is to bless and heal—to bless the earth and the fruits of the earth, to bless the animals, to bless mankind, and to heal the sick in body and mind, to heal by prayer and blessing to heal through the liturgy which has such power to restore and integrate the unconscious" (289). The life of faith, Vann asserts, involves the necessity to "put on Christ" and thereby "to be made whole." Baptism, "the sacrament of the child," is provided by the Church, who is the "mother" (290). Unlike Parker's own strictly fundamentalist mother and unlike his wife, Sarah Ruth, the Church offers through the liturgy and through its guidance the essential comfort that Parker needs.

Parker's childlike stance at the conclusion of the story signals that, in putting on the image of Christ, he is ready for spiritual guidance and direction that only "Mother Church" can provide. Sarah Ruth is therefore the antithesis of what O. E. Parker needs. To my way of thinking, this story may be O'Connor's most clearly Catholic narrative, though the Catholicism presented here is a gentler, more mellow one than we have previously seen. Rebuking the Manichaean heresy (of which *Wise Blood* and other early works stand accused), O'Connor presents a character whose simplicity and instinctive urge for the holy are compelling. If Parker's attraction to Sarah Ruth and his clinging to her for something she can never provide are misguided, Parker is nonetheless to be commended for following his spiritual instinct. The "all-demanding eyes" of Christ present Parker with a far more significant challenge than Sarah Ruth's "icepick" eyes. Sight and vision are obviously as important in O'Connor's last work as these images were in *Wise Blood*. Like Paul who was knocked flat by his blinding vision, O. E. Parker and Hazel Motes are returned to true vision only when they are able to see themselves for what they really are, spider webs of sin.

O'Connor suggests that Parker will find the opportunity for true obedience only within the Church. Like Hazel Motes, he sees the error of his life and seeks to correct it in the only way he knows how. Unlike Hazel, however, Parker loves the world and seeks a binding connection to it. That, in both instances, O'Connor uses a male protagonist for the spiritual quest does not surprise us. That she sees the female as ancillary to the quest, suggesting, as Sarah Ruth does, both the temptress (or a comic version thereof) *and* the naysayer should also not surprise us. Such is the air O'Connor breathed, as a Roman Catholic and by this time as a member of the patriarchal literary establishment. Nevertheless, I see "Parker's Back" as a decided softening on O'Connor's part, as a moving acceptance of this world, as a true comedy in its celebration of divine love. It is as though O'Connor can envision the inhabitants of Taulkinham now looking up at the night sky and actually seeing the "vast construction work that involve[s] the whole of creation and [will] take all time to complete" (*Wise Blood* 19). As Gerald Vann observes, "The modern West has reached a chilly cerebral state in its evolution; think how it might be helped and perhaps be saved from complete dessication by the might of the seraphs, those spirits whom Christian tradition associates especially with fire, with the burning love which is the power of wonder" (294). We might speculate that because this story comes at the end of her career and of her life, O'Connor in her last illness saw in sharpest clarity the wonders of creation.

Flannery O'Connor's O. E. Parker presents us with the strongest affirmation of the might of the seraphs. Somehow I do not worry about what will become of him. And as for what would have become of O'Connor's fiction had she lived, I can only conclude that "Parker's Back" seems to anticipate a new direction and a fuller acceptance of that love which, in poet Richard Wilbur's words, "calls us to the things of this world."

Notes

1. Questions of Authority and Power

1. A shorter version of this chapter, "'The Crop': Limitation, Restraint, and Possibility," appeared in *Flannery O'Connor: New Perspectives*, ed. Sura Rath and Mary Neff Shaw (Athens: U of Georgia P, 1996), 96–121.

2. Excerpts from the unpublished work of Flannery O'Connor are used by permission of the literary executor, Robert Giroux. Copyright © 2000 by the Estate of Flannery O'Connor. Location in the Flannery O'Connor Collection at Georgia College & State University will be indicated parenthetically in the text with the citation *Collection* followed by the file number.

3. Gilbert and Gubar provide illuminating commentary on the impact of *The Waste Land*, especially its treatment of the fear of gender blurring. They conclude that Woolf's *Mrs. Dalloway* was, in part, a "revision" of *The Waste Land*, although still reflective of the "postwar misogyny" internalized by many women writers (*War of the Words* 311). They also cite the misogyny and fear of sexual confusion in Joyce's *Ulysses*, D. H. Lawrence's "The Fox," West's *Miss Lonelyhearts*, Sherwood Anderson's "The Man Who Became a Woman," James T. Farrell's "Just Boys," and Hemingway's posthumous *Garden of Eden* (341–66).

2. The Case of the Fierce Narrator

1. See my essay "Maryat and Julian and the 'Not So Bloodless Revolution,'" *Flannery O'Connor Bulletin* 21 (1992): 25–36, which explores the idea that Julian is, in large measure, *both* Flannery O'Connor, in her relationship with her mother, and Maryat Lee, whose actual experience on a bus during the civil rights movement in all likelihood inspired the plot of the story.

2. Virginia Wray's essay "'An Afternoon in the Woods': Flannery O'Connor's Discovery of Theme," in the *Flannery O'Connor Bulletin* 20 (1991): 45–53, is most helpful in describing this story's evolution.

3. Literary Lessons: The Male Gaze, the Figure Woman

1. See Sally Fitzgerald's essay "The Owl and the Nightingale," *Flannery O'Connor Bulletin* 13 (1984): 44–58, esp. 57.

2. As indicated in chapter 1, n. 2, excerpts from the unpublished work of Flannery O'Connor are used by permission of the literary executor, Robert Giroux. Copyright © 2000 by the Estate of Flannery O'Connor. When the text is clear, I will not repeat the word *Collection* in the parenthetical reference; I will include only file and page numbers.

3. I will develop Lynch's theory and the idea of incarnational art in chapter 4.

4. Many modernist works also contain that aridity and chaos found in the modern landscape, perhaps most significantly for our purposes Graham Greene's *Heart of the Matter*. Descriptions of landscape in this work also bear strong resemblance to landscape descriptions in *Wise Blood*.

5. Although several critics have commented on O'Connor's indebtedness to Nathanael West's *Miss Lonelyhearts* for the name Shrike, no critic has remarked that James Thurber wrote a tale called "The Shrike and the Chipmunks" and, more significantly, created a male character named Shrike in his cartoons.

6. The similarity between the image of Christ's whip or scourge in this passage and the whiplike power of Sabbath's gaze in 97, 9—"the look of her eyes was deep and hard like the cut of leather across the skin"—would seem to underscore both Sabbath's fierce belief in a punitive Christ and the association of fleshly punishment with the religious impulse.

7. Haze Motes in *Wise Blood* is repeatedly described as straining forward, as in this passage in the final chapter, in which Mrs. Flood observes her blind tenant: "His face had a peculiar pushing look, as if it were going forward after something it could just distinguish in the distance. Even when he was sitting motionless in a chair, his face had the look of straining toward something. But she knew he was totally blind" (214).

4. The Gentleman Caller and the Anagogical Imagination

1. Perhaps O'Connor here inadvertently reveals her own assumption that the writer is male by her use of the metaphor of the Medusa, whose look turned *men* to stone. As we have seen, such an assumption was the rule, not the exception, among most women writers of O'Connor's time, and it continues among some writers even today. May Sarton's poem "The Muse as Medusa" and Sylvia Plath's "Medusa" may be seen as attempts to adapt the role of the gorgon—with very different effects—to the role of the *woman* writer.

2. Hopkins's journal contains a vivid description of the inscape of the peacock in the following passage:

May 17 etc—I have several times seen the peacock with train spread lately. It has a very regular warp, like a shell, in which the bird embays himself, the bulge being inwards below but the hollow inwards above, cooping him in and only opening towards the brim, where the feathers are beginning to rive apart. The eyes, which lie alternately when the train is shut, like scales or gadroons, fall into irregular rows when it is opened, and then it thins and darkens against the light, it loses the moistness and satin it has when in the pack but takes another grave and expressive splendour, and the outermost eyes, detached and singled, give with their corner fringers the suggestion of that inscape of the flowing cusped trefoil which is often effective in art. He shivers it when he first rears it and then again at intervals and when this happens the rest blurs and the eyes start forward.—I have thought it looks like a tray or green basket or fresh-cut willow hurdle set all over with Paradise fruits cut through—first through a beard of golden fibre and then through wet flesh greener than greengages or purpler than grapes—or say that the knife had caught a tatter or flag of the skin and laid it flat across the flesh—and then within all a sluggish corner drop of black or purple oil. (208–9)

3. In a note to this chapter, Ragen cites a conversation with feminist critic Elaine Showalter in which she stressed that "automobiles often appear as images of the female body." Ragen counters, however, by asserting that the automobile is "like the West itself" and "cannot involve the male, through procreation, in history or the ties of society" (212, n. 5). Thus he argues that in the traditional American plot only actual human females can link the male protagonist to the responsibility of his humanity. As I stated before, Ragen asserts that O'Connor is parodying this common plot in American literature. However, I cannot find convincing evidence of such intent, and I call attention once again to the ancillary function of the female in assisting the salvation of the male.

4. See my essay "The News from Afar: A Note on Structure in O'Connor's Narratives," *Flannery O'Connor Bulletin* 14 (1985): 80–87.

5. Although there are hints throughout the story that Joy/Hulga possesses a dissociated sensibility, perhaps nowhere is that idea more evident than in the "seduction" scene with Manley Pointer in the hayloft. The Bible salesman's kiss is described as producing "that extra surge of adrenalin" that, in Joy/Hulga's case, created a "power [that] went at once to the brain." In her initial need for power and control, Joy/Hulga decides that the kiss is "an unexceptional experience and all a matter of the mind's control" (*O'Connor* 278). Later, as the physical encounter intensifies, the young woman is surprised at Manley Pointer's request to see where her wooden leg joins on. She is convinced of his sincerity and innocence, however, when he assures her that the leg is "what makes [her] different," proving that she is as susceptible to flattery—or the power of words to manipulate—as anybody else. The following sentences underscore her dissociated sensibility: "She sat staring at him. There was nothing about her face or her round freezing-blue eyes to indicate that this had moved her, but she felt as if her heart had stopped and left her mind to pump her blood" (281). And when she begins to realize that her lover is not going to reattach the leg, Joy/Hulga recognizes her weakened state: "Without the leg she felt entirely dependent on him. Her brain seemed to have stopped thinking and to be about some other function that it was not very good at" (282).

6. Mrs. Hopewell's discovery of Joy/Hulga's reading matter is further evidence of her fearful perception that her own view of reality—as circumscribed by her platitudinous language—is threatened by her daughter. The quotation from Heidegger that Mrs. Hopewell reads—asserting in its circuitous way that science is interested only in tangible reality—is described as "work[ing] on Mrs. Hopewell like some evil incantation in gibberish." She immediately closes the book and leaves the room "as if she were having a chill" (*O'Connor* 269).

7. As if in further underscoring the importance of language and the power it possesses for distortion, Mr. Shortley learns that he has "a gift" for talking and begins to

tell his "story" to anyone who will listen, particularly the blacks. Indeed, his words are a wildly comic distortion of the banal and the historic, as this passage indicates:

> "All men was created free and equal," he said to Mrs. McIntyre, "and I risked my life and limb to prove it. Gone over there and fought and bled and died and come back on over here and find out who's got my job — just exactly who I been fighting. It was a hand-grenade come that near to killing me and I seen who throwed it — little man with eyeglasses just like his. Might have bought them at the same store. Small world," and he gave a bitter little laugh. (*O'Connor* 323)

Mr. Shortley maintains, furthermore, that language differences are often the only way to distinguish between "us" and "them." He informs Sulk that if he ever travels again, he will visit either China or Africa because, he says, "You go to either of them two places and you can tell right away what the difference is between you and them. You go to these other places and the only way you can tell is if they say something. And then you can't always tell because about half of them know the English language. That's where we make our mistake," he says, "letting all them people onto English. There'd be a heap less trouble if everybody only knew his own language. My wife said knowing two languages was like having eyes in the back of your head. You couldn't put nothing over on her." Thus, in his view, language serves as an indicator of power and trust, with the English language being the standard. That non-native speakers have appropriated the language with our permission (we let them "onto English") is, in Mr. Shortley's view, the source of much of our difficulty. Sulk's own ignorance and fear are reflected in his response praising Mrs. Shortley: "She was fine. She was sho fine. I never known a finer white woman than her" (*O'Connor* 324). In these statements Sulk demonstrates his own skill in adopting a cliché for the purposes of appeasement.

8. Asals's contention is a questionable one if we consider Hazel Motes's death; surely Haze "pays" for his vision with his life.

5. Communities: The Historic, the Orthodox, the Intimate

1. See Allen Tate's "Religion and the Old South" in *Reactionary Essays on Poetry and Ideas* (New York: Scribner's, 1936), 167–90, esp. 175–76, for a full explanation of "the long view" and "the short view." Essentially Tate defines the long view as one of cultural relativism by means of which, for example, the Resurrection of Christ is seen as simply another manifestation of the dying god of eastern vegetation myths. The "short view," on the other hand, places ultimate value on the Christian mystery, evidence of God's only entry into human history. It is appropriately deemed the eschatological vision.

2. See Tate's essay "The Man of Letters in the Modern World," in *Essays of Four Decades* (Chicago: Swallow, 1968), 3–16.

3. For a discussion of O'Connor's literary group in Milledgeville, see Jean Cash, "Milledgeville, 1957–1960: O'Connor's 'Pseudo-Literary and Theological Gatherings,'" *Flannery O'Connor Bulletin* 18 (1989): 13–27.

4. Sarah Gordon, "Maryat and Julian and the 'Not So Bloodless Revolution,'" *Flannery O'Connor Bulletin* 21 (1992): 25–36.

Works Cited

Acocella, Joan. "After the Laughs." *New Yorker* August 16, 1993: 76–81.

Asals, Frederick. *Flannery O'Connor: The Imagination of Extremity.* Athens: U of Georgia P, 1982.

Bacon, Jon Lance. *Flannery O'Connor and Cold War Culture.* New York: Cambridge UP, 1993.

Baym, Nina. "Melodramas of Beset Manhood: How Theories of American Fiction Exclude Women Authors." *The New Feminist Criticism: Essays on Women, Literature, Theory.* Ed. Elaine Showalter. New York: Pantheon, 1985. 63–80.

Brinkmeyer, Robert H. *The Art and Vision of Flannery O'Connor.* Baton Rouge: Louisiana State UP, 1989.

Brooks, Cleanth, and Robert Penn Warren. *Understanding Fiction*. New York: Appleton-Century-Crofts, 1943.

Carroll, James. "The Silence." *New Yorker* April 7, 1997: 52–68.

Cash, Jean. "Maryat and 'Flanneryat': An Antithetical Friendship." *Flannery O'Connor Bulletin* 19 (1990): 56–74.

———. "Milledgeville, 1957–1960: O'Connor's 'Pseudo-Literary and Theological Gatherings.'" *Flannery O'Connor Bulletin* 18 (1989): 13–27.

Cash, W. J. *The Mind of the South*. New York: Knopf, 1941.

Clark, Katerina, and Michael Holquist. *Mikhail Bakhtin*. Cambridge: Harvard UP, 1984.

Crews, Frederick. "The Power of Flannery O'Connor." *New York Review of Books* 26 April 1990: 49–55.

Desmond, John. *Risen Sons: Flannery O'Connor's Vision of History*. Athens: U of Georgia P, 1987.

Dunn, Robert, and Stephen Driggers, eds., with Sarah Gordon. *The Manuscripts of Flannery O'Connor at Georgia College*. Athens: U of Georgia P, 1989.

Eagleton, Terry. *Literary Theory: An Introduction*. Minneapolis: U of Minnesota P, 1983.

Eliot, T. S. *Four Quartets. T. S. Eliot: The Complete Poems and Plays*. New York: Harcourt, 1962. 117–45.

———. "Hysteria." *T. S. Eliot: Collected Poems, 1909–1935*. New York: Harcourt, 1936. 37.

———. *The Waste Land. T. S. Eliot: The Complete Poems and Plays*. New York: Harcourt. 37–55.

Fetterley, Judith. "Reading about Reading: 'A Jury of Her Peers,' 'The Murders in the Rue Morgue,' 'The Yellow Wallpaper.'" *Gender and Reading: Essays on Readers, Texts, and Contexts*. Ed. Elizabeth A. Flynn and Patrocinio P. Schweikart. Baltimore: Johns Hopkins UP, 1986. 147–64.

———. *The Resisting Reader: A Feminist Approach to American Fiction*. Bloomington: Indiana UP, 1978.

Fitzgerald, Sally. "An Interview with Sally Fitzgerald." Susan Elizabeth Howe et al. *Flannery O'Connor and the Christian Mystery. Literature and Belief* 17 (1997): nos. 1, 2. 1–20.

———. "Letter to the Editor." *Flannery O'Connor Bulletin* 23 (1995): 175–82.

———. "The Owl and the Nightingale." *Flannery O'Connor Bulletin* 13 (1984): 44–58.

Friedman, Melvin J. "Introduction." *Critical Essays on Flannery O'Connor*. Ed. Melvin J. Friedman and Beverly Lyon Clark. Boston: Hall, 1985. 1–15.

Gentry, Marshall Bruce. *Flannery O'Connor's Religion of the Grotesque*. Jackson: U of Mississippi P, 1986.

Giannone, Richard. *Flannery O'Connor and the Mystery of Love*. Urbana: U of Illinois P, 1989.

Gilbert, Sandra, and Susan Gubar. *The War of the Words*. Vol. 1 of *No Man's Land: The Place of the Woman Writer in the Twentieth Century*. New Haven: Yale UP, 1988.

———. *Sexchanges*. Vol. 2 of *No Man's Land: The Place of the Woman Writer in the Twentieth Century*. New Haven: Yale UP, 1989.

Gish, Nancy K. "T. S. Eliot (1888–1965)." *The Gender of Modernism: A Critical Anthology*. Ed. Bonnie Kime Scott. Bloomington: Indiana UP, 1990. 139–55.

Gittings, Robert. *The Nature of Biography*. Seattle: U of Washington P, 1978.

Gopnik, Alan. "The Great Deflator." *New Yorker* June 27, July 4, 1994: 169–77.

Gordon, Caroline. "Old Red." *Understanding Fiction*. Ed. Cleanth Brooks and Robert Penn Warren. New York: Appleton-Century-Crofts, 1943. 124–47.

Gordon, Caroline, and Allen Tate, eds. *The House of Fiction: An Anthology of the Short Story with Commentary by Caroline Gordon and Allen Tate*. 2nd ed. New York: Scribner's, 1960.

Gordon, Mary. "Getting Here from There: A Writer's Reflections on a Religious Past." *Good Boys and Dead Girls and Other Essays*. New York: Viking, 1991. 160–75.

———. "Good Boys and Dead Girls." *Good Boys and Dead Girls and Other Essays*. New York: Viking, 1991. 3–23.

Gordon, Sarah. "Flannery O'Connor, the Left-Wing Mystic, and the German Jew." *Flannery O'Connor Bulletin* 16 (1987): 43–51.

———. "Maryat and Julian and the 'Not So Bloodless Revolution.'" *Flannery O'Connor Bulletin* 21 (1992): 25–36.

———. "The News from Afar: A Note on Structure in O'Connor's Narratives." *Flannery O'Connor Bulletin* 14 (1985): 80–87.

Haggard, H. Rider. *She: A History of Adventure*. Mattituck, N.Y.: Amereon House, 1976.

Hamilton, Barbara Tunnicliff. "Flannery in Iowa City." Unpublished essay. Flannery O'Connor Collection. Ina Dillard Russell Library, Georgia College & State University, Milledgeville.

Harrison, Beverly Wildung. "The Power of Anger in the Work of Love: Christian Ethics for Women and Other Strangers." *Weaving the Visions: New Patterns in Feminist Spirituality*. Ed. Judith Plaskow and Carol P. Christ. San Francisco: Harper, 1989. 214–25.

Hawkes, John. "Dark Landscapes." *In Praise of What Persists*. Ed. Stephen Berg. New York: Harper, 1983. 135–47.

———. "Flannery O'Connor's Devil." *Sewanee Review* 70 (1962): 395–407.

Hendin, Josephine. *The World of Flannery O'Connor*. Bloomington: Indiana UP, 1970.

Hopkins, Gerard Manley. *Gerard Manley Hopkins*. Ed. Catherine Phillips. Oxford: Oxford UP, 1986.

Jacobus, Mary. "The Difference of View." *The Feminist Reader: Essays in Gender and the Politics of Literary Criticism*. New York: Blackwell, 1989.

James, Henry. "The Art of Fiction." *Norton Anthology of American Literature*. Shorter 3rd ed. Ed. Baym et al. New York: Norton, 1989. 1472–86.

Jones, Anne Goodwyn. *Tomorrow Is Another Day: The Woman Writer in the South*. Baton Rouge: Louisiana State UP, 1981.

Kahane, Claire Katz. "The Gothic Mirror." *The (M)other Tongue: Essays in Feminist Psychoanalytic Interpretation*. Ed. Shirley Nelson Garner et al. Ithaca: Cornell UP, 1985. 334–52.

Kazin, Alfred. *Writing Was Everything*. Cambridge: Harvard UP, 1995.

Kinney, Arthur F. *Flannery O'Connor's Library: Resources of Being*. Athens: U of Georgia P, 1985.

Lodge, David. *After Bakhtin: Essays on Fiction and Criticism*. London: Routledge, 1990.

Lynch, William F. *Christ and Apollo: The Dimensions of the Literary Imagination*. New York: Mentor-Omega, 1963.

———. "Theology and the Imagination." *Thought* 29 (Spring 1954): 61–86.

MacKethan, Lucinda H. *Daughters of Time: Creating Woman's Voice in Southern Story*. Athens: U of Georgia P, 1990.

Marcus, Jane. "Antonia White (1899–1980)." *The Gender of Modernism: A Critical Anthology*. Ed. Bonnie Kime Scott. Bloomington: Indiana UP, 1990. 597–612.

May, John R. *The Pruning Word: Parables of Flannery O'Connor*. Notre Dame: U of Notre Dame P, 1976.

Michaels, J. Ramsey. "'The Oldest Nun at the Sisters of Mercy': O'Connor's Saints and Martyrs." *Flannery O'Connor Bulletin* 13 (Autumn 1984): 80–86.

Miles, Margaret R. *Carnal Knowing: Female Nakedness and Religious Meaning in the Christian West*. Boston: Beacon, 1989.

Moirai, Catherine R. Review of *The Habit of Being: Letters of Flannery O'Connor*. *Feminary* (Fall 1982): 129–46.

Mossberg, Barbara A. C. *Emily Dickinson: When a Writer Is a Daughter*. Bloomington: Indiana UP, 1982.

Ochs, Carol. *Women and Spirituality*. Totowa, NJ: Rowman, 1983.

O'Connor, Flannery. "Biologic Endeavor." *Corinthian* (Spring 1944): 7, 18.

———. *The Complete Stories*. New York: Farrar, 1971.

———. "Education's Only Hope." *Corinthian* (Spring 1945): 14–15.

———. *Flannery O'Connor: Collected Works*. Ed. Sally Fitzgerald. New York: Library of America, 1988.

———. *The Habit of Being: Letters*. Ed. Sally Fitzgerald. New York: Farrar, 1979.

———. *Mystery and Manners: Occasional Prose*. Ed. Sally and Robert Fitzgerald. New York: Farrar, 1969.

———. "Peabodite Reveals Strange Hobby." *Peabody Palladium*. Tuesday, December 16, 1941. Rpt. in *Flannery O'Connor Bulletin* 19 (1990): 54.

———. *The Presence of Grace and Other Book Reviews*. Comp. by Leo J. Zuber. Ed. Carter W. Martin. Athens: U of Georgia P, 1983.

———. *The Violent Bear It Away. Flannery O'Connor: Collected Works*. Ed. Sally Fitzgerald. New York: Library of America, 1988.

———. *Wise Blood. Flannery O'Connor: Collected Works*. Ed. Sally Fitzgerald. New York: Library of America, 1988.

Park, Clara Claiborne. "Crippled Laughter: Toward Understanding Flannery O'Connor." *American Scholar* 51 (Spring 1982): 249–57.

Parker, Dorothy. *Here Lies: The Collected Stories of Dorothy Parker*. New York: Literary Guild, 1939.

Percy, Walker. "Notes for a Novel about the End of the World." *The Message in the Bottle: How Queer Man Is, How Queer Language Is, and What One Has to Do with the Other*. New York: Farrar, 1975. 101–18.

Poe, Edgar Allan. *The Complete Tales and Poems of Edgar Allan Poe*. Introd. Hervey Allen. New York: Modern Library, 1938.

Prenshaw, Peggy Whitman, ed. *Conversations with Eudora Welty*. Jackson: U of Mississippi P, 1984. 131–41.

Pyron, Darden Asbury. *Southern Daughter: The Life of Margaret Mitchell*. New York: Oxford UP, 1991.

Ragen, Brian Abel. *A Wreck on the Road to Damascus: Innocence, Guilt, and Conversion in Flannery O'Connor*. Chicago: Loyola UP, 1989.

Rubin, Louis D., Jr. "Flannery O'Connor's Company of Southerners; or, 'The Artificial Nigger' Read as Fiction Rather than Theology." *Flannery O'Connor Bulletin* 6 (1977): 47–71.

Russ, Joanna. *How to Suppress Women's Writing*. Austin: U of Texas P, 1983.

Scarry, Elaine. *The Body in Pain: The Making and Unmaking of the World*. Oxford: Oxford UP, 1987.

Scott, Anne Firor. *The Southern Lady: From Pedestal to Politics*. Chicago: U of Chicago P, 1970.

Scott, Bonnie Kime. "Introduction." *The Gender of Modernism: A Critical Anthology.* Ed. Bonnie Kime Scott. Bloomington: Indiana UP, 1990. 1–18.

Sewell, Elizabeth. "The Imagination of Graham Greene." *Thought* 29 (Spring 1954): 51–60.

Shloss, Carol. *Flannery O'Connor's Dark Comedies: The Limits of Inference.* Baton Rouge: Louisiana State UP, 1980.

Simpson, Lewis. *The Brazen Face of History: Studies in the Literary Consciousness of America.* Baton Rouge: Louisiana State UP, 1980.

Smith, Lillian. *Killers of the Dream.* New York: W. W. Norton, 1949.

———. *Strange Fruit.* New York: Reynal and Hitchcock, 1944.

Stephens, Martha. *The Question of Flannery O'Connor.* Baton Rouge: Louisiana State UP, 1973.

Tate, Allen. "The Man of Letters in the Modern World." *Essays of Four Decades.* Chicago: Swallow, 1968. 3–16.

———. *Ode to the Confederate Dead. The Fugitive Poets: Modern Southern Poetry in Perspective.* Ed. William Pratt. Nashville: Sanders, 1991. 67–69.

———. "The Profession of Letters in the South." *Reactionary Essays on Poetry and Ideas.* New York: Scribner's, 1936. 145–66.

———. "Religion and the Old South." *Reactionary Essays on Poetry and Ideas.* New York: Scribner's, 1936. 167–90.

Tate, J. O. "The Essential Essex." *Flannery O'Connor Bulletin* 12 (1983): 47–59.

———. "O'Connor's Confederate General: A Late Encounter." *Flannery O'Connor Bulletin* 8 (1979): 45–53.

———. "On Flannery O'Connor: Citizen of the South and Citizen of the World." *Flannery O'Connor Bulletin* 13 (1984): 26–43.

Thurber, James. "After Cato, What?" *My World and Welcome to It.* New York: Harcourt, 1942. 288–99.

———. "The American Literary Scene." *Thurber Country.* New York: Simon, 1953. 189–97.

———. "The Car We Had to Push." *My Life and Hard Times.* London: Penguin, 1948. 31–42.

———. "The Case of Dimity Ann." *Thurber Country.* New York: Simon, 1953. 106–21.

———. "Courtship Through the Ages." *My World and Welcome to It.* New York: Harcourt, 1942. 9–17.

———. "Draft Board Nights." *My Life and Hard Times.* London: Penguin, 1948. 115–27.

———. "A Final Note on Chanda Bell." *Thurber Country.* New York: Simon, 1953. 151–63.

———. "Footnote on the Future." *My World and Welcome to It*. New York: Harcourt, 1942. 111–18.

———. "The Night the Ghost Got In." *My Life and Hard Times*. London: Penguin, 1948. 57–67.

———. "Preface to a Life." *My Life and Hard Times*. London: Penguin, 1948. 13–21.

———. "See No Weevil." *Thurber Country*. New York: Simon, 1953. 253–58.

———. "University Days." *My Life and Hard Times*. London: Penguin, 1948. 101–14.

———. "*What* Cocktail Party?" *Thurber Country*. New York: Simon, 1953. 219–29.

———. "What's So Funny?" *Thurber Country*. New York: Simon, 1953. 1–7.

———. "The Whip-Poor-Will." *Thurber on Crime*. New York: Warner, 1991. 191–200.

Vann, Gerald, O. P. "The Vision of the Way." *The Idea of Catholicism: An Introduction to the Thought and Worship of the Church*. Eds. Walter J. Burghardt and William F. Lynch. Cleveland: Meridian, 1964. 281–94.

Walker, Alice. "Beyond the Peacock: The Reconstruction of Flannery O'Connor." *In Search of Our Mothers' Gardens*. New York: Harcourt, 1984.

Welty, Eudora. "A Memory." *The Collected Stories of Eudora Welty*. New York: Random, 1980. 75–80.

West, Nathanael. *Miss Lonelyhearts*. New York: Avon, 1964.

Westling, Louise. *Sacred Groves and Ravaged Gardens: The Fiction of Eudora Welty, Flannery O'Connor, and Carson McCullers*. Athens: U of Georgia P, 1985.

Wood, Ralph C. *The Comedy of Redemption: Christian Faith and Comic Vision in Four American Novelists*. Notre Dame: U of Notre Dame P, 1988.

———. "Where Is the Voice Coming From? Flannery O'Connor on Race." *Flannery O'Connor Bulletin* 22 (1994): 90–118.

Woolf, Virginia. "Professions for Women." *The Death of the Moth and Other Essays*. New York: Harcourt, 1970.

Wray, Virginia. "'An Afternoon in the Woods': Flannery O'Connor's Discovery of Theme." *Flannery O'Connor Bulletin* 20 (1991): 45–53.

Index